Adobe

Classroom in a Book

W9-BLB-515

Adobe® Premiere®

version

5.0

Library of Congress Catalog No.: 98-84556

ISBN: 1-56830-467-6

10 9 8 7   . First Printing: June 1998

Published by Adobe Press, Adobe Systems Incorporated, San Jose, California. For information on becoming an Adobe Certified Expert (ACE) with Adobe Premiere 5.0, send an e-mail to certification@adobe.com or visit the U.S. Adobe Web site at (http://www.adobe.com).

Direct to plate pre-press and printing by GAC Shepard Poorman, Indianapolis, Indiana. Printed in the United States of America

Published simultaneously in Canada.

Adobe Press books are published and distributed by Macmillan Computer Publishing USA. For individual, educational, corporate, or retail sales accounts, call 1-800-428-5331, or 317-581-3500. For information on Adobe Press books address Macmillan Computer Publishing USA, 201 West 103rd Street, Indianapolis, Indiana, 46290 or visit Macmillan's World Wide Web page (http://www.mcp.com/hayden/adobe).

Part number: 9001 1559 (6/98 MW)

Contents

Adding Transitions

Adding Audio

Applying Video and Audio Filters

Lesson 11

Subclips and Virtual Clips

Lesson 12

Introduction

Adobe® Premiere® 5.0 is a powerful program for editing digital video. Premiere helps you create dynamic video or film, whether you're creating long video programs and motion-picture films or short movies for CD-ROM or the Web. You'll find precise tools like those available on traditional nonlinear editing systems—tools that allow 3-point editing and other professional techniques.

About Classroom in a Book

Adobe Premiere 5.0 Classroom in a Book® is part of the official training series for Adobe software developed by experts at Adobe Systems. The lessons are designed for you to learn at your own pace. If you're new to Adobe Premiere, you'll learn the fundamental concepts and features you'll need to master the program. If you've been using Adobe Premiere for a while, you'll find *Classroom in a Book* teaches many advanced features, including tips and techniques for using the latest version of Adobe Premiere.

Although each lesson provides step-by-step instructions for creating a specific project, there's room for exploration and experimentation. You can follow the book from start to finish or do only the lessons that correspond to your interests and needs. Each lesson concludes with review questions and answers summarizing what you've covered.

Prerequisites

Before beginning to use *Adobe Premiere 5.0 Classroom in a Book*, you need to have a working knowledge of your computer and its operating system. Make sure you know how to use the mouse and standard menus and commands, and how to open, save, and close files. If you need to review these techniques, see the printed or online documentation included with your system.

It's helpful, but not necessary, for you to have experience with Adobe Illustrator®, Adobe Photoshop®, and Adobe After Effects®.

Checking system requirements

Before you begin using *Adobe Premiere 5.0 Classroom in a Book*, make sure that your system is set up correctly and that you've installed the required software and hardware. For space requirements for the Classroom in a Book lessons, see "Using the Classroom in a Book files" on page 4.

Windows® system requirements

You need the following components:

• Intel® Pentium® processor (or 100% compatible)

• Microsoft® Windows® 95 (or later) or Windows NT® 4.0 (or later) operating system

• QuickTime 3.0 (installed with Premiere)

• 32 MB of RAM installed

• 60 MB of available hard-disk space for installation (30 MB for application)

• 256-color display adapter and compatible monitor

• CD-ROM drive

For best results, Adobe Systems recommends the following hardware and software:

• Multi-processor system (Windows NT only)

• 64 MB or more of RAM

• Large capacity hard disk or hard-disk array

• 24-bit color display adapter

• Microsoft Video for Windows®-compatible or Apple QuickTime for Windows-compatible video capture card

• Apple QuickTime for Windows 3.0 (optionally installed with Premiere), Microsoft DirectX® Media 5.1 (optionally installed with Premiere), or other video software supported by your video-capture hardware

• Sound card (recommended if your video capture card does not contain on-board sound circuitry)

Mac OS system requirements

You need the following components:

- PowerPC™ processor
- Mac OS 7.5.5 or later (or 7.5.1 with Radius™ VideoVision™ only)
- 16 MB of application RAM
- 30 MB of disk space for installation
- CD-ROM drive

For best results, Adobe Systems recommends the following:

- Multiprocessor system
- QuickTime 3.0 (installed with Premiere)
- 48 MB or more of application RAM
- Large capacity hard disk or hard-disk array
- QuickTime-compatible video capture card
- 24-bit color display adapter

Installing the Adobe Premiere program

You must purchase the Adobe Premiere software separately. See the *Adobe Premiere 5.0 User Guide* that comes with the Adobe Premiere software for instructions on installing the application.

Installing QuickTime

QuickTime 3.0 is required to play the QuickTime movies you create in Adobe Premiere on both Windows and Mac OS systems. In addition, to play sound:

- On a Windows system, a sound card and speakers must be installed.
- On a Mac OS system, sound playback hardware is built in, though the quality varies by model. For best quality when previewing audio, you may want to connect external speakers to your system.

If QuickTime 3.0 is not already installed on your system, you can install it from the Adobe Premiere application CD-ROM. See the *Adobe Premiere 5.0 User Guide* for installation instructions.

Installing lesson fonts

Lesson 8 and Lesson 9 of the *Classroom in a Book* require the fonts News Gothic and OCRA Alternate, respectively. These Adobe PostScript fonts are included on the Classroom in a Book CD-ROM along with other bonus fonts.

In Windows, you install Adobe PostScript fonts using Adobe Type Manager (ATM). An ATM installer is included on the Adobe Premiere CD-ROM. In Windows and Mac OS, ATM draws PostScript fonts smoothly at any size on your monitor and on any printer. To install fonts on Mac OS, see the Mac OS documentation.

Using the Classroom in a Book files

The Classroom in a Book CD-ROM includes source files for the lessons. Each lesson has its own folder that contains source files and (in some cases) a Premiere project file for the beginning of the lesson, as well as a QuickTime movie of the finished version of the lesson. At any time, you can refer to the finished movie to help you understand the objective of a task or lesson.

Note: Files on the Classroom in a Book CD-ROM are protected by copyright law. They may be used for lessons but may not be redistributed.

You can choose from two ways to work through the lessons:

• Use the lesson files directly from the CD-ROM while saving your own work to your hard disk. This will save space on your hard disk but can slow performance.

• Copy the lesson files to your hard disk. This will provide the best performance but will require some disk space for the lesson files. If disk space is a problem, you can copy one lesson folder to your hard disk and delete it when you're finished with the lesson before copying the next lesson folder. You will need approximately 55 MB to copy the largest lesson folder to your hard disk, or less if you don't copy a lesson's final QuickTime movie (.mov) file.

Note: When you open a project file at the beginning of a lesson, a message may appear asking for the location of a file. This is because Premiere expects to find the project files in their original location, and that location changes if you copy the folder to your hard disk or use the files directly from the CD-ROM disc. If this message appears, select the file in question in the lesson folder and click OK to continue opening the project.

To use lesson files directly from the CD-ROM disc:

1 On your Windows or Mac OS desktop, create a new folder and name it Lessons. Inside Projects, create a folder for each lesson you plan to do, for example 03Lesson, 04Lesson, and so on.

2 Do the lesson using the lesson files on the CD-ROM disc. When a lesson tells you to save a file, save it to one of the folders you created in the Projects folder. (You cannot save to a CD-ROM disc.)

To use lesson files copied to your hard disk:

1 On your Windows or Mac OS desktop, create a new folder and name it Lessons.

2 Open the Lessons folder on the CD-ROM disc. Copy the lesson folders you need to the Lessons folder you just created on your desktop.

3 Do the lesson using the lesson files you copied to the Lessons folder on your desktop. When a lesson tells you to save a file, you can save it in the same folder as the other lesson files, or to another location of your choice.

Restoring default preferences

Like many software programs, Adobe Premiere maintains a *preferences file* that stores the settings you last used in the program. As you begin each lesson project, you'll see a step telling you to delete your Adobe Premiere preferences file. This step returns Premiere options to their *default*, or factory preset, settings. This ensures that your settings match those needed at the start of a lesson. Deleting the preferences file also resets the window and palette positions.

To quickly locate and delete the Premiere preferences file in Windows, choose Start > Find > Files or Folders and search for prem50.prf. Choose Options > Save Results and then File > Save Search. In Mac OS, create an alias for the Preferences folder. Afterward, you can double-click the saved search file (Windows) or alias (Mac OS) any time you want to delete the preferences file.

To restore default preferences for Premiere:

1 If Premiere is running, exit Premiere.

2 Do one of the following:

• In Windows, delete the Prem50.prf file from the folder containing the Premiere program.

• In Mac OS, delete the Adobe Premiere 5.0 Prefs file from the Preferences folder in the System Folder.

Additional resources

Adobe Premiere 5.0 Classroom in a Book is not meant to replace the documentation that comes with the program. Only the commands and options used in the lessons are explained in this book. For comprehensive information about all of Adobe Premiere's features, refer to these resources:

• The Adobe Premiere User Guide. Included with the Adobe Premiere software, the User Guide contains complete descriptions of all features. For your convenience, you will find excerpts from these guides, including the Tour, in this Classroom in a Book.

• The Tour Movie, available on the Adobe Premiere 5.0 CD-ROM.

• The Quick Reference Card, a useful companion as you work through the lessons in this book. You can view an online version by choosing Help > Keyboard in Premiere.

• Online Help, an online version of the User Guide and Quick Reference Card, which you can view by choosing Help > Contents in Premiere.

• The Adobe Web site, which you can view by choosing File > Adobe Online in Premiere if you have a connection to the World Wide Web.

Adobe certification

The Adobe certification program offers users, instructors, and training centers the opportunity to demonstrate their product proficiency and promote their software skills as Adobe Certified Experts, Adobe Certified Instructors, or Adobe Authorized Learning Providers. Visit the U.S. Web site at www.adobe.com to learn how you can become certified.

A Tour of
Adobe Premiere

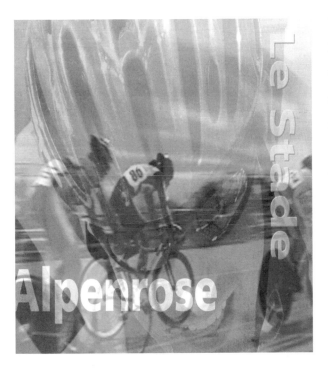

This tour, excerpted from the Adobe Premiere 5.0 User Guide, *helps you understand and work with basic concepts and features of the Adobe Premiere program. You'll run through a typical series of steps for creating a video piece, including basic editing techniques, adding transitions, motion, and transparency. Completing the video piece should take approximately one hour.*

Over the course of this tour, you'll create a promotional television spot for a fictional bicycle company using video and audio clips provided on the CD-ROM. You'll be working with clips that have already been digitized as QuickTime files. If you were actually producing this project from the start, you would likely capture clips from the original video tapes and digitize them yourself, using Premiere.

Starting the project

To begin, you need to create a new project and then import the video clips.

1 Make sure you know the location of the files used in this lesson. Insert the CD-ROM disc if necessary. If desired, copy the Tour folder to your hard drive. For help, see "Using the Classroom in a Book files" on page 4.

2 To ensure that the Premiere preferences are set to the default values, exit Premiere, and then delete the preferences file as explained in "Restoring default preferences" on page 5.

3 Start Premiere. If it is already running, choose File > New > Project.

4 In the New Project Settings dialog box, choose QuickTime for the Editing Mode.

5 Choose 30 for the Timebase.

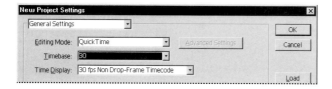

The Timebase menu specifies the frames per second for your project. If you were producing the final version of your video program for broadcast, you would choose 29.97, which is the National Television Standards Commission (NTSC) standard for television, or 25, for the PAL (Phased Alternating Line) standard, depending on the part of the world in which you were broadcasting.

6 Click Next to open the Video Settings section of the New Project Settings dialog box.

7 For Frame Size, type **240** in the leftmost box to set the width of the preview.

Because the 4:3 Aspect option is checked, 180 appears automatically for the height of the preview frame. This setting controls how the project is previewed on your monitor.

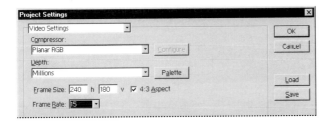

8 For Frame Rate, specify 15, and then click OK.

Many of the project settings you just defined determine how the video program will be built and exported. Before you create your own videos, read Chapter 2, "Working with Projects," in the *Adobe Premiere 5.0 User Guide* for a better understanding of the available settings and their importance to the success of your work.

Viewing the finished movie

If you'd like to see what you'll be creating, you can take a look at the finished movie.

1 Choose File > Open and double-click the zfinal.mov file in the Tour folder in your Premiere folder (if you installed the Tour with Premiere) or on the Adobe Premiere Application CD-ROM disc (if you did not install the Tour).

The video program opens in the Source view.

2 Click the Play button (▶)to view the video program.

Importing clips

Now you're ready to import the clips you'll be using for your video program. A clip can be digitized film, video, audio, a still image, or sequence of still images; a video or audio clip might be only a few seconds long.

There are several ways to bring clips into a project. In this tour you'll import clips directly into the Project Window, the one place where Premiere lists each clip associated with a project.

1 Depending on your system, do one of the following:

• In Windows, Choose File > Import > File, and then open the Tour folder you copied or installed from the Premiere Application CD-ROM disc. Select the Boys.mov file, hold down the Shift key, and then select the Finale.mov file. This selects the first four movie files in the folder. Then click Open.

• In Mac OS, choose File > Import > Multiple, open the Tour folder you copied or installed from the Premiere Application CD-ROM disc, and then open the Clips folder. Then select Boys.mov and click Import. Do the same for the Cyclers.mov, Fastslow.mov, and Finale.mov files, and then click Done.

The files appear in the Project window. For each file that you import, the Project window lists its name, type, and duration. Other columns let you add your own descriptions or labels. You can scroll or enlarge the window if necessary.

Before you continue, save the project and give it a name.

2 Choose File > Save.

3 In the Save File dialog box, type **Cycling.ppj** for the file name, and specify a location on your hard disk. Click Save.

Premiere saves the project file to your hard disk.

Creating a rough cut

For many projects, you may want to begin by creating a *rough cut* of your video program. A rough cut is simply a sequence of clips assembled in the general sequence you want, with little or no editing. A rough cut can quickly give you some sense of your video program's effectiveness, letting you start making decisions about where to cut, trim, and add transitions and special effects.

1 If the Timeline window is not open, choose Window > Timeline.

The clips you imported do not become part of the video program until you place them into the Timeline. The Timeline window is where you'll construct and edit your video program—adding, copying, and moving clips, adjusting their lengths, and so on. The Timeline provides an overview of your work by showing where in time each clip begins and ends, as well as the relationships between clips.

It's important to understand that just as there are different ways to import a clip, there is more than one approach to editing a video in Premiere. Experienced video-editors, for example, might prefer to rely on the Monitor window (described later in this tour) rather than the Timeline. The method of editing described in this tour is appropriate for novice users creating a relatively simple project. Chapter 4, "Editing Video," in the *Adobe Premiere 5.0 User Guide* describes more advanced approaches to editing in Premiere, such as 3-point editing.

When you first open the Timeline window, it displays seven separate rows, called *tracks*, underneath the time ruler. The tracks act as containers for the clips; by involving multiple tracks and arranging clips within the tracks, you create sequences and effects that become the video program you are making. This tour introduces you to each kind of track and to the kinds of controls available for all tracks.

2 In the Project window, select the Boys.mov clip and drag it into the Video 1A track. As you drag into the Video 1A track, the clip appears as a darkened box. Before releasing the mouse, make sure that the left end of the box is up against the left side of the Video 1A track.

Note: If the Video 1A track is not expanded (that is, set to show the Transition track and the Video 1B track with which it is associated), click the arrow to the left of the track label so that the tracks appear as they do in the following illustration.

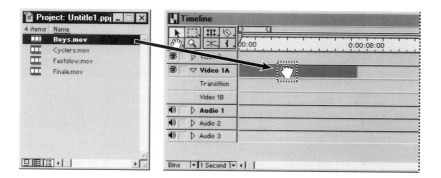

3 Select the Cyclers.mov clip and drag it into the Video 1A track, this time positioning it just after the Boys.mov clip, so that the beginning of the Cyclers clip is up against the end of the Boys clip.

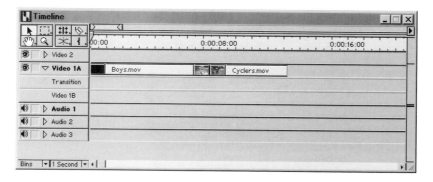

4 Select the Fastslow.mov clip, drag it into the Video 1A track, and position it after the Cyclers.mov clip. Do the same with Finale.mov clip, dragging it just after the Fastslow.mov clip.

Now you have four clips in your Video 1A track, forming a video program about 32 seconds in length. This is a rough cut, giving you some idea of how your sequence works and what needs to be trimmed, edited, and modified. In the next section, you'll preview this sequence. Before moving on, though, you'll change how the clips are represented in the Timeline.

5 Click the Timeline window title bar to make sure the window is active, and choose Window > Timeline Window Options.

6 For Icon Size, select the middle option, and then click OK.

The clip representations in the Timeline change size accordingly. Now change the unit of time displayed throughout the Timeline.

7 From the Time Units pop-up menu in the lower left of the Timeline window, choose 2 Seconds.

The clips now take up less horizontal space, since you're now displaying the Timeline contents in a time unit requiring less detail.

Now it's time to play the sequence of clips you've imported.

Previewing in the Monitor window

To see how your work is progressing, you can preview one or more clips in the Monitor window.

1 If the Monitor window is not already open, choose Window > Monitor.

The Monitor window displays two views:

• Source view (on the left side of the window) lets you preview a clip, trim it, and then insert it into the Timeline window. This view can store many clips at a time, but you can view and trim only one clip at a time.

• Program view (on the right) lets you preview your entire video program, at any time. This view displays the sequence of clips currently in the Timeline window. You can also use the Program view to edit your video program.

2 In the Monitor window, click the Play button underneath the Program view, or press the spacebar.

The rough cut of your video program plays until the end.

Note that the edit line in the Timeline moves in tandem with the preview. This edit line indicates the active frame—the frame being edited or previewed.

3 To replay it, click the Play button again, or click the Loop button (↻)to play the video program in a continuous loop. To stop the action, click the Stop button (■) or press the spacebar.

Now that you've got a general idea of the video program, you'll trim the video clips and add audio, transitions, special effects, and superimposing to create the finished version.

Trimming clips in the Monitor window

When you shoot footage with your camera, you almost always produce much more material than you'll actually use in your video program. To create scenes, cuts, and transitions, you'll need to trim your clips, removing the parts that you don't need. Trimming clips is an essential part of creating a video program, something you'll do many times. Premiere provides a number of different ways to trim clips, including quick rough-cut tools and more precise frame-by-frame views.

You'll start editing the bicycle video by trimming the Boys.mov clip, the first clip in the video program.

1 Make sure that both the Timeline window and the Monitor window are visible and that they don't overlap one another. Then click the Timeline window title bar to make the Timeline active.

2 In the Video 1A track of the Timeline window, double-click the Boys.mov clip.

The first frame of the Boys.mov clip appears in the Source view of the Monitor window.

Before you trim, first play the clip.

3 Click the Play button (▶) underneath the Source view, or press the spacebar.

As it is, the clip is a little long, so you'll trim it somewhat. Trimming a clip involves setting a new *In point*, *Out point*, or both. An In point is the frame at which a clip begins; an Out point is the last frame of the clip. You'll change the Out point for the Boys.mov clip.

4 To get an idea of exactly where you'll trim the clip, click the Play button and look for the point at which the first bike rider stops moving forward (just over 4 seconds into the clip): That is where you'll set the Out point.

The controls for both views in the Monitor window also contain a shuttle slider, which lets you *scrub* clips. Scrubbing—advancing or reversing a clip manually—lets you precisely identify and mark events.

5 Under the Source view, drag the shuttle slider until you see the first bike rider at the end of his ride. (The time below the shuttle slider should read between 4:20 and 5:00 seconds.)

6 Click the Mark Out point button (**┃**).

After you've positioned the Out point correctly, you need to apply the change to the clip in the Timeline. Note that the Apply button is now visible above the Source view. This button appears whenever you mark a new In or Out point for a clip in the Timeline.

7 To apply the trim, click the Apply button.

Premiere trims the end of the clip to give the clip a new Out point. It's important to understand that the trimmed area has not been deleted; Premiere has merely hidden the trimmed frames so that they don't appear in the Timeline and will not appear when you preview or export the video program. You can easily restore any trimmed frames by resetting the Out point using any trimming method.

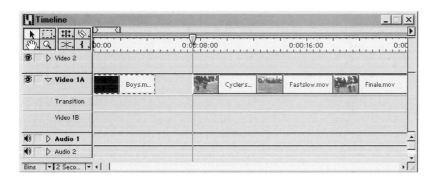

Because you set a new Out point, there is now a gap in the Timeline between the first and second clips. To preserve a continuous flow from one clip to the next, you need to close this gap by moving the other clips to the left. To do this, you'll use the track selection tool (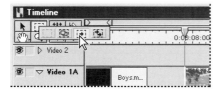). This tool selects all the clips in a track to the right of where you click. (Later in the lesson you'll learn how to automatically close gaps when you trim.)

8 In the Timeline window, select the track selection tool.

9 Click the Cyclers.mov clip in track 1A. This clip, and the clips to the right, are selected.

10 Drag the selection to the left, until it is up against the Boys.mov clip.

11 Click the selection tool (▶), since you are through with the track selection for now.

12 In the Monitor window, click the Program view Play button to preview the changes you've made.

13 Save the project.

Adding audio

Now you'll add some music to the project by importing and placing an audio file in the first audio track. The music in the audio file was recorded in a studio, digitized, and then assembled and rendered in Premiere.

1 Choose File > Import > File, and double-click the Music.aif file in the Clips folder within the Tour folder. The file appears in the Project window.

2 Drag the Music.aif icon from the Project window to the Audio 1 track.

3 Click the arrow to the left of the track to expand it.

The expanded view shows the waveform of the clip. The waveform displays the volume of the audio over time. Higher peaks in the waveform indicate greater volume. In the next section, you'll come back to the audio track to synchronize events in the video with the music. For now, you'll lock the track so it doesn't get repositioned later.

4 Click in the box next to the speaker icon to lock the audio track.

5 Click the Program view Play button in the Monitor window to preview the video and the audio together.

Trimming clips in the Timeline window

In addition to trimming clips in the Monitor window, you can trim clips in the Timeline window using a number of different methods. To edit more precisely in the Timeline window, it's often easier to view a wider range of frames. By default, the Timeline window displays the frame at each second.

1 From the Time Units pop-up menu in the lower left of the Timeline window, choose 8 Frames.

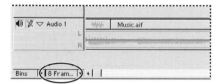

The Timeline window now displays every eighth frame.

First, you'll adjust the trim you made to the Boys.mov clip so that its Out point is synchronized with the first spike in the audio track.

2 Select the ripple edit tool (◄▮►) in the Timeline window.

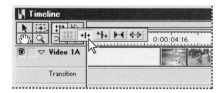

A *ripple edit* trims the specified clip, but keeps the duration of all other clips the same. The trim, however, "ripples" through the project; other clips are pulled in or pushed out, depending on whether you shorten or lengthen the clip. The duration of the entire video program, therefore, changes.

3 Move the pointer across the line where the first two clips join. Notice how the pointer changes into the icon representing a ripple edit.

4 Drag the ripple edit tool until it is positioned over the first spike in the audio track, and then release the mouse button.

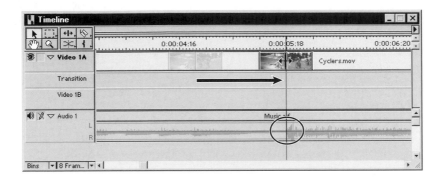

Now you'll trim the Cyclers.mov clip so that its endpoint corresponds with an exact point in the Timeline. To trim the Cyclers.mov clip to this time, you'll use the Info palette.

5 Select the Cyclers.mov clip and choose Window > Show Info.

The Info palette displays the name, duration, and the starting and ending points of the selected clip. In addition, it displays the current location of the pointer; you'll use the pointer information to help you trim.

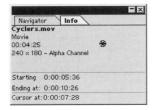

6 With the ripple edit tool still selected, move the pointer across the line where the Cyclers.mov and Fastslow.mov clips join.

7 Drag the ripple edit tool to the left, until the position of the pointer in the Info palette reads 0:00:08:01, and then release the mouse button.

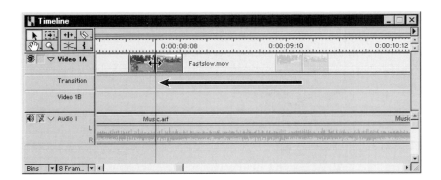

You have trimmed the Out point of the Cyclers.mov clip. Since you trimmed the clip using a ripple edit, the subsequent clips have followed suit, shifting to the left.

8 Select the selection tool ( ), since you are done with ripple editing.

Now you'll move on to applying a transition between clips.

Adding a transition

A *transition* is a change from one scene to the next, or from one clip to another. The simplest transition is the *cut*, where the last frame of one clip leads directly into the first frame of the next. By placing the first two clips together—Boys.mov and Cyclers.mov— you created a cut between them.

To add texture, nuance, or attention-getting special effects between scenes, you can use special transitions available in Premiere 5.0, such as dissolves, wipes, and zooms. In this tour, you'll use the Cross Dissolve transition.

1 If the Transitions palette is not open, choose Window > Show Transitions.

The Transitions palette appears, displaying the available transitions. Each icon graphically represents how the transition works. You can also animate these icons to see a dynamic view of each transition. Do that now.

2 Click the small black arrow (▸) in the upper right corner of the Transitions palette, and then choose Animate.

If you find the animation distracting, you can turn it off by once again choosing Animate from the Transitions palette menu to deselect the option.

3 If the Video 1 track is not expanded, click the arrow to the left of the track.

To create a transition, you first need to overlap two clips in the Video 1A and Video 1B tracks. The overlapping portion of the clips are used in the transition. Typically, the overlapping portions of the clips are not essential to your project, since the transition will obscure them both somewhat.

4 In the time ruler, drag the edit line to one second before the Out point of the Cyclers.mov clip (0:00:07:01); you'll use this as a kind of guide for repositioning the Fastslow clip in the next step.

Note: *To locate the desired frame, watch the timecode display below the Program view as you drag the edit line.*

5 Now drag the Fastslow.mov clip down to the Video 1B track, snapping its In point to the edit line.

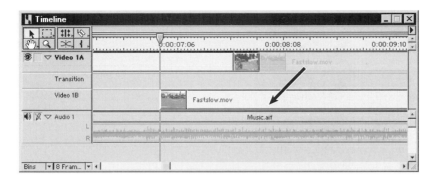

The two clips are now overlapping for a one-second duration.

6 In the Transitions palette, find the Cross Dissolve transition, scrolling if necessary.

This transition, frequently used in video and film, "dissolves" one scene into another, over a brief duration.

7 Drag the Cross Dissolve transition into the Timeline window, placing it in the *Transition* track (the area where the two clips overlap).

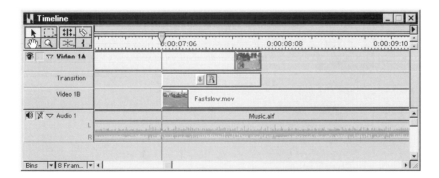

When you release the mouse, the transition is automatically sized to the overlap and displayed as an icon. This Cross Dissolve begins one second prior to the end of the Cyclers.mov clip and ends one second into the Fastslow.mov clip.

Previewing transitions and other effects

The Program view play button previews only the video clips in the Video 1 track and the audio clips but does not play transitions, filters, or superimposed clips (ones placed on the Video 2 track) unless a *preview file* has been created. Once the preview file has been created, the Program view shows the additional effects.

1 Hold down the Alt key (Windows) or the Option key (Macintosh) and move the pointer into the time ruler within the Timeline window. The pointer changes into a small downward arrow (↓).

2 Drag the pointer in the time ruler over the transition, keeping the Alt or Option key held down.

The Cyclers.mov clip dissolves into the Fastslow.mov clip, over a duration of one second.

Dragging in this fashion provides a quick method for previewing your video program but cannot give you a precise frame rate, since you're moving it by hand. To preview effects at a specified frame rate, you need to generate a preview file.

Before you generate it, however, you need to adjust the *work area bar*—the topmost section of the Timeline window—to cover the area you want to preview. The work area bar specifies the portion of your project that you want to preview (with transitions, filters, and other effects) or output. In this case, you'd like to preview the first three clips of your project, including the transition effect you just added.

3 To view the first three clips in their entirety, choose 1 Second from the Time Units pop-up menu. Now it will be easy to extend the work area by the correct amount.

Note: Depending on the size and resolution of your monitor, the 1 Second setting might not make the first three clips entirely visible; in that case, choose another setting from the Time Units pop-up menu. Doing so will not affect your ability to follow the remaining procedures in this tour, although the illustrations may not exactly match what you see on your screen.

4 Drag the right end of the work area bar so that it extends the length of the first three clips and aligns with the end of the Fastslow.mov clip.

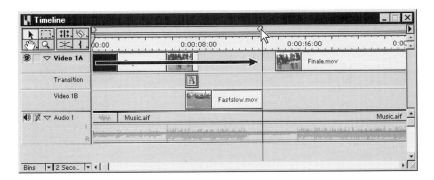

5 Choose Project > Preview or press Enter (Windows) or Return (Mac OS) on the keyboard.

Premiere displays a status bar as it generates a preview file. When complete, the preview of your video program plays in the Program view of the Monitor window.

Splitting a clip

Sometimes you may want to superimpose a portion of a clip. To do this, you need to split the clip to create two or more separate clips. Here you'll split the Fastslow.mov clip so that you can make a particular portion of it change speed and fade out.

1 In the Timeline window, move the edit line across the Fastslow.mov clip until you see the shot of the unobstructed bleachers (about 11:18). Leave the edit line positioned at this point.

2 In the Timeline window, select the razor tool (✄).

3 Position the pointer over the Fastslow.mov clip at the current edit line, and click.

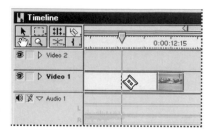 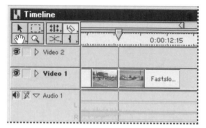

Premiere cuts the Fastslow.mov clip at the point where you clicked, creating two separate clips.

Changing the speed of a clip

You can change the playback speed of a clip to make it play slower or faster. Changing the speed changes its duration without adding or removing any frames. To make the bike sequence more interesting and attention-getting, you'll slow down the second portion of the clip you just cut, increasing its duration.

Since you also want to fade out the same clip, which requires it to be placed in a super-impose track, you'll place it there now.

1 Collapse the Video 1 track by clicking the downward pointing arrow to the left of the track.

2 Click the selection tool ( ) to select it, and then drag the second portion of the Fastslow clip upward into the Video 2 track.

Make sure to keep the position of the clip at exactly the same point in time; the edges of the clip snap to its same location in the Video 2 track.

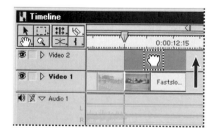 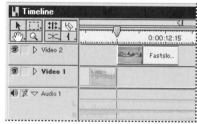

Now you'll change its speed.

3 Select the clip you just moved (if it is not already selected), and choose Clip > Speed.

4 In the dialog box, type **30** in the New Rate box. Click OK.

The playback speed of the clip is now at 30% of its original speed. Accordingly, the duration of the clip has increased proportionally, approximately tripling in length.

Note that this clip now overlaps some of the Finale.mov clip. Because you want the slowed-down clip to fade to black, you need to move the Finale.mov clip to the right.

5 Drag the Finale.mov clip to the right until its left edge snaps to the Out point of the slowed-down clip.

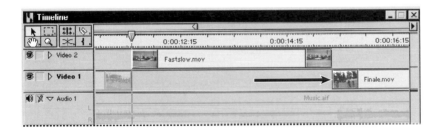

Now let's generate another preview.

6 Drag the right end of the work area bar to the right so that it extends to the end of the Fastslow clip in the Video 2 track.

7 Choose Project > Preview or press Enter (Windows) or Return (Mac OS) on the keyboard. To preview more than once, just repeat this step.

8 Save the project.

Changing a clip's opacity

If a clip is on Video 2 track or higher, you can make it partially transparent by changing its opacity. The opacity option lets you fade into or out of a clip and superimpose one or more clips on top of others, so that two or more clips are visible at the same time. You'll superimpose clips later in the tour. For now, you'll use the superimpose track to fade out a clip by manually adjusting its opacity over time.

By default, Premiere includes one superimpose track, Video 2, above the Video 1 track. You can add others, as needed. Once a clip has been placed in a superimpose track, an opacity control bar, or a "rubber band," becomes available. To see the bar, you need to expand the Video 2 track.

1 Click the arrow to the left of the Video 2 track.

The opacity bar shows the clip's opacity. Right now, the opacity is at 100%.

2 Now move the pointer onto the opacity bar (where the pointer changes into a pointing finger), and click about three-quarters of the way into the clip to create a small box called a *handle*.

The handle divides the control bar into sections that you can adjust by dragging. A control bar includes a handle at each end to define the beginning and ending opacity settings.

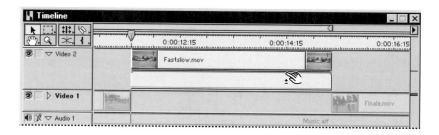

3 In the Video 2 track of the Timeline window, click the rightmost handle. Keep the mouse button depressed throughout the next step.

4 Press Shift, and then drag the selected opacity handle down until the value beside the handle displays 20%.

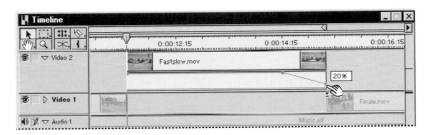

This creates a downward slope in the control bar, starting at the first handle you created. A downward slope decreases opacity. In this case, the opacity of the clip begins at 100% and decreases to 20%. (Make sure you press the Shift key after you select the handle, otherwise the change applies starting with the leftmost handle in the control bar.)

Note: *You can also drag handles without holding down Shift, but that limits you to 5-percent increments and does not produce a pop-up display. You can, however, use the Info palette to view the opacity setting if you drag without holding down the Shift key.*

Preview what you've done.

5 Hold down the Alt key (Windows) or the Option key (Macintosh) and slowly drag in the time ruler above the clip you just adjusted. The preview plays in the Monitor window. Because this clip is the only one playing in the Timeline, it fades into the background color, which is black.

6 Save the project.

Adding special effects to a video clip

Premiere 5.0 lets you create many different kinds of special effects using video filters. For the last clip in the video program, you'll add the Camera Blur effect, which blurs a clip as if it were leaving the focal range of the camera.

1 Select the Finale.mov clip in the Timeline window.

2 Choose Clip > Filters.

3 Move the Filters window so that you can see both it and the Monitor window.

4 In the Filters window, select Camera Blur from the Available column, and then click the Add button.

The Camera Blur control window appears, displaying the first frame of the Finale.mov clip.

5 Drag the slider bar to zero, and then click OK.

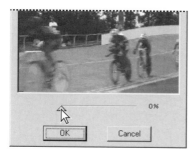

The Camera Blur filter appears in the Current column of the Filters window. Filters listed in this column are applied to the currently selected clip.

To create an effect of changing focus, you can vary the Camera Blur effect over time. To do this, you set *keyframes*. A keyframe specifies a control value at a specific point in time.

The lower portion of the Filters window now displays a timeline, representing the duration of the Finale.mov clip. The triangular keyframes at each end of the timeline control when the effect begins and ends, and with what amount of blurring. Since you'd like the blurring to start about midway through the Finale.mov clip, you move the first keyframe. Moving a keyframe scrubs the clip in the Program view of the Monitor window.

6 Arrange the Filters window so that the program view in the Monitor window is visible. Then drag the first keyframe (the triangle on the left) to the right until you reach the point in the clip where the bikes are perpendicular to the camera.

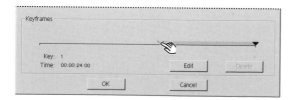

7 Click the Edit button.

8 Make sure the slider is set at zero. Click OK.

Now you'll create a new keyframe and increase the amount of blurring.

9 In the Filters window, click in the middle of the two keyframes.

The Camera Blur Settings edit box appears.

10 Drag the slider bar until the Blur is at 80%, and then click OK.

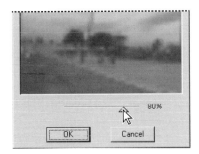

In the Filters window, you can now see the triangle indicating the new keyframe you just created. Now you'll position this keyframe at an exact time.

11 Drag the keyframe you just created until the timecode reads 00:00:25:00 (25 seconds).

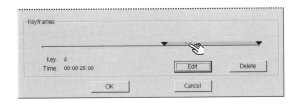 

12 Now select the last keyframe (the triangle at the far right) and click Edit.

13 Once again, drag the slider bar until the Blur is at 80%. Click OK.

14 In the Filters window, click OK.

Let's briefly review what you've just done. By setting three keyframes—the first at 0%, the second at 80%, and the third at 80%—you have specified that the Camera Blur effect begins at 0% at the point in time you specified, increases to 80% at 25 seconds, and then remains at 80% for the duration of the clip.

Why not just use two keyframes—the first at 0% and the last at 80%? Premiere always creates a linear change between keyframes. Therefore, if you used only two keyframes, the blurring would gradually increase over the duration of the clip. This is not the effect you want; rather, you want the blur to happen fairly quickly, and then remain at that level for its duration.

Preview your work again.

15 Drag the right end of the work area bar so that it aligns with the end of the Finale.mov clip. Press Enter (Windows) or Return (Mac OS).

It's starting to look like something now!

16 Save the project.

Superimposing an image

In the previous section, you used the Camera Blur filter to blur the second half of the final clip. Now you'll superimpose a company logo on top of this clip, making it appear as if the camera is now focusing on the image.

1 Choose File > Import > File. Then locate and select the Veloman.eps file in the Clips folder within the Tour folder. Click Open.

2 From the Project window, drag the Veloman.eps image into the Video 2 track.

3 Choose Window > Show Info if the palette is not already open, and adjust the image so that its In point is set to 0:00:25:00 (shown as "Starting at: 0:00:25:00" in the Info palette).

By default, the duration of a still image is set in the General Preferences at 30 frames. Because the frame rate of your video program is 15 frames per second, the duration of the image is 2 seconds. To keep the image visible until the end of the video program, you'll need to extend its duration. Unlike a motion clip, a still image duration can be specified by stretching the clip representation in the Timeline.

4 In the Timeline window, select the selection tool.

5 Drag the right edge of the Veloman.eps image to the right until it snaps to the end of the Finale.mov clip.

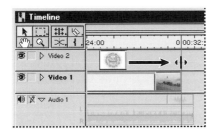

The image now overlaps the Finale.mov clip in the Timeline window. The overlapping area is where the logo will be superimposed on the bike race.

Note: Hold down the Alt key (Windows) or the Option key (Mac OS) and drag in the time ruler over the area where the two clips overlap.

As expected, all you see is the Veloman.eps image; you don't see the Finale.mov clip at all. That's because the Veloman.eps image is still fully opaque. Now you'll make the background of the Veloman.eps image transparent.

To specify that certain areas of a clip become transparent and other areas remain opaque, you need to use a *transparency key*. A transparency key (often referred to simply as a key) makes designated colors (or a range of colors) in a clip transparent or partially transparent. A blue screen key, for example, makes a shade of blue transparent; in this way, an actor can be filmed in the studio against a blue screen, and then superimposed on an outdoor action scene. Creating transparency with a particular color is called *keying out* that color. To superimpose the Veloman.eps image, you need to key out the white background.

6 Select the Veloman.eps image in the Timeline window, and then choose Clip > Video > Transparency.

The Transparency Settings dialog box shows the selected clip in the Sample area. The key you choose is applied to the clip, and the resulting effect is displayed in this area.

7 Select the Page Peel icon, which displays the actual clips in the Sample area.

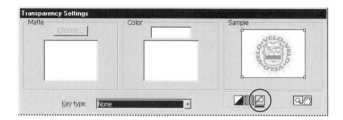

8 In the Transparency Settings dialog box, choose White Alpha Matte for the Key Type. The White Alpha Matte key will key out any areas of alpha white in an image that contains an alpha channel.

In the Sample area of the dialog box, the white areas of the Veloman.eps image are now transparent, letting the underlying image—the Finale.mov clip—show through.

9 Click OK.

10 To preview the effect, hold down the Alt key (Windows) or the Option key (Macintosh) and drag in the time ruler over the area where the superimposition occurs.

11 Save the project.

Animating a clip

For additional special effects, Premiere lets you move, rotate, or zoom a clip within the area bounded by the video program's frame. You cannot add motion to elements within the clip; you can add motion only to the clip itself.

To add more visual interest to the Veloman.eps image, you'll make it zoom into the frame, from the left.

1 If the Veloman.eps image is not still selected in the Timeline window, select it now.

2 Choose Clip > Video > Motion.

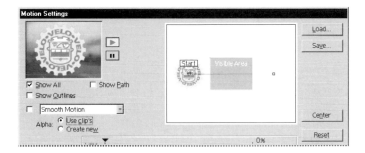

In the middle of the dialog box is the motion path for the clip. By default, the path is a straight line, starting outside the frame on the left, and ending outside the frame on the right. The area on the left half of the dialog box previews the motion for you.

You'll now define a new motion path.

3 In the Motion path area, drag the Start point to the right, so that approximately half of the image overlaps the Visible Area.

You can also specify the position of the image by entering coordinates. You'll do that now.

4 Select the End point, and then enter 26 and -8 in the two text boxes below the line that reads "Click on a point above." Then press Tab on your keyboard.

The End point moves to the specified location.

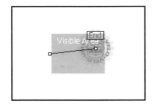 

By default, the Motion Area provides two motion points, Start and End, which you have just modified for position. You can also specify zooming, rotation, and distortion at these points, and you can create other motion points, each with particular animation values. Like keyframes for filters, motion points let you specify a particular value at a point in time.

In order to manipulate the Veloman.eps image in an eye-catching way, you'll add a new motion point, specify new zoom values for the start and end points, and, finally, apply a rotation value so that the logo spins as it appears to recede into the distance.

5 In the Motion Path area, click on the path approximately halfway between the Start and End points.

A new motion point is created.

6 Move the new motion point down and to the right as shown below.

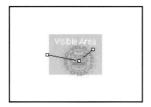

Now you'll specify zoom values for the start and end points.

7 In the Motion Path area, select the Start point.

8 In the Zoom box at the bottom of the dialog box, type **0**, and then press Tab.

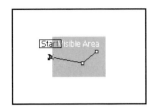 

9 Select the end point, type **0** in the Zoom edit box, and press Tab.

The settings you just entered make the logo appear to zoom in from the left side of the frame and then recede into the distance.

10 With the end point still selected, type **720** in the Rotation text box near the bottom of the dialog box, and press Tab.

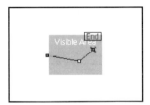 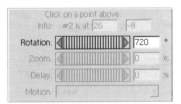

Rotation values are specified in degrees. The value of 720 (360 x 2) defines two complete circles or rotations from one point to the next.

The image now follows the motion you defined earlier as it zooms and rotates across the screen.

11 Click OK to close the Motion Settings dialog box.

Let's preview the end of the video program to see the superimposed image moving through the frame.

12 Move the work area bar to cover the last portion of your video program, where the image begins.

13 Press Enter (Windows) or Return (Mac OS) and watch the preview.

14 Save the project.

All you need to do now is make the QuickTime movie.

Exporting the movie

To complete the tour, you'll make the project into a QuickTime movie. The QuickTime format is a standard format for both Windows and Mac OS systems.

1 Choose File > Export > Movie.

2 Click the Settings button.

3 Make sure QuickTime is selected for File Type, and Entire Project is selected for Range.

4 Also make sure that the Export Video and Export Audio options are selected. The default values for other settings, including those for compression, are fine for this project.

5 Click OK to close the Export Movie Settings dialog box.

6 In the Export Movie dialog box, specify a filename (be sure to add the .MOV file extension to the end) and a folder in which to store the movie.

7 Click Save.

Premiere starts making the movie, displaying a status bar that provides an estimate for the amount of time it will take to render or output the movie. The output time always depends on the capabilities of your computer. On most systems, Premiere should finish making the movie within 7 minutes. You can cancel the output process by pressing the Esc key.

When the movie is complete, it opens in its own window.

8 Click the Play button to watch the show.

Congratulations on completing the Tour!

Lesson 1

Getting to Know the Work Area

Premiere organizes editing functions into specialized windows. This gives you the flexibility to arrange a window layout that matches your editing style. Floating palettes give you information and quick access to any part of your video program. You can arrange windows and palettes to make the best use of your computer and television monitors.

In this introduction to the work area, you'll learn how to do the following:

- Start Adobe Premiere and open a project file.
- Work with Project, Library, and Bin windows.
- Work with the Timeline window.
- Work with the Monitor window.
- Navigate to a specific time in your video program.
- Work with palettes.
- Discover keyboard shortcuts.

Starting the Adobe Premiere program

Every Adobe Premiere movie starts as a project—a collection of video clips, still images, and audio that you organize along a timeline. In this lesson, you'll explore palettes and windows using a project that has already been constructed. Make sure you know the location of the files used in this lesson. For help, see "Using the Classroom in a Book files" on page 4.

To ensure that the Premiere preferences are set to the default values, exit Premiere, and then delete the preferences file as explained in "Restoring default preferences" on page 5.

1 Double-click 01Lesson.ppj in the 01Lesson folder to open it in Premiere.

Note: Premiere remembers the original location of each clip in a project. Because you are using the project file on a computer other than the one that created it, Premiere may prompt you to find a file when you open a lesson project. Locate and select the file in the appropriate project folder and click OK.

2 If necessary, rearrange windows and palettes so they don't overlap one another.

A new project appears with the following windows open by default:

• The Project window, which lets you import, organize, and store references to clips. It lists all source clips you import into a project, though you don't have to use every clip you import.

• The Monitor window, which includes the Source and Program views. Use the Source view to see an individual video clip and the Program view to see the current state of the video program being edited in the Timeline.

• The Timeline window, which provides a schematic view of your program, including all video, audio, and superimposed video tracks. Changes you make appear in the Program view.

The following palettes also open by default, in two tabbed groups:

• The Navigator palette provides a convenient way to move around the Timeline.

• The Info palette provides information about the selected clip, transition, selected area in the Timeline, or operation you are performing.

• The Transitions palette lets you add transitions between clips in the Timeline.

• The Commands palette lets you create a button list of frequently used commands, and assign keyboard shortcuts to them.

You work with clips and assemble your program in windows. In contrast, palettes don't contain clips. Palettes always float above windows, and can be combined.

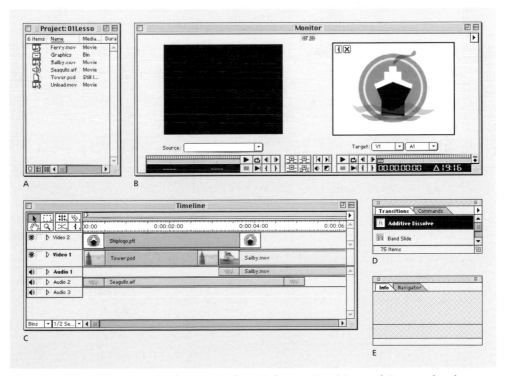

*A. Project window B. Monitor window C. Timeline window D. Transitions and Commands palettes
E. Navigator and Info palettes*

Premiere also provides specialized windows for tasks such as capturing video and creating titles; those windows are described with their tasks elsewhere in this book. As you develop a working style in Premiere, arrange the windows and palettes in a way that works best for you.

Working with Project, Library, and Bin windows

The filenames in the Project window identify the files imported into the project. Icons next to each filename indicate the file type. Video and audio files are large, so copying each one into a project would waste disk space. Instead, a Premiere project stores only references to the clips you import, not the clips themselves. This means a 5 MB source clip always occupies just 5 MB on your hard disk whether you use it in one project or ten. When you edit your video program, Premiere retrieves frames from the original files as needed.

A. Video with audio B. Bin C. Audio D. Title E. Still image

You can organize clips in a project or library using *bins*, just as you organize folders on your hard drive. Bins are useful for organizing a project or library that contains a large number of clips. At the end of this section you'll also use a library, which is similar to a bin but exists outside the project. A bin can exist inside a project or library, or inside another bin. Now you'll open a bin to see what's inside it.

1 Double-click the Graphics bin icon in the Project window. This bin contains a graphics file. You can organize all your graphics files in this bin.

Note: Be sure to position the pointer over the icon (not its name) when double-clicking or dragging.

2 Move the Graphics Bin window so you can see both it and the Project window at once.

3 Drag Shiplogo.ptl from the Project window to the Graphics bin.

4 Close the Graphics bin.

Using libraries

A *library* is a storage window similar to a Project or Bin window. While a Project window contains a file list specific to one project, a library contains a file list independent of any project. A library is useful for storing a set of clips that you want to have available for several projects.

1 Choose File > New > Library. An untitled Library window appears.

2 Move the Library window so that you can also see the contents of the Project window.

3 Drag any clip from a Project or Bin window to the Library window you created.

Note: Remember that when working with icons in the Project window, you must position the pointer over the icon (not its name) before you begin dragging.

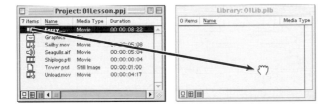

4 Make sure the Library window is active, and then choose File > Save As.

5 Save the library to your project folder with the name basiclib.plb, and click Save.

You can freely drag files among Project, Bin, and Library windows. The way you organize source files in these windows doesn't affect edits in the Timeline or the locations of the original files on disk. Note that dragging to or from a Library window makes a copy of the file reference in the destination window and doesn't remove the file from the original window. On the other hand, dragging between Project and Bin windows moves the clip from the original window. That's because a library is independent of a project, whereas a bin is part of the project.

Customizing Project, Bin, and Library windows

By default, Premiere displays the file list as the list of files with small icons that you see in the Project and Bin windows. You can customize the way a Project, Bin, or Library window displays the file list. The settings can be unique for each window.

1 Double-click the Graphics bin icon in the Project window to open the Graphics Bin window.

2 Choose Window > Bin Window Options.

3 Choose Thumbnail View from the menu at the top of the Bin Window Options dialog box.

Now you'll customize one of the four customizable fields. In this example you'll use the field to track the person responsible for providing the file.

4 In the Fields section, highlight the text **Label 1** in the second box and type **From** to replace the existing text.

5 Click OK.

You have changed the Bin window to Thumbnail view, which lists files using large icons. You can change options for most windows in Premiere by choosing the first command under the Window menu, as you did here. You can now use the field you customized.

6 Drag the lower right corner of the Bin window to the right to reveal the From column next to the Comment column.

7 In the From box for the clip Sun.ai, type **Maria.**

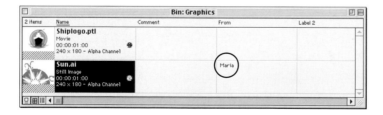

Premiere can also display the list as loose icons, which you can arrange by dragging. This time you'll use a faster method to change the view.

8 Click the Icon View icon at the bottom of the Bin window.

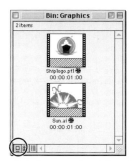  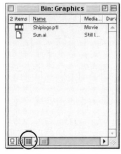

Click the Icon View, Thumbnail View, or List View buttons at the bottom left of a Project, Bin, or Library window to change the view (the same Bin window is shown).

◯ *If you can't see one or more icons in icon view, try choosing Project > Clean Up.*

Comments don't appear in icon view, but you can quickly see them by changing back to the list view again. You can use a different view button to do this.

9 Click the List View button at the bottom of the Bin window.

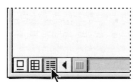

In list view, you can change the sort order directly. You'll sort this list by name.

10 Click the Name heading just under the title bar.

11 The work area has become a little cluttered. To clean it up, close the Library and Bin windows. If you made any changes to your library, you'll be prompted whether to save the changes. Click Yes if you want to preserve the changes.

The techniques you've learned to change the Bin window options also apply to the Project and Library windows. Although you can use these windows to manage source clips, you don't use them to edit the actual video program. In the following sections you'll learn about the windows you use for editing.

Saving and autosaving a project

Saving a project saves your editing decisions, references to source files, and the most recent arrangement of the program's windows. Protect your work by saving often. If you prefer, you can choose File > Preferences > Auto Save/Undo to make Premiere save your project automatically at a specified interval. Premiere can either save the project to the same file each time or to a new file. For example, you can set Premiere to save a new archive of your project every 15 minutes, producing a series of files that represent the state of your project at each interval. In this way, automatic archiving can serve as an alternate form of the Undo command, depending on how much the project changed between each save. Because project files are quite small compared to source video files, archiving many iterations of a project consumes relatively little disk space. Archived files are saved in the Project-Archives folder inside the Adobe Premiere 5.0 folder.

—From the Adobe Premiere User Guide, Chapter 2

Working with the Timeline window

You can assemble and edit your video in the Timeline window, a time-based representation of your project. When you start a new project, the Timeline is empty. In this project, clips exist in the Timeline because we've already started the project for you. The Timeline also includes a toolbox containing editing tools. In this section you'll learn how to locate controls for navigating time and editing.

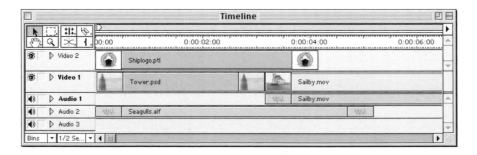

The Timeline window represents time horizontally. Clips earlier in time appear to the left, and clips later in time appear to the right. Time is indicated by the time ruler near the top of the Timeline window.

The Time Unit menu at the bottom of the Timeline indicates the time scale currently in use. You can change the time scale when you want to view time in more detail or see more of the video program.

1 Choose 4 Seconds from the Time Unit menu. The Timeline changes so that four seconds of video are shown for every major division in the time ruler.

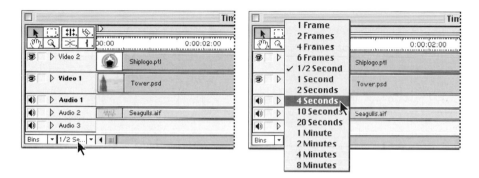

2 Choose 1 Frame from the Time Unit menu.

The Timeline now displays one frame at every time ruler division. At the time scale of 1 Frame you can make very precise edits in the Timeline, but you can't see very much of the video program at once.

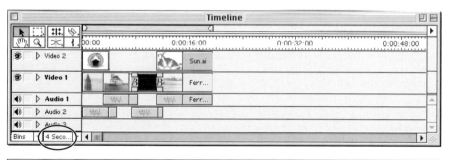

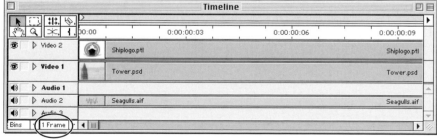

3 Click and hold the right scroll arrow at the bottom of the Timeline window to see parts of the video that are later in time. Because you're now using a highly magnified time scale, scrolling through the Timeline takes longer.

You can also use handy keyboard shortcuts to zoom in and out relative to the current time scale.

4 Press - (hyphen key) to zoom out one level.

The Time Unit menu now indicates a time scale of 2 Frames. Press the same key again to zoom out one more level. You can zoom out to a time scale of 8 minutes per time ruler division, which lets you view an entire 3-hour program at once.

5 Press = (equal sign key) to zoom in one level. The Time Unit menu changes to indicate the new time scale.

6 Press \ (backslash key) to fit the entire video within the visible area of the Timeline.

Working with tracks

The Timeline window includes tracks where you arrange clips. Tracks are stacked vertically. When one clip is above another, both clips play back simultaneously.

Tracks are divided into three sections:

• In the center of the window, the Video 1 track is the main video editing track.

• All tracks above Video 1 are for superimposing clips over the Video 1 track.

• All tracks below Video 1 are for audio.

You can *expand* the superimposition and audio tracks, revealing controls such as those for fading opacity or audio gain.

1 Click the triangle next to the Video 1 track name.

Premiere expands the Video 1 track into the Video 1A, Transition, and Video 1B tracks so that the relationship between clips and transitions is clearer. You'll work with transitions in Lesson 4, "Adding Transitions."

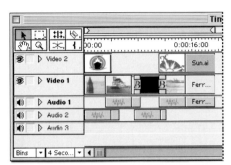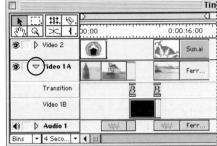

The Video 1 track collapsed (left) and expanded (right).

2 Click the triangle next to the Video 2 track name. Premiere expands the Video 2 track. Two clips exist on the Video 2 track:

• Shiplogo.ptl is a still image with transparency settings applied to it so that another clip (Tower.psd on track Video 1A) is visible under the later end of the clip. You'll work with transparency in Lesson 9, "Superimposing."

• Sun.ai is a still image created in Adobe Illustrator with transparency settings to reveal another clip (Ferry.mov on track Video 1A) underneath. The red line sloping upward is the clip's opacity control, indicating that Sun.ai starts completely transparent and gradually becomes completely opaque.

3 Click the triangle next to the Video 2 track name to collapse the track.

Notice the red line along the bottom edge of the clip Shiplogo.ptl. This indicates that motion settings are applied to the clip. You'll work with motion settings in Lesson 10, "Adding Motion."

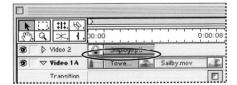

Similarly, a blue line appears along the top edge of the clip Sailby.mov. This indicates that a filter is applied to the clip. You'll work with filters in Lesson 11, "Applying Video and Audio Filters."

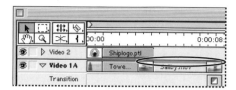

4 Click the triangle next to the Audio 1 track name.

Premiere expands the Audio 1 track and reveals the red fade and blue pan controls for the audio clips on that track. The red line in the audio track indicates the audio gain level at any point in time. You'll work with audio in Lesson 5, "Adding Audio."

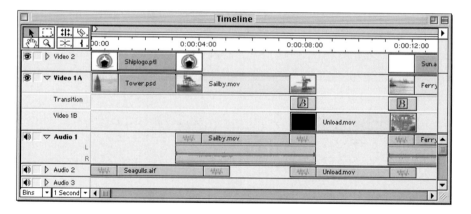

5 Click the triangle next to the Audio 1 track name to collapse the track.

The Timeline also includes editing tools, which are covered in more detail throughout this book. As you learn tools, you can use Tool Tips to identify them and their keyboard shortcuts; see "Learning keyboard shortcuts" on page 64.

Working with the Monitor window

In addition to the Timeline, you can assemble clips in the Monitor window, which includes the Source view and the Program view:

• The Source view displays a single clip. You use the Source view to prepare a clip for inclusion in the video program or to edit a clip you've opened from the video program.

• The Program view displays the current state of the video program you are building. When you play the video program in Premiere, it appears in the Program view. You can think of it as an alternate view of the Timeline—the Timeline displays a time-based view of your video program, and the Program view displays a frame-based view of your video program.

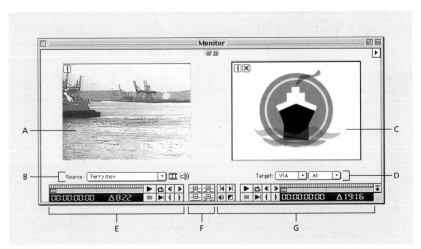

*A. Source view **B**. Source controls **C**. Program view **D**. Target controls **E**. Source controller*
*F. Controls for inserting a source clip into existing Timeline track **G**. Program controller*

The Monitor window includes controllers at the bottom of the window. The controls are grouped according to their function. Some controls work like the tape transport controls on a video deck.

It can be helpful to think of the Source view as a viewer for the Project window and the Program view as a viewer for the Timeline. When you open a project, by default the Source view is blank because you haven't worked with any source clips in the session yet, and the Program view displays the first frame in the Timeline if at least one clip is in the Timeline.

1 In the Project window, double-click the Ferry.mov icon.

The Source view displays the clip you double-clicked in the Project window. Double-clicking a clip in the Project window like this displays the uncut clip as it appears before any editing. However, if you double-click a clip in the Timeline, you see only those frames that are included in your video program. You'll try that now.

2 In the Timeline, double-click the file Sailby.mov.

Now the Source view displays a clip that was in the Timeline. You'll do this when you want to make changes to a clip that you previously added to the Timeline. You've viewed two clips in the Source view in this session, and Premiere remembers them in the Source view menu below the Source view in the Monitor window.

3 Position the pointer over the Source view menu and hold down the mouse button. The two clips you've viewed in this session are listed so that you can go back to them at any time. When you close this project, the Source view menu will be reset.

Because the Program view and the Timeline are different views of the same video program, you can edit video using either window. If you're learning how to edit video, you may find it easier to edit in the more graphical Timeline. Editors experienced in using high-end video-editing systems may be able to edit faster and more precisely using the Source and Program controllers instead.

Navigating to a specific time

The edit line in the Timeline window indicates the frame displayed in the Program view in the Monitor window and the point in time where the next edit will apply when using a command or a control in the Monitor window. Using the Program controller affects the Timeline, and editing the Timeline updates the Program view.

1 In the Timeline window, click in the ruler at the top of the window or drag in the ruler to move the edit line right or left (a technique called *scrubbing*). Both the Program view and the timecode display below the Program view change to represent the current frame.

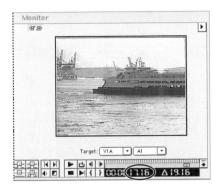

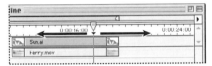

You may have noticed that when the Program view changed, the only frames visible were those of the topmost clips in the Timeline. Simply dragging the edit line doesn't display opacity, transitions, or filter effects. You can view those effects using another method.

2 Hold down Alt (Windows) or Option (Mac OS) as you drag in the ruler. There may be a slight delay as effects are processed.

Note: You must press and Alt/Option key before you begin dragging in the ruler.

Now the Program view displays frames with opacity, transitions, and effects of filters you've applied to a clip.

Using palettes

Adobe Premiere provides several palettes to display information and help you modify the Timeline. By default, all palettes are open. You can open, close, or group palettes as you work. The palettes work the same way as the palettes in Adobe Photoshop, Illustrator, and PageMaker.

If you have more than one monitor connected to your system and your operating system supports a multiple-monitor desktop, you can drag palettes to any monitor.

Using the Info palette

The Info palette displays information about a selected clip or transition. The information displayed in the palette may vary depending on the media type and the current window. The Info palette can be helpful in identifying the many kinds of content you can include in your project and the attributes of those contents.

1 Make sure the Info palette is visible. If necessary, click the Info tab (if visible) or choose Window > Show Info.

2 Select the audio clip Seagulls.aif in the Timeline. The Info palette reports the clip's name, duration, and audio attributes, its location in the Timeline, and the position of the cursor.

3 Drag the audio clip Seagulls.aif to the right. As you drag, the Info palette continuously updates the clip's position so that you can move it precisely.

4 Choose Edit > Undo Move to return the clip you dragged to its original position.

If you dragged the clip multiple times, just choose the Undo command multiple times until it returns to its original position.

5 Select the clip Sun.ai in the Timeline. This time the Info palette identifies the clip as a still image.

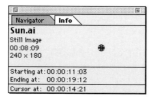

6 Select the gap between the first and second clips on the Video 2 track. The Info palette indicates the duration of the gap in the Timeline.

Using the Navigator palette

The Navigator palette is an interactive miniature view of the entire Timeline, providing convenient ways to quickly change your view of the Timeline. It's especially useful when you work with a long video program that extends far beyond the edges of the Timeline window.

1 Make sure both the Timeline and the Navigator palette are visible. If necessary, click the Navigator tab (if visible) or choose Window > Show Navigator.

The Navigator palette represents all tracks in your video program. The controls in the Navigator palette let you change the time scale at which the Timeline is displayed. The Navigator palette is color-coded to indicate various parts of the Timeline, as shown below.

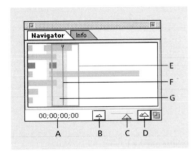

A. Double-click, type a time to position the edit line, and press Enter or Return.
B. Click to reduce the Timeline (zoom out).
C. Drag left to reduce or right to magnify the Timeline.
D. Click to magnify the Timeline (zoom in).
E. Drag the green rectangle to see the hidden areas of the Timeline.
F. Press Shift and drag to move the edit line, indicated in red.
G. The blue area indicates the current work area, which will play back during a preview.

The Navigator palette also color-codes track types to help you identify them. Video tracks are yellow, transitions are blue, and audio tracks are green.

2 Click the zoom-in (bottom right) button in the Navigator palette.

The Timeline zooms in to the next higher time scale. As you do this, the green rectangle becomes narrower, because you're now seeing less of the video program in the Timeline.

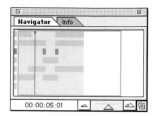 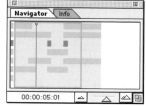

3 Drag the green rectangle. As you drag, the visible area in the Timeline changes accordingly.

4 Press and hold Shift as you drag the green rectangle.

This time, the visible area doesn't change, but as you drag, the Timeline edit line moves and the Program view in the Monitors window displays the frame at the edit line.

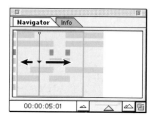

5 Highlight the time display at the bottom of the Navigator palette, type **200**, and press Enter (Windows) or Return (Mac OS). The edit line moves to frame 00:00:02:00 in the Timeline, the Navigator palette, and in the timecode display in the Program view.

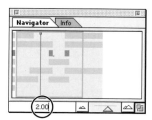

Using the Commands palette

The Commands palette comes with a list of preset commands that you can modify to suit your needs. You can create a custom set of buttons for fast access to your favorite menu commands, and assign a function key to each button for instant keyboard access. In this section you'll add a button that performs the Select All command. In your own work, you'll want to add the commands you use most frequently.

1 Make sure the Commands palette is visible. If necessary, click the Commands tab (if visible) or choose Window > Show Commands.

2 Choose Edit Command Set from the Commands palette menu.

3 Click Add. A new, unassigned button labeled "None" (Windows) or "Undefined" (Mac OS) appears above the selected command.

4 With the new None or Undefined button selected, choose Edit > Select All from the menu bar. When you're in this dialog box, choosing a command adds the command to the palette.

5 For Key, choose any available keyboard shortcut, such as Shift + F7. The menu displays only keys that are not already assigned to other commands (Windows) or dims keys that are already assigned to other commands (Mac OS). Click OK.

Note: In Windows, the F1 key is reserved for online Help by the system.

You're ready to try your new button.

6 Click to activate a window that allows clip selection, such as the Project window or the Timeline.

7 In the Commands palette, click the Select All button you just created or press the keyboard shortcut you chose. All the clips in the window are selected.

You've added this command as an exercise for this lesson. It now exists in Premiere for any project you open. If you don't want to keep it, do the next two steps.

8 Choose Edit Command Set from the Commands palette menu.

9 Make sure Select All is selected, click Delete, and click OK.

💡 *If you don't like the default keyboard shortcut for a command, you can use the Commands palette to override it: A keyboard shortcut in the Commands palette takes precedence over a corresponding built-in shortcut.*

Learning keyboard shortcuts

Premiere provides keyboard shortcuts for most commands and buttons, so it is possible to edit a video program with minimal use of the mouse. As you develop a working style, you can speed up your work by learning the keyboard shortcuts for the commands and buttons you use the most. Some experienced video editors can edit faster using the keyboard than the mouse. In this section you'll learn how to find the keyboard shortcuts you need.

As in other software, if a menu command has a keyboard shortcut, you'll find it next to the command on its menu.

1 In the Timeline, click any clip.

2 Click the Clip menu to view the menu commands. Note the keyboard shortcuts to the right of most commands.

Premiere also contains many tools and buttons, and you can find their keyboard shortcuts just as easily. Now you'll find the shortcut for a button in the Monitors window.

3 Click the Monitors window to activate it.

4 Move the pointer over the Mark Out button (⊦) on the Source controller, and hold the pointer over the button until its Tool Tip appears. The keyboard shortcut appears in parentheses after the tool description. (If Tool Tips do not appear, choose File > Preferences > General / Still Image and make sure Show Tool Tips is selected.)

Now you'll find a keyboard shortcut in online Help.

5 Choose Help > Keyboard (Windows) or Help > Keyboard Shortcuts (Mac OS).

6 Use the controls to find the shortcut you want.

An equally complete listing of keyboard shortcuts appears on the *Quick Reference Card*, included in the Adobe Premiere package.

Review questions

1 What can you do with the Source view in the Monitors window?

2 What can you do with the Program view in the Monitors window?

3 What's the difference between a bin and a library?

4 What are two ways to see finer increments of time in the Timeline window?

5 How can you customize a keyboard shortcut for a command?

Answers

1 You can view a clip from a Project, Bin, or Library window, prepare a clip for inclusion in the Timeline, or edit a clip you opened from the Timeline.

2 You can edit clips already added to the Timeline.

3 A bin exists inside a specific project. A library exists independently of all projects.

4 Any of these are correct: You can choose a time scale from the Time Unit menu, press = (equal sign key), click the zoom-in button, or drag the magnification slider in the Navigator palette.

5 Add a command to the Commands palette and then assign a keyboard shortcut to the command.

Lesson 2

1. Create

6. CD-ROM

3. Deluxe

Assemble

Acrobat

4. World Wide Web

1. Create

About Digital Video Editing

When you edit video, you arrange source clips so that they tell a story. That story can be anything from a fictional television program to a news event and more. Understanding the issues that affect your editing decisions can help you prepare for successful editing and save you valuable time and resources.

This lesson describes Premiere's role in video production and introduces a variety of key concepts:

• Measuring video time.

• Measuring frame size and resolution.

• Compressing video data.

• Capturing video.

• Superimposing and transparency.

• Using audio in a video.

• Creating final video.

How Premiere fits into video production

Making video involves working through three general phases:

• *Pre-production* involves writing the script, visualizing scenes by sketching them on a storyboard, and creating a production schedule for shooting the scenes.

• *Production* involves shooting the scenes.

• *Post-production* involves editing the best scenes into the final video program, correcting and enhancing video and audio where necessary. Editing includes a first draft, or *rough cut*, where you can get a general idea of the possibilities you have with the clips available to you. As you continue editing, you refine the video program through successive iterations until you decide that it's finished. At that point you have built the *final cut*. Premiere is designed for efficient editing, correcting, and enhancing of clips, making it a valuable tool for post-production.

The rest of this chapter describes fundamental concepts that affect video editing and other post-production tasks in Premiere. All of the concepts in this section and the specific Premiere features that support them are described in more detail in the *Adobe Premiere 5.0 User Guide*.

If any stage of your project involves outside vendors, such as video post-production facilities, consult with them before starting the project. They can help you determine what settings to use at various stages of a project and avoid time-consuming, costly mistakes. For example, if you're creating video for broadcast, you should know whether you are creating video for the NTSC (National Television Standards Committee) standard used primarily in North America and Japan, the PAL (Phase Alternate Line) standard used primarily in Europe, Asia, and southern Africa, or the SECAM (Sequential Couleur Avec Memoire) standard used primarily in France, the Middle East, and North Africa.

Measuring video time

In the natural world, we experience time as a continuous flow of events. However, working with video requires precise synchronization, so it's necessary to measure time using numbers. Familiar time divisions—hours, minutes, and seconds—are not precise enough for video editing, because a single second might contain several events. This section describes how Premiere and video professionals measure time, using standard methods which count fractions of a second in frames.

How the timebase and frame rates affect each other

You determine how time is divided in your project by specifying the project *timebase*. For example, a timebase of 30 means that each second is divided into 30 units. The exact time at which an edit occurs depends on the timebase you specify, because an edit can only occur at a time division, and using a different timebase causes the time divisions to fall in different places.

The time divisions in a source clip are determined by the *source frame rate*. For example, when you shoot source clips using a video camera with a frame rate of 30 frames per second, the camera records the scene every 1/30th of a second. Note that whatever was happening between those 1/30th of a second intervals is not recorded, so a higher frame rate provides higher time resolution.

You determine how often Premiere generates frames from your project by specifying the *project frame rate*. For example, a frame rate of 30 frames per second means that Premiere will create 30 frames from each second of your project.

For smooth and consistent playback, the timebase, the source frame rate, and the project frame rate should be identical. In general, use 24 fps (frames per second) for editing motion-picture film, 25 fps for editing PAL and SECAM video, 29.97 fps for editing NTSC video, and 30 fps for other video types. (NTSC was originally designed for a black-and-white picture at 30 fps, but signal modifications made in the mid-20th century to accommodate color pictures altered the standard NTSC frame rate to 29.97 fps.)

Sometimes the time systems don't match. For example, you might be asked to create a video intended for CD-ROM distribution that must combine motion-picture source clips captured at 24 fps with video source clips captured at 30 fps, using a timebase of 30 for a final CD-ROM frame rate of 15 fps. When any of these values don't match, it is mathematically necessary for some frames to be repeated or omitted; the effect may be distracting or imperceptible depending on the differences between the timebase and frame rates you used in your project.

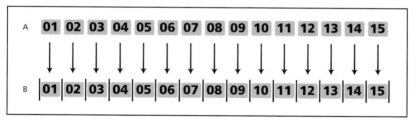

A. 30 fps video clip (one-half second shown). *B. Timebase of 30, for a video production. When the source frame rate matches the timebase, all frames display as expected.*

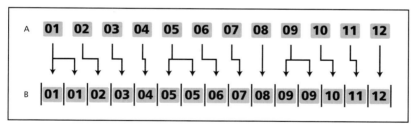

A. 24 fps motion-picture source clip (one-half second shown). *B. Timebase of 30, for a video production. To play one second of 24 fps frames at a timebase of 30, source frames 1, 5, and 9 are repeated.*

💡 *Always capture your clips at the same frame rate at which you plan to export it. For example, if you know your source clips will be exported at 30 fps, capture the clips at 30 fps instead of 24 fps.*

When time systems don't match, the most important value to set is the timebase, which you should choose appropriately for the most critical final medium. For example, if you are preparing a motion picture trailer that you also want to show on television, you might decide that motion picture is the most important medium for the project, and specify a timebase of 24.

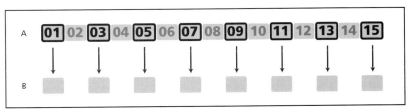

A. Timebase of 30 (one-half second shown). ***B.*** *Final frame rate of 15, for a Web movie. When the timebase is evenly divisible by the frame rate, timebase frames are included evenly.*

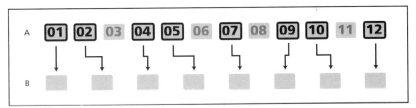

A. Timebase of 24 for a motion-picture film (one-half second shown). ***B.*** *Final frame rate of 15, for a Web movie. The time is not evenly divisible by the frame rate, so frames are included unevenly. A final frame rate of 12 fps would generate frames more evenly.*

The important thing to remember is this: You'll get the most predictable results if your timebase and frame rate are identical, or are at least even multiples of each other.

[?] For more information, see "Measuring time" in online Help, or Appendix A in the Adobe Premiere User Guide.

Counting time with timecode

Timecode defines how frames are counted and affects the way you view and specify time throughout a project. Timecode never changes the timebase or frame rate of a clip or project—it only changes how frames are numbered.

You specify a timecode style based on the media most relevant to your project. For example, you count frames differently when editing video for television than when editing for motion-picture film. By default, Premiere displays time using the SMPTE (Society of Motion Picture and Television Engineers) video timecode, where a duration of 00:06:51:15 indicates that a clip plays for 6 minutes, 51 seconds, and 15 frames. At any time, you can change to another system of time display, such as feet and frames of 16mm or 35mm film. Professional videotape decks and camcorders can read and write timecode directly onto the videotape, which lets you synchronize audio, video, and edits, or edit offline (see page 84).

When you use the NTSC-standard timebase of 29.97, the fractional difference between this timebase and 30 fps timecode causes a difference between the displayed duration of the program and its actual duration. While tiny at first, this difference grows as program duration increases, preventing you from accurately creating a program of a specific length. *Drop-frame timecode* is a SMPTE standard for 29.97 fps video that eliminates this error, preserving NTSC time accuracy. When you use drop-frame timecode, Premiere renumbers the first two frames of every minute except for every tenth minute. For example, the frame after 59:29 is labeled 1:00:02. No frames are lost, because drop-frame timecode doesn't actually drop frames, only frame numbers. Premiere indicates drop-frame timecode by displaying semicolons between the numbers in time displays throughout the software, and displays non-drop-frame timecode by displaying colons between numbers in timecode displays.

Drop-frame timecode uses semicolons (left) and non-drop-frame timecode uses colons (right).

Interlaced and non-interlaced video

A picture on a television or computer monitor consists of horizontal lines. There is more than one way to display those lines. Most personal computers display using *progressive scan* (or non-interlaced) display, in which all lines in a frame are displayed in one pass from top to bottom before the next frame appears. Television standards such as NTSC, PAL, and SECAM standards are *interlaced*, where each frame is divided into two *fields*. Each field contains every other horizontal line in the frame. A TV displays the first field of alternating lines over the entire screen, and then displays the second field to fill in the alternating gaps left by the first field. One NTSC video frame, displayed approximately every 1/30th of a second, contains two interlaced fields, displayed approximately every 1/60th of a second each. PAL and SECAM video frames display at 1/25 of a second and contain two interlaced fields displayed every 1/50th of a second each. The field that contains the topmost scan line in the frame is called the *upper field*, and the other field is called the *lower field*. When playing back or exporting to interlaced video, make sure the field order you specify matches the receiving video system, otherwise motion may appear stuttered, and edges of objects in the frame may break up with a comb-like appearance.

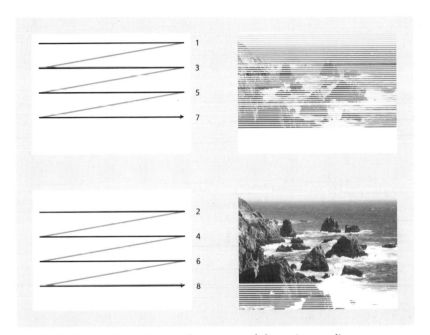

Interlaced video describes a frame with two passes of alternating scan lines.

Progressive-scan video describes a frame with one pass of sequential scan lines.

> ### Deinterlacing video
>
> *If you plan to slow down or hold a frame in an interlaced video clip, you may want to prevent flickering or visual stuttering by* deinterlacing *its frames, which converts the interlaced fields into complete frames. If you're using progressive-scan source clips (such as motion-picture film or computer-generated animation) in a video intended for an interlaced display such as television, you can separate frames into fields using a process known as* field rendering *so that motion and effects are properly interlaced.*
>
> —From the Adobe Premiere User Guide, Appendix A

For more information, see "Processing interlaced video fields" in online Help, or Chapter 4 in the Adobe Premiere User Guide.

Measuring frame size and resolution

Several attributes of frame size are important when editing video digitally: pixel (picture element) and frame aspect ratio, clip resolution, project frame size, and bit depth. A *pixel* is the smallest unit that can be used to create a picture; you can't accurately display anything smaller than a pixel.

Aspect ratio

The *aspect ratio* of a frame describes the ratio of width to height in the dimensions of a frame. For example, the frame aspect ratio of NTSC video is 4:3, whereas some motion-picture frame sizes use the more elongated aspect ratio of 16:9.

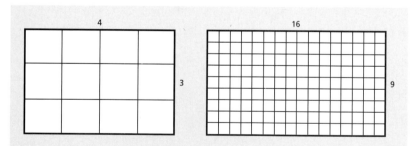

A frame using a 4:3 aspect ratio (left), and a frame using the wider 16:9 aspect ratio (right).

Some video formats use a different aspect ratio for the pixels that make up the frame. When a video using non-square pixels is displayed on a square-pixel system, or vice versa, shapes and motion appear stretched. For example, circles are distorted into ellipses.

A frame with square pixels (left), a frame with tall horizontal pixels (center), and the center frame again displayed using square pixels (right).

Frame size

In Premiere, you specify a *frame size* for playing back video from the Timeline, and if necessary, for exporting video to a file. Frame size is expressed by the horizontal and vertical dimensions of a frame; for example, 640 by 480 pixels. In digital video editing, frame size is also referred to as *resolution*. In general, higher resolution preserves more image detail and requires more memory to edit. As you increase frame dimensions, you increase the number of pixels Premiere must process and store for each frame, so it's important to know how much resolution your final video format requires. For example, a 640 by 480 pixel NTSC frame contains 307,200 pixels, while a 720 by 576 PAL image contains 349,920 pixels. If you specify too low a resolution, the picture will look coarse and pixelated; specify too high a resolution and you'll use more memory than necessary.

Overscan and safe zones

Frame size can be misleading if you're preparing video for television. Most NTSC consumer television sets enlarge the picture; however, this pushes the outer edges of the picture off the screen. This process is called *overscan*. Because the amount of overscan is not consistent across all televisions, you should keep action and titles inside two safe areas—*action-safe* and *title-safe*. The action-safe zone is a margin, about the width of a typical amount of overscan, around all sides of a frame. The title-safe zone is a margin that extends further into the frame than the action-safe zone. The title-safe zone helps ensure that text and important graphics are completely displayed, and avoids the distortion of text and graphics which can occur toward the edges of many televisions. Always anticipate overscan by using safe zones, keeping important action and text within them, and testing the video on an actual television monitor.

A. A title-safe zone *B. An action-safe zone*

Safe zones are indicated by dotted lines in Premiere's Title window. See "About titles" on page 225.

Bit depth

In a computer, a *bit* is the most basic unit of information storage. The more bits are used to describe something, the more detailed the description can be. *Bit depth* indicates the number of bits set aside for describing the color of one pixel. The higher the bit depth, the more colors the image can contain, which allows more precise color reproduction and higher picture quality. For example, an image storing 8 bits per pixel (8-bit color) can display 256 colors, and a 24-bit color image can display approximately 16 million colors.

How much is enough?

The bit depth required for high quality depends on the color format used by the video-capture card. Many capture cards use the YUV color format, which can store high-quality video using 16 bits per pixel. Before transferring video to your computer, video-capture cards that use YUV convert it to the 24-bit RGB color format which Premiere uses. For the best RGB picture quality, save source clips and still images with 24 bits of color (although you can use clips with lower bit depths). If the clip contains an alpha channel mask, save it from the source application using 32 bits per pixel (also referred to as 24 bits with an 8-bit alpha channel, or Millions of Colors+). For example, QuickTime movies can contain up to 24 bits of color with an 8-bit alpha channel, depending on the exact format used. Internally, Premiere always processes clips using 32 bits per pixel regardless of each clip's original bit depth. This helps preserve image quality when you apply effects or superimpose clips.

—From the Adobe Premiere User Guide, Appendix A

If you're preparing video for NTSC, keep in mind that although both 16-bit YUV and 24-bit RGB provide a full range of color, the color range of NTSC is limited in comparison. NTSC cannot accurately reproduce saturated colors and subtle color gradients. The best way to anticipate problems with NTSC color is to preview your video on a properly calibrated NTSC monitor during editing.

For more information, see "Previewing on another monitor" in online Help or in Chapter 4 of the Adobe Premiere User Guide.

Understanding video data compression

Editing digital video involves storing, moving, and calculating extremely large volumes of data compared to other kinds of computer files. Many personal computers, particularly older models, are not equipped to handle the high *data rates* (amount of video information processed each second) and file sizes of uncompressed digital video. Use *compression* to lower the data rate of digital video into a range that your computer system can handle. Compression settings are most relevant when capturing source video, previewing edits, playing back the Timeline, and exporting the Timeline. In many cases, the settings you specify won't be the same for all situations:

• It's a good idea to compress video coming into your computer. Your goal is to retain as much picture quality as you can for editing, while keeping the data rate within your computer's limits.

• You should also compress video going out of your computer. Try to achieve the best picture quality for playback. If you're creating a videotape, keep the data rate within the limits of the computer that will play back the video to videotape. If you're creating video to be played back on another computer, keep the data rate within the limits of the computer models you plan to support.

Applying the best compression settings can be tricky, and the best settings can vary with each project. If you apply too little compression, the data rate will be too high for the system, causing errors such as dropped frames. If you apply too much compression, lowering the data rate too far, you won't be taking advantage of the full capacity of the system and the picture quality may suffer unnecessarily. You can use the Data Rate Analyzer to evaluate any video file.

For information on the Data Rate Analyzer, see "Analyzing clip properties and data rate" in online Help or in Chapter 3 of the Adobe Premiere User Guide.

Choosing a video compression method

The goal of data compression is to represent the same content using less data. You can specify a compressor/decompressor, or *codec*, that manages compression. A codec may use one or more strategies for compression because no single method is best for all situations. The following list describes the most common strategies used by codecs and the kinds of video they are intended to compress:

Spatial compression Spatial (space) compression looks for ways to compact a single frame by looking for pattern and repetition among pixels. For example, instead of describing each of several thousand pixels in a picture of a blue sky, spatial compression can record a much shorter description, such as "All the pixels in this area are light blue." *Run-length* *encoding* is a version of this technique that is used by many codecs. Codecs that use spatial compression, such as QuickTime Animation or Microsoft RLE, work well with video containing large solid areas of color, such as cartoon animation.

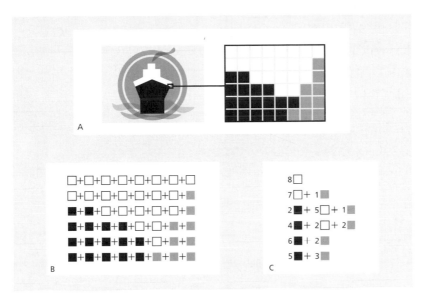

*Digital images are composed of pixels (**A**), which consume a lot of disk space when stored without compression (**B**). Applying run-length encoding stores the same frame data in much less space (**C**).*

In general, as you increase spatial compression, the data rate and file size decrease, and the picture loses sharpness and definition. However, some forms of run-length encoding preserve picture quality completely, but require more processing power.

Temporal compression Temporal (time) compression compacts the changes during a sequence of frames by looking for patterns and repetition over time. In some video clips, such as a clip of a television announcer, temporal compression will notice that the only pixels that change from frame to frame are those forming the face of the speaker. All the other pixels don't change (when the camera is motionless). Instead of describing every pixel in every frame, temporal compression describes all the pixels in the first frame, and then for each frame that follows, describes only the pixels that are different from the previous frame. This technique is called *frame differencing*. When most of the pixels in a frame are different from the previous frame, it's preferable to describe the entire frame again. Each whole frame is called a *keyframe*, which sets a new starting point for frame differencing. You can use Premiere to control how keyframes are created (see the *Adobe Premiere 5.0 User Guide*). Many codecs use temporal compression, including Cinepak. If you can't set keyframes for a codec, chances are it doesn't use temporal compression. Temporal compression works best when large areas in the video don't change, and is less effective when the image constantly changes, such as in a music video.

In this clip, the only change is the circle around the ship.

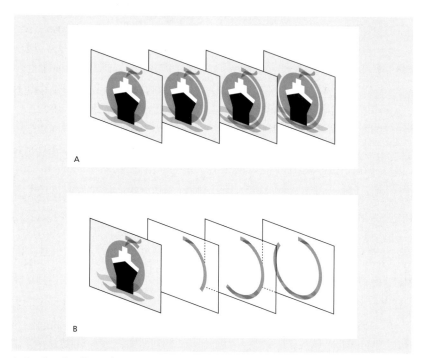

A. Storing the clip without compression records all pixels in all frames. B. Applying temporal compression creates a keyframe from the first frame, and subsequent frames record only the changes.

Lossless and lossy compression Some codecs use *lossless* compression, which ensures that all of the information—and thus all of the quality—in the original clip is preserved after compression. However, preserving the original level of quality limits the degree to which you can lower the data rate and file size, and the resulting data rate may be too high for smooth playback. Other compression methods use *lossy* compression, which discards some of the original data during compression. For example, if the pixels making up a sky actually contain 78 shades of blue, a lossy codec set for less than best quality may record 60 shades of blue. Lossy compression allows much lower data rates and file sizes than lossless compression, so lossy codecs such as Cinepak or Sorenson Video are commonly used for final production of video delivered using CD-ROM or the Internet. Lossless codecs such as Animation (at the Best quality setting) are used to preserve maximum quality during editing or for still images where data rate is not an issue.

Asymmetrical and symmetrical compression The codec you choose affects your production workflow, not just in file size or playback speed, but in the time required for a codec to compress a given number of frames. Fast compression helps video production, and fast decompression makes viewing easier, but many codecs take far more time to compress frames than to decompress them during playback. This is why a 30-second clip may take a few minutes to process before playback. A codec is considered *symmetrical* when it requires the same amount of time to compress as to decompress a clip. A codec is *asymmetrical* when the times required to compress and decompress a clip are significantly different.

Compressing video is like packing a suitcase—you can pack as fast as you unpack by simply throwing clothes into the suitcase, but if you spend more time to fold and organize the clothes in the suitcase, you can fit more clothes in the same space.

Capturing video

Before you can edit your video program, all source clips must be instantly accessible from a hard disk, not from videotape. You import the source clips from the source videotapes to your computer through a post-production step called *video capture*. You must have a hard disk big enough to store all the clips you want to edit, so to save space, capture just the clips you know you want to use.

Capturing to support online or offline editing

Depending on the level of quality you want and the capabilities of your equipment, you may be able to use Premiere for either online or offline editing. The settings you specify for video capture are different for offline or online editing.

About online and offline editing

Online editing *is the practice of doing all editing (including the rough cut) on the same computer that will produce the final cut. Previously, online editing had to be done on expensive high-end workstations designed to handle the picture quality and high volumes of data created by broadcast-quality video. Today, continuing improvements in the speed of personal computers make online editing increasingly practical for broadcast television or motion-picture film productions. For online editing, you capture clips once at the highest level of quality your computer and its connected hardware can handle.*

In offline editing, *you edit video using lower-quality copies of the original clips and produce the final version on a high-end system using the original clips. When you capture video for offline editing, you specify settings that emphasize editing speed over picture quality. In most cases you need only enough quality to mark the beginning and ending frames for each scene. Once you have completed the offline edit in Premiere, you export a text file of scene sequences called an* edit decision list, *or EDL. You then move the EDL to an* edit controller *on a high-end system, which applies the sequence worked out in Premiere to the original high-quality clips. In this way, the editing work done on a slower, less-expensive workstation is used to create the final cut on a more expensive, higher-quality workstation.*

—From the Adobe Premiere User Guide, Chapter 3

Offline editing requires clips captured with frame-accurate timecode (see "Counting time with timecode" on page 73). To do this, use device control to capture clips (see "Using device control to capture or export video" on page 87).

Components that affect video capture quality

Video capture requires a higher and more consistent level of computer performance—far more than you need to run general office software, and even more than you need to work with image-editing software. Getting professional results depends on the performance and capacity of all of the components of your system working together to move frames from the video-capture card to the processor and hard disk. The ability of your computer to capture video depends on the combined performance of the following components:

Video-capture card You need video-capture hardware—either a video-capture card or equivalent capability built into your computer—to transfer video between a videotape deck (or other video source) and your computer. Note that a video-capture card is not the same as the video card that drives your computer monitor. Premiere is sold with many video-capture cards, which usually include non-Premiere software written by the card manufacturer to control the specific card type.

Your video-capture card must be fast enough to capture video at the level of quality that your final medium requires. For full-screen, full-motion NTSC video, the card must be capable of capturing thirty frames (sixty fields) per second at 640 by 480 pixels without dropping frames; for PAL and SECAM, twenty-five frames (fifty fields) per second at 720 by 576 pixels (see "Interlaced and non-interlaced video" on page 74). However, if you're capturing video for a project requiring a smaller frame size or lower frame rate than those listed here, such as for Internet video, save processing time and disk space by specifying the lower values more appropriate to your medium.

Hard disk The hard disk stores the video frames you capture. It must be fast enough to store captured video frames as quickly as they arrive from the video card, otherwise frames will be dropped as the disk falls behind. For capturing at the NTSC video standard of just under 30 frames per second, your hard disk should have an average (not minimum) access time of 10 milliseconds (ms) or less, and a sustained (not peak) data transfer rate of at least 3 MB per second but preferably around 6 MB per second. (The *access time* is how fast a hard disk can reach specific data. The *data transfer rate* is how fast the hard disk can move data to and from the rest of the computer.) Due to factors such as system overhead, the actual data transfer rate for video capture is usually about half the stated data transfer rate of the drive. For best results, capture to a separate high-performance hard disk intended for use with video capture and editing, such as an AV (audio-video)-certified hard disk configuration with a SCSI 2, Ultra SCSI, or Ultra DMA IDE drive, or a disk array. The state of high-end video hardware changes rapidly; consult the manufacturer of your video-editing card for suggestions about appropriate video storage hardware.

Central processing unit (CPU) Your computer's processor—such as a Pentium or PowerPC chip—handles general processing tasks in your computer. It must be fast enough to process captured frames at the capture frame rate. A faster CPU or using multiple CPUs in one computer (multiprocessing) is better. However, other system components must be fast enough to handle the CPU speed. Using a fast CPU with slow components is like driving a sports car in a traffic jam.

Codec (compressor/decompressor) Most video-capture cards come with a compression chip that keeps the data rate within a level your computer can handle (see "Understanding video data compression" on page 79). If your video-capture hardware doesn't have a compression chip, capture using a fast, high-quality codec such as Motion JPEG. If you capture using a slow-compressing or lossy codec such as Cinepak, you'll drop frames or lose quality.

Processing time required by other software If you capture video while several other programs are running (such as virtual memory, network connections, non-essential system enhancers, and screen savers), the other programs will probably interrupt the video capture with requests for processing time, causing dropped frames. Capture video while running as few drivers, extensions, and other programs as possible. In Mac OS, turn off AppleTalk. See the Mac OS documentation or online Help.

Data bus Every computer has a data bus that connects system components and handles data transfer between them. Its speed determines how fast the computer can move video frames between the video-capture card, the processor, and the hard disk. If you purchased a high-end computer or a computer designed for video editing, the data bus speed is likely to be well matched to the other components. However, if you've upgraded an older computer with a video-capture card, a faster processor, or a hard disk, an older data bus may limit the speed benefits of the new components. Before upgrading components, review the documentation provided by the manufacturer of your computer to determine whether your data bus can take advantage of the speed of a component you want to add.

Using device control to capture or export video

You can control some videotape decks from within Premiere by using device control. This lets you use the source playback controller in Premiere to operate a deck directly, making it much easier to capture video into your computer or print your project to videotape. To use device control, you'll need the following items:

• A frame-accurate videotape deck that supports external device control.

• A cable that connects the deck to your computer.

• Premiere-compatible plug-in software that lets you control the tape deck directly from Premiere (usually included by the deck manufacturer).

• Source videotape recorded with timecode (see "Counting time with timecode" on page 73).

Device control is not available on consumer videocassette recorders (VCRs). Device-control decks are sold by dealers of professional video equipment, and are more expensive than VCRs.

[?] For more information, see "Capturing video with device control" in online Help or in Chapter 3 of the Adobe Premiere User Guide.

Understanding transparency and superimposing

Transparency allows a clip (or any part of it) to reveal a second, underlying clip, so that you can create composites, transitions, or other effects. Several kinds of transparency are possible in Premiere:

Matte or mask A matte or mask is an image that specifies transparent or semitransparent areas for another image. For example, if you want to superimpose an object in one clip over the background of another clip, you can use a mask to remove the background of the first clip. You can use other still-image or motion graphics software to create a still-image or moving (traveling) matte and apply it to a clip in your Premiere project. In a mask, black areas are transparent, white areas are opaque, and gray areas are semitransparent—darker areas are more transparent than lighter areas. You can use shades of gray to create feathered (soft-edged) or graduated masks.

Alpha channel Color in an RGB video image is stored in three color *channels*—one red, one green, and one blue. An image can also contain a mask in a fourth channel called the *alpha channel*. By keeping an image together with its mask, you don't have to manage two separate files. (Saving a mask as a separate file can be useful in some cases, such as when creating a track matte effect. That's because the mask must be placed in a separate track in Premiere's Timeline. See "Applying the Track Matte transparency key type" on page 268.)

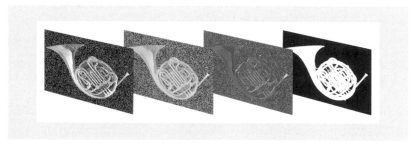

A 32-bit frame consisting of four 8-bit channels: red, green, blue, and an alpha channel mask.

Programs such as Adobe Photoshop and Adobe After Effects let you paint or draw a mask and use the alpha channel to keep the mask with the image or movie. Premiere uses the alpha channel for compositing.

The Photoshop image (left) contains an alpha channel mask (center) which Premiere uses to composite the subject against another background (right).

Keying Keying finds pixels in an image that match a specified color or brightness and makes those pixels transparent or semitransparent. For example, if you have a clip of a weatherman standing in front of a blue-screen background, you can *key out* that blue and replace it with a weather map.

Opacity You can control the degree of overall transparency for a clip. You can use opacity to fade a clip in or out.

You can combine the transparency options described here. For example, you can use a matte to remove the background from one clip and superimpose it over a second clip, and then use opacity to fade in the first clip's visible area.

Using audio in a video

In a video, audio can play an equally important role in telling your story. You can use Premiere to *mix* audio tracks. For example, you might combine each character's dialogue clips with ambient background sounds and a musical soundtrack. Mixing in Premiere can include any combination of the following tasks:

• Fading, or increasing or decreasing the level of an audio clip.

• Panning, or positioning audio anywhere to the left or right within a stereo field.

• Sweetening, or removing noise, enhancing frequency response and dynamic range, and adding sound effects.

When you import a video clip that contains audio, the audio track is *linked* to its video track by default so that they move together. When you edit superimposed video tracks, remember to consider the effects of your edits on the audio tracks.

Understanding digital audio

You hear sounds because your ear recognizes the variations in air pressure that create sound. *Analog audio* reproduces sound variations by creating or reading variations in an electrical signal. *Digital audio* reproduces sound by sampling the sound pressure or signal level at a specified rate and converting that to a number.

The quality of digital audio depends on the sample rate and bit depth. The *sample rate* is how often the audio level is digitized. A 44.1 kHz sample rate is audio-CD-quality, while CD-ROM or Internet audio often uses a sample rate of 22 kHz or below. The *bit depth* is the range of numbers used to describe an audio sample; 16 bits is audio-CD-quality. Lower bit depths and sample rates are not suitable for high-fidelity audio, but may be acceptable (though noisy) for dialogue. The file size of an audio clip increases or decreases as you increase or decrease the sample rate or bit depth.

Keeping audio in sync with video

Be mindful of audio sample rates in relation to the timebase and frame rate of your project. The most common mistake is to create a movie at 30 fps with audio at 44.1 kHz, and then play back the movie at 29.97 fps (for NTSC video). The result is a slight slowdown in the video, while the audio (depending on your hardware) may still be playing at the correct rate and therefore will seem to get ahead of the video. The difference between 30 and 29.97 results in a synchronization discrepancy that appears at a rate of 1 frame per 1000 frames, or 1 frame per 33.3 seconds (just under 2 frames per minute). If you notice audio and video drifting apart at about this rate, check for a project frame rate that doesn't match the timebase. Although the best solution for NTSC is to build all video and animation at 29.97 fps, you can also alter your audio sample rate from 44.1 kHz to 44.056 kHz (slowing audio playback by 0.1%), or build the audio source clip at 44.144 kHz at 30 fps (speeding up the original audio clip by 0.1%).

A similar problem can occur when editing motion-picture film after transferring it to video. Film audio is often recorded on a digital audio tape (DAT) recorder at 48 kHz synchronized with a film camera running at 24 fps. When the film is transferred to 30 fps video, the difference in the video frame rate will cause the audio to run ahead of the video unless you slow the DAT playback by 0.1% when transferring to the computer. Using your computer to convert the sample rate after the original recording doesn't help with this problem; the best solution is to record the original audio using a DAT deck that can record 0.1% fast (48.048 kHz) when synchronized with the film camera.

Older CD-ROM titles sometimes used an audio sample rate of 22.254 kHz; today, a rate of 22.250 kHz is more common. If you notice audio drifting at a rate accounted for by the difference between these two sample rates (1 frame every 3.3 seconds), you may be mixing new and old audio clips recorded at the two different sample rates.

Creating final video

Premiere provides a number of ways to create final video. If you want to create videotape or motion-picture film from a Premiere project, you must have either the proper hardware for video or film transfer or have access to a service provider that offers the equipment and services you require.

Exporting a video file You can export a file for viewing from a hard disk, removable cartridge, CD-ROM, or the World Wide Web. Through plug-in software modules, Premiere can also export formats provided by other software manufacturers. Some video-capture cards include plug-ins that export formats to Premiere. When exporting for hard disk or cartridge playback, you can use high quality settings. When exporting for low-bandwidth media such as CD-ROM or the World Wide Web, you'll lower the frame size and picture quality to achieve a low data rate.

Recording directly to videotape You can play a completed video program while a connected videotape deck records the video. Device control makes this easy. See "Using device control to capture or export video" on page 87. You'll specify the highest quality frame size and picture quality settings your system can handle.

Creating an edit decision list (EDL) You can have Premiere generate an EDL when you require a level of quality that your system cannot provide. An EDL creates a list of edits, synchronized to the original clips using timecode. This lets you re-create your edits precisely for the final cut using the high-quality original tapes in an online edit bay. Edit bays generally don't include the same feature set as Premiere, so some effects and transitions won't translate into the EDL.

🗈 You'll learn to export in many of the lessons in this book. For more information on the other output paths, see "Producing Final Video" in online Help or Chapter 11 in the Adobe Premiere User Guide.

Review questions

1 What's the difference between the timebase and the project frame rate?

2 Why is non-drop-frame timecode important for NTSC video?

3 How is interlaced display different from progressive scan?

4 Why is data compression important?

5 What's the difference between applying a mask and adjusting opacity?

6 What is an EDL and why is it useful?

Answers

1 The timebase specifies the time divisions in a project. The project frame rate specifies the final number of frames per second that are generated from the project. Movies with different frame rates can be generated from the same timebase; for example, you can export movies at 30, 15, and 10 frames per second from a timebase of 30.

2 Counting NTSC frames using 30 fps timecode will cause an increasingly inaccurate program duration due to the difference between 30 fps and the NTSC frame rate of 29.97 fps. Drop-frame timecode ensures that the duration of NTSC video is measured accurately.

3 Progressive scan displays a frame's scan lines in one pass. Interlacing displays a frame's scan lines in two alternating passes.

4 Without data compression, digital video and audio often produce a data rate too high for many computer systems to handle smoothly.

5 A mask is a separate channel or file that marks transparent or semitransparent areas within a frame. In Premiere, opacity specifies the transparency of an entire frame.

6 An EDL is an edit decision list, or a list of edits marked by timecode. It's useful whenever you have to transfer your work to another editing system because it lets you re-create a program using the timecode on the original clips.

Lesson 3

Basic Editing

Editing a video program is at the heart of the work you'll do with Adobe Premiere. Adobe Premiere makes it easy to trim video clips or other source files. You can then assemble the polished result for playback on a variety of media.

In this lesson, you'll create a 20-second video program about a horse training technique called *dressage*. You'll use these basic editing techniques:

- Assembling clips in the Timeline.
- Using the Monitor window to trim and insert clips.
- Previewing the video program.
- Setting In and Out points.
- Performing a ripple edit and a rolling edit.
- Making a QuickTime movie.

Getting started

For this lesson, you'll create a new project and then import the video clips. Make sure you know the location of the files used in this lesson. Insert the CD-ROM disc if necessary. For help, see "Using the Classroom in a Book files" on page 4.

To ensure that the Premiere preferences are set to the default values, exit Premiere, and then delete the preferences file as explained in "Restoring default preferences" on page 5.

1 Start Premiere.

2 In the New Project Settings dialog box, choose QuickTime for the Editing mode, and choose 30 for the Timebase.

The timebase specifies the frame rate (number of frames per second) that Premiere uses to calculate the precision of your editing.

Let's set some options Premiere will use when you export a movie at the end of this lesson.

3 Click the Next button to display the video settings.

4 (Windows only) Choose Video for the Compressor.

5 Type **240** in the first Frame Size field. Premiere automatically inserts 180 in the second field.

6 Choose 15 for the Frame Rate.

7 Click OK to close the New Project Settings dialog box.

The three main windows appear: the Project window, the Monitor window, and the Timeline window.

8 If necessary, rearrange windows and palettes so they don't overlap.

Before importing files, you'll simplify the interface by closing several palettes that you don't need right now.

9 Click the close box on the Transitions/Commands palette and on the Navigator/Info palette.

Viewing the finished movie

If you'd like to see what you'll be creating, you can take a look at the finished movie.

1 Choose File > Open and double-click the 03Final.mov file in the Final folder, inside the 03Lesson folder.

The video program opens in the Source view.

2 Click the Play button (▶) to view the video program.

Importing clips

Now you'll add files to the Project window.

1 Import files in one of the following ways, depending on your system:

• In Windows, choose File > Import > File and open the 03Lesson folder. Select all the files (but not the Final folder) by selecting the first file, holding down the Shift key, and then selecting the last file. Then click Open.

• In Mac OS, choose File > Import > Multiple, open the 03Lesson folder, select Field.mov, and then click Import. Do the same for the remaining files, but do not import the Final folder. Then click Done.

The video files are added to the Project window.

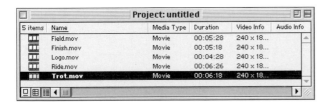

To make your clips a little easier to see in the Timeline, you'll change the view somewhat.

2 Click the title bar of the Timeline window to make it active. Then choose Window > Timeline Window Options. Select the medium icon size on the left and click OK.

3 Click the arrow next to the Video 1A track to collapse it.

Now you'll save and name the project.

4 Choose File > Save, type **Dressage.ppj** for the name, and 04Lesson folder for the location. Then click Save.

In Windows, the default file extension for Premiere projects, ppj, is added to your filename automatically. In Mac OS, type the extension as part of the filename.

Note: Each step in this lesson that directs you to make an edit includes the exact timecode used in the final movie. We recommend you locate the general area described in the step, then fine-tune the edit point by going to the timecode given. Using the timecode enables you to check your results against the figures in the procedure.

Methods of working in Premiere

Premiere provides two fundamental ways of assembling and trimming clips: dragging clips directly into the Timeline and trimming them there, and trimming clips in the Monitor window and then adding them to the Timeline. The method you use depends on your specific situations and tasks. You'll use the Source view of the Monitor window in this lesson. Throughout the Classroom in a Book lessons, you'll use both methods.

Dragging clips into the Timeline

When you want to quickly assemble a series of clips with little or no trimming (usually called a *rough cut*), you simply drag clips from the Project window directly into the Timeline. For this project, you'll use this method to assemble three clips as a way of evaluating an opening sequence. In a later exercise, you'll trim these clips to remove portions of them.

1 In the Project window, position the pointer on the Logo.mov clip icon and drag it into the Timeline, positioning it at the beginning of the Video 1 track. To drag files from the Project window, you must drag the file icon, not the filename.

2 In the same way, drag Field.mov from the Project window to the Timeline, snapping it to the end of the Logo.mov clip.

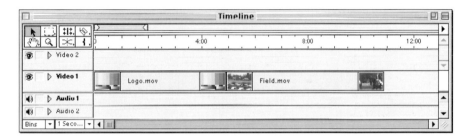

This time, you'll drag a clip into the Timeline and insert it between the two clips you just added.

3 Drag the Trot.mov clip into the Timeline, positioning it between Logo.mov and Field.mov so that a bar icon appears between the two clips.

When you release the mouse button, the Trot.mov clip is inserted between the other two clips. Using the same method, you can also insert a clip at the beginning of the Timeline, in front of a previously inserted clip.

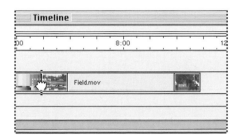
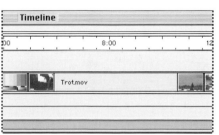

4 Choose File > Save to save the project.

You've just assembled a short rough cut. Next, you'll find out how to preview the cut.

A clip in the Timeline can include the clip name, but it may not be displayed if the clip is too short or if you select the track format that does not include a name. To see the name of a clip in the Timeline, click the Timeline title bar to activate it, if necessary, and then simply position the pointer on the clip.

Previewing

Editing a video program requires a lot of previewing. You need to know how the video program looks in its current version so you can make any necessary changes. Or you might make a change, preview it, and then decide to undo the change because the video program looks better without it.

Premiere lets you preview your video program in a few different ways. For now, we'll preview what you've done so far using two simple methods: dragging the edit line and using the Play button.

Scrubbing in the Timeline ruler

For quick previewing, you can drag the edit line in the Timeline window. This method of previewing by dragging is called *scrubbing* because of the back-and-forth motion you use. Because this method plays your video program at the rate at which you move your hand, it's best for checking your changes quickly, rather than as a way to view editing accuracy.

1 Position the pointer in the time ruler of the Timeline window at the point where you want to start previewing, and then begin scrubbing.

The edit line jumps to the pointer location as soon as you click in the Timeline ruler.

2 Continue scrubbing across the clips in the Timeline window.

The clips appear in the Program view of the Monitor window as you scrub through them.

Using the Play button

The controls below the Program view are the same as those for the Source view. The difference is that you use the Source view to work with individual clips; you use the Program view to work with the assembly of clips in the Timeline window. Consequently, clicking the Program view Play button plays the clips in the Timeline window.

1 To start the preview from the beginning of the project, drag the edit line all the way to the left so that it is positioned at the beginning of the timeline.

2 Below the Program view, click the Play button (▶).

Your video program plays in the Program view of the Monitor window.

Trimming assembled clips

Once you have clips assembled in the Timeline, you can trim them using two different methods: trimming in the Timeline, or trimming in the Source view of the Monitor window. To quickly trim clips, you can work in the Timeline. For greater control during critical editing, use the controls for trimming clips in the Source view.

Trimming clips in the Timeline

Now that you have some clips assembled in the Timeline, you'll trim one of them there. In this exercise, you'll trim the end of the Field.mov clip in the Timeline to remove an extra shot in this clip.

1 Scrub in the Timeline time ruler to move the edit line through the last half of the Field.mov clip to locate the close-up of a single rider. Position the edit line so that the Program view shows the last frame of the long shot of three riders. For more precision, you can advance or go back one frame at a time using the Frame Forward (▶) and Frame Back (◀) buttons under the Program view. Each time you click one of these buttons, the clip backs up or advances one frame.

A. Program Frame Back button
B. Program Frame Forward button

The edit line marks the last frame of the Field.mov clip that you want to use in your project. Now you'll trim to this point.

2 Select the selection tool (▶) in the Timeline window (if it is not already selected) and position the pointer on the right edge of the Field.mov clip so that it turns into a trim pointer (◀▐▶). Drag the edge to the left until the trim pointer snaps to the edit line.

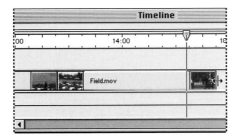 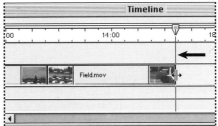

You've just trimmed Field.mov to the edit line.

Using the Monitor window controllers

The Monitor window displays individual frames of clips and the video program, with one monitor for the source, or source clip, and another for the program, or edited video. (A source clip is a clip outside the Timeline or in the Source view of the Monitor window; a program clip is a clip in the Timeline or Program view of the Monitor window.) The controllers beneath the Source and Program views serve the following purposes:

• Use the Source controller (under the Source view) to play or view the frames of a source clip and to specify the clip's source In and Out points. (The first frame that will be added is the source In point and the last frame that will be added is the source Out point.)

• Use the Program controller (under the Program view) to play or view the video program in the Timeline and to specify a clip's program In and Out points, which define where the clip's source In and Out points are located on the Timeline.

When you want to use a controller to navigate a clip or the program, first make sure the correct controller is active. When a controller is active, its timecode readout is green, and the view above it is outlined with the highlight color set for your computer. The number at the bottom left of each controller is the current time position for that view (the location timecode). The number preceded by a delta symbol (△) at the bottom right of each controller is the time difference between the In point and the Out point of the currently displayed source clip or video program (the duration timecode).

—From the Adobe Premiere User Guide, Chapter 4

Trimming in the Source view

As you've just seen, you can do simple trimming in the Timeline window. To perform more complex editing and make use of additional tools, however, the Source view of the Monitor window is usually a better choice. Here, you'll use the Source view and its controls to trim the Logo.mov clip that is already in the Timeline. Then you'll trim and assemble two more clips.

1 Copy the Logo.mov clip to the Source view by double-clicking the clip in the Timeline.

The Logo.mov clip is an animation created in Adobe After Effects®, using Adobe Illustrator® and Adobe Photoshop® files. The clip contains color bars at the beginning and end. Since you don't want the color bars to appear in your video program, you need to trim them.

2 Drag the shuttle slider below the Source view until the first frame of the actual logo portion of the clip appears. Use the Frame Forward (▶) and Frame Back (◀) buttons to display this frame.

The shuttle slider under the Source view

3 In the Source view, set the In point by clicking the Mark In button (**{**) located at the right end of the controls.

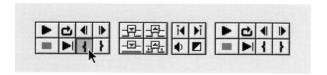

The In point icon appears both in the current location of the shuttle slider and in the upper left corner of the frame displayed in the Source view.

4 Drag the shuttle slider to find the last frame of the actual logo portion of the clip.

5 Click the Mark Out button (}) to set the Out point.

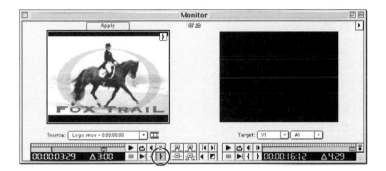

Note that an Apply button now appears above the Source view. This button appears after you have edited a clip that has already been placed in the Timeline window. By clicking it, you apply the changes you've made.

6 Click the Apply button located directly above the Source view.

The Logo.mov clip in the Timeline has been trimmed to the In point and Out point you set in the Source view. Trimming this clip, however, has left a gap between it and the Trot.mov clip. You'll now use the track select tool ([+]), which enables you to select all clips to the right of any clip in a track. With this tool, you'll select the clips to the right of the Logo.mov clip and move them to close the gap.

7 In the Timeline window, select the track select tool by positioning the pointer on the range select icon ([:]), pressing and holding down the mouse button, and then dragging right to the track select icon.

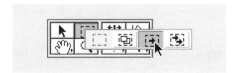

8 Position the pointer anywhere on the Trot.mov clip so that it turns into the track select pointer. Drag left until the Trot.mov clip snaps to the Logo.mov clip.

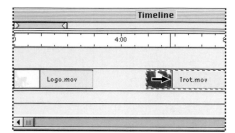 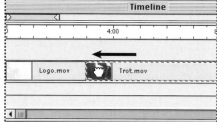

When you release the mouse button, all subsequent clips in the selected tracks move to the left. All three clips in the Timeline should now be edge-to-edge, with no space between them. Note that these clips are still selected. It's a good idea to get in the habit of deselecting clips when you are finished with a task so that the next task doesn't affect these selected clips.

9 Select the selection tool (⬉) in the Timeline window to deselect the clips you just moved.

10 Choose File > Save to save the project.

Trimming and assembling using the Source view

At the beginning of the lesson, you added clips to the project by dragging them directly into the Timeline. You can also add clips to the project by first dragging one or more clips into the Source view, where you can trim them using the controls available in the Monitor window. You can then add the clips to the video program.

Dragging clips to the Source view

First, you'll move two clips into the Source view.

1 In the Project window, select Ride.mov, and then hold down the Control key
(Windows) or Shift key (Mac OS) and click Finish.mov to select it also. Drag them to the
Source view. Remember to drag the file icon, not the filename.

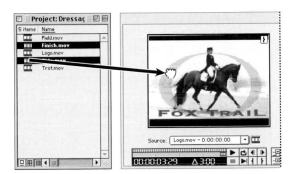

Both clips are copied into the Source menu, and the last selected clip in the Project
window, Ride.mov, appears in the Source view.

Trimming, inserting, and overlaying

Before you start trimming the clips in the Source view, let's look at the controls you'll use
to add them to the project once they have been trimmed. When working in the Source
view, you can add clips in two ways: inserting and overlaying. The Insert button and the
Overlay button are at the bottom of the Monitor window.

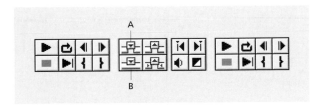

A. Insert button B. Overlay button

The Insert button inserts the clip at the edit line by splitting any existing material in two; none of the existing material is replaced. In contrast, the Overlay button places a clip at the edit line by replacing any existing material for the duration of the clip you are placing.

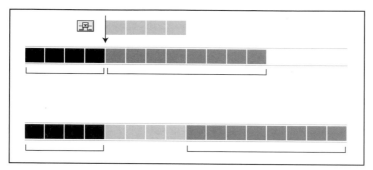

Inserting a clip makes a break in existing material and moves it aside.

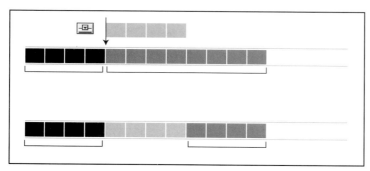

Overlaying a clip replaces an equal amount of existing video.

Now that you understand the concepts of inserting and overlaying clips, you'll trim each of the clips you dragged into the Source view and add them to the project. Let's take a look at the clip you're about to trim.

♀ *To move and view one frame at a time in either the Source view or the Program view, use the left and right arrow keys.*

1 Play the Ride.mov clip by clicking the Play button (▶) below the Source view.

You'll be inserting Ride.mov at the beginning of the project, but first you'll trim it to remove some extra footage included at the end of this clip.

2 Drag the shuttle slider below the Source view to locate the point in the last half of Ride.mov where the scene changes to an open track with a horse galloping in from the left. Display the last frame of the first shot in this clip (at 04:12) using the Frame Forward (▶) and Frame Back (◀) buttons.

3 To mark this frame as the Out point, click the Mark Out button (▸) below the Source view.

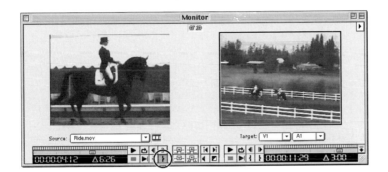

Now that you've set the new Out point for the clip, you'll insert it at the beginning of your project. This is a common editing decision—one you might make after deciding that the project would work better with additional material at the beginning. First, you'll set the insert point using the Program view.

4 Display the first frame of the Logo.mov clip in the Program view by dragging its shuttle slider all the way to the left.

By dragging the Program view's shuttle slider, you positioned the edit line at the beginning of the Timeline.

5 Click the Insert button (⊞) to place the trimmed clip into the Video 1 track in the Timeline window at the edit line position.

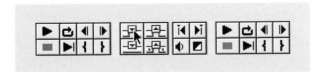

The trimmed Ride.mov clip is inserted at the beginning of the project. You used the Insert button because you didn't want to replace any existing material. Clicking the Overlay button would have replaced some of the Logo.mov clip.

6 Preview the first few clips by dragging the edit line to the beginning of the Timeline and clicking the Play button below the Program view in the Monitor window. Click the Stop button (■) when you are finished previewing.

Next, you'll overlay the Finish.mov clip over part of the Field.mov clip at the end of the project.

7 Choose Finish.mov from the Source menu under the Source view.

The Finish.mov clip appears in the Source view. Before you can overlay this clip, you need to trim about two seconds from the beginning of it. You'll use a new method to move to a location in the project.

8 Click the Source view to make it active, click the location timecode (the left set of green numbers below the Source view) to highlight all the digits, and then type **128**. Then press Enter (Windows) or Return (Mac OS) on your keyboard. Premiere interprets 128 as 01:28 (1 second and 28 frames).

The Source view advances to the specified time. Next, you'll set this point as the new In point.

9 Click the Mark In button (⁍).

Now you'll find the point in Field.mov at which you want to overlay the Finish.mov clip.

10 Drag the shuttle slider below the Program view to find the point in Field.mov where the single rider moving to the left starts passing between the other two riders (at 17:00).

11 Click the Overlay button () to place the trimmed clip in the Timeline window in the Video 1 track.

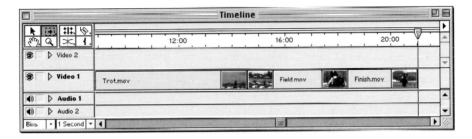

The Finish.mov clip replaces the end of the Field.mov clip.

12 If you like, you can preview this sequence of clips by dragging the edit line to the beginning of Field.mov and clicking the Play button below the Program view in the Monitor window.

13 Save the project.

Fine-tuning in the Timeline

Often you'll need to adjust In and Out points after you've placed a number of clips in the Timeline window. Adjusting any clip that's part of a sequence will affect the entire video program. Special tools in the Timeline window let you specify how your adjustments affect the other clips.

Performing a ripple edit

In this section, you'll perform what's called a *ripple edit*. A ripple edit adjusts the In or Out point of one clip and shifts other clips in or out accordingly, changing the total duration of your video program, but preserving the duration of the other clips.

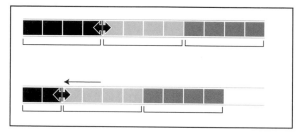

In a ripple edit, all subsequent clips move in response to the change.

Remember that you need to make this project 20 seconds long. Notice that the current duration is somewhat longer. To bring the project to 20 seconds, you'll trim Trot.mov, a clip in which the In point, Out point, and timing are not critical.

Project duration is indicated by the duration timecode, the right set of green numbers marked by a delta symbol (Δ) under the Program view. If you used the exact timecodes given for edit points in previous steps, the overall duration of the project at this point should be 20:20. If this timecode is 20:20 on your system, the current project duration is 20 frames too long. To set the length of the project precisely, you'll trim 20 frames from the end of Trot.mov.

Note: *If your project is not exactly 20 frames too long, use the numbers appropriate for your project in place of the 20-frame value and the numbers you'll derive from it in this exercise.*

1 Use the controls under the Program view to move the edit line to the first frame of Field.mov (at 14:01). The edit line is now at the cut between Trot.mov Field.mov.

The location timecode (the left set of green numbers) displayed under the Program view indicates the time at the beginning of Field.mov (14:01). You'll determine where to place a new Out point for Trot.mov by subtracting 20 frames from its current Out point.

2 Subtract 20 frames from 14:01.

An easy way to do this is to convert 14:01 to an equivalent from which you can subtract 20 frames. Our timebase for this project is 30 fps, so 1 second = 30 frames. Borrow 1 second from 14 seconds, and add it (as 30 frames) to the frames portion of our existing timecode (:01 + :30 = :31). This gives you a timecode of 13:31, which is equivalent to 14:01. Now subtract 20 frames (:20) from 13:31. The result, 13:11, is where you'll set the new Out point for Trot.mov.

3 Click the Program view to make it active, click the location timecode to highlight it, and then type **1311** and press Enter (Windows) or Return (Mac OS).

The edit line jumps to 13:11 in the Timeline.

In the Timeline window, select the ripple edit tool by positioning the pointer on the rolling edit icon (⁙), pressing and holding down the mouse button, and then dragging right to the ripple edit icon.

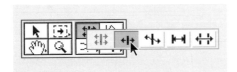

4 In the Timeline window, move the pointer to the right edge of the cut between Trot.mov and Field.mov. The pointer changes into the ripple edit pointer. Be sure the ripple edit pointer is over Trot.mov and not Field.mov. Drag left until the end of Trot.mov snaps to the edit line.

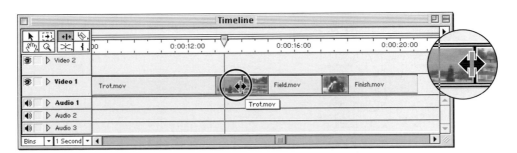

When you release the mouse button, all the other clips shift to the left, following the trim you just made to the Trot.mov clip. In a ripple edit, the total duration of your project changes. The project is now exactly 20:00 in duration.

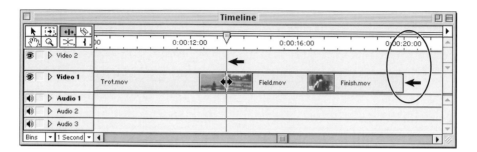

5 If you like, you can view your change by clicking the Play button (▶) below the Program view in the Monitor window.

6 Save the project.

Performing a rolling edit

Another editing method that acts on a sequence of clips is called the *rolling edit*. A rolling edit adjusts the In or Out point of one clip but also adjusts the duration of the adjacent clip, keeping the total duration of the two clips the same. As you shorten one clip, the adjacent clip is extended to maintain the total duration of the two clips. Note, however, that you can extend a clip only if the clip was previously trimmed. In other words, you cannot make a clip longer than it is—you can only restore frames that were previously trimmed.

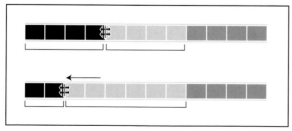

A rolling edit changes two clips at once to preserve the project's duration.

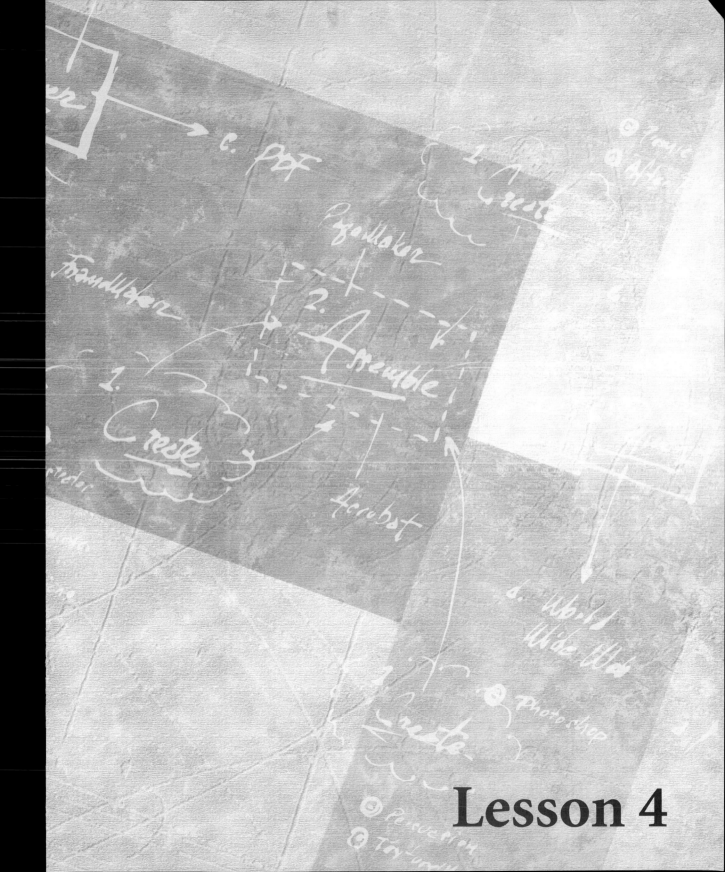

Lesson 4

1. Create

b. CD-ROM

3. Deliver

Ensemble

Acrobat

d. World Wide Web

1. Create

Adding Transitions

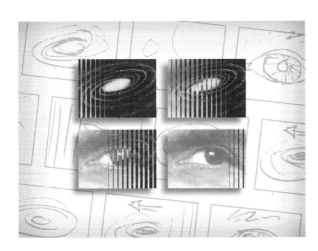

Although the instantaneous switch from one clip to another is the most common and simple way to combine video clips, Adobe Premiere also gives you dozens of options for varying the change from one clip to another. Such transitions can provide texture, nuance, and special effects.

In this lesson, you'll create a short prelude to a television program about dreams, using *transitions* between clips. Since the subject of dreams lends itself well to the use of transitions, you'll use a variety of transitions in this lesson in interesting ways. Specifically, you'll learn how to do the following:

- Place a transition using the Transitions palette.
- Preview transitions.
- Adjust transition controls.
- Trim a transition.

About transitions

In the previous lesson, you assembled a sequence of clips using the simplest of transitions: the cut. A cut is simply a sudden change to another clip. It's the most-used transition in video and film and is often the most effective. However, there may be certain projects, such as this one, that require more specialized transitions, such as dissolves, wipes, or zooms. Premiere provides a wide variety of transitions for many different creative effects.

Getting started

To begin, you'll create a new project and then import the video clips. Make sure you know the location of the files used in this lesson. Insert the CD-ROM disc if necessary. For help, see "Using the Classroom in a Book files" on page 4.

To ensure that the Premiere preferences are set to the default values, exit Premiere, and then delete the preferences file as explained in "Restoring default preferences" on page 5.

1 Start Premiere. If Premiere is already running, choose File > New > Project.

2 In the New Project Settings dialog box, choose QuickTime for the Editing mode, and choose 30 for the Timebase.

Let's set some additional options Premiere will use when you export a movie at the end of this lesson.

3 Click the Next button to display the video settings.

4 (Windows only) Choose Video for the Compressor.

5 Type **240** in the first Frame Size field. Premiere automatically inserts 180 in the second field.

6 Choose 15 for the Frame Rate.

7 Click OK to close the New Project Settings dialog box.

Viewing the finished movie

If you'd like to see what you'll be creating, you can take a look at the finished movie.

1 Choose File > Open and select the 04Final.mov file in the Final folder, inside the 04Lesson folder.

The video program opens in the Source view of the Monitor window.

2 Click the Play button to view the video program.

Importing clips

Now you're ready to import the source files for your project.

1 Import files in one of the following ways, depending on your system:

• In Windows, Choose File > Import > File and open the 04Lesson folder. Select all the files (but not the Final folder) by selecting the first file, holding down the Shift key, and then selecting the last file. Then click Open.

• In Mac OS, choose File > Import > Multiple, open the 04Lesson folder, select Earth.mov, and then click Import. Do the same for the Eye.mov, Solar1.mov, and Solar2.mov. Then click Done.

The video files are added to the Project window.

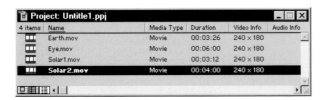

To open the Import dialog box quickly, double-click in an empty area of the Project window.

To make the clips in the Project window easier to identify, let's change the view for the window.

2 Choose Window > Project Window Options, select Thumbnail View from the menu at the top of the dialog box, and then click OK.

Now you'll save and name the project.

3 Choose File > Save, type **Dream.ppj** for the name. Then click Save.

In Windows, the default file extension for Premiere projects, ppj, is added to your filename automatically. In Mac OS, type the extension as part of the filename.

Overlapping clips

To create a transition between two clips, you need to overlap them in the Video 1A and Video 1B tracks in the Timeline window. Only the overlapping area—the end of one clip and the beginning of the next—is involved in the transition. Typically, you overlap portions of the clips that are not essential to the video program, since they will likely be obscured by the effect of the transition.

1 In the Timeline window, make sure the Video1 track is expanded so that it displays the Video1A, the Transition, and the Video1B tracks. If it's not expanded, click the arrow to the left of the Video1 track.

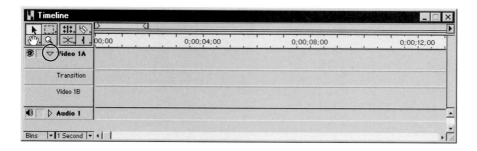

To make your clips a little easier to see in the Timeline, you'll change the view.

2 Click the title bar of the Timeline window to make it active. Choose Windows > Timeline Window Options. Then select the medium-sized icon size. Click OK.

3 In the lower left corner of the Timeline window, choose 1/2 Second from the Time Units pop-up menu.

4 Drag Solar1.mov from the Project window to the Video1A track in the Timeline window, placing its In point at the very beginning of the timeline.

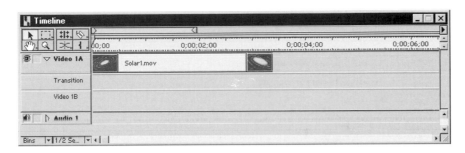

Now you'll overlap the beginning of the Earth.mov clip with the end of the Solar1.mov clip.

5 Under the Program view of the Monitor window, drag the shuttle slider until the location timecode (the left set of green numbers) reads 02:04.

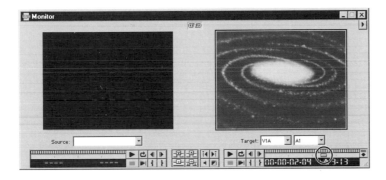

6 Drag Earth.mov into the Video1B track, snapping its In point to the edit line.

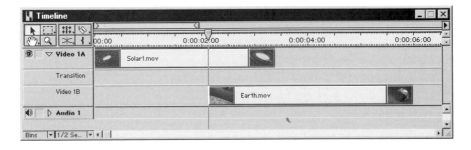

7 Choose File > Save.

Adding the Cross Dissolve transition

1 If the Transitions palette is not open, choose Windows > Show Transitions.

Each transition is represented by an icon next to the transition name.

2 In the upper right corner of the Transitions palette, click the small black arrow and deselect Hide Descriptions in the menu.

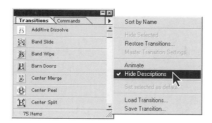

The icons in the palette are shown at a larger size.

3 Click the black arrow again and this time choose Animate from the menu.

The icons for each transition are now animated, showing you more precisely how the transitions work.

4 Scroll down to the Cross Dissolve transition in the Transitions palette, and then drag it into the Transition track of the Timeline window, in the area where the two clips overlap.

Premiere places the transition between the two clips, automatically sizing it to the duration of the overlapping area, which is 1 second.

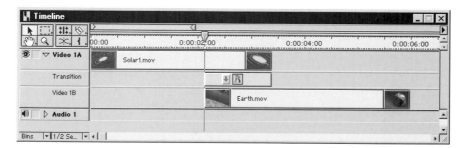

The arrow button (⬇) (called the *Track Selector*) in the transition icon is used to set the direction of the transition (from Video 1A to Video 1B, or from Video 1B to Video 1A).

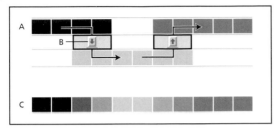

Transitions operate from one track to another (A) in the direction set by the Track Selector (B), producing a specific effect in the exported video program (C).

In most cases, Premiere sets the direction of the transition automatically, and you won't have to worry about it. Later in this lesson, you'll use the Track Selector and other controls to modify transitions.

To preview transitions (and other effects) by scrubbing (dragging) in the Timeline ruler, you need to hold down a modifier key. Otherwise, Premiere previews only the video clips, without any transitions or effects.

5 Hold down the Alt key (Windows) or the Option key (Mac OS) and then scrub in the Timeline ruler to move the edit line across the transition. Note that the pointer has changed into a smaller arrow, indicating that you are previewing effects. The preview plays in the Program view of the Monitor window.

6 Save the project.

Using the Transitions palette

Premiere includes 75 transitions, which you choose from the Transitions palette. In the palette, icons represent the way each transition works, where A is the first clip and B is the second. To help you choose, you can animate these icons and display brief descriptions.

• To animate the icons, choose Animate from the Transitions palette menu.

• To stop icon animation, deselect Animate on the Transitions palette menu.

• To display large icons and brief descriptions, choose Hide Descriptions from the Transitions palette menu to deselect it.

• To hide selected transitions, select one or more transitions in the Transitions palette, and then choose Hide Selected from the Transitions palette menu.

• To restore hidden transitions, choose Restore Transitions from the Transitions palette menu. Select those you want to display, and then click Show.

• To reorder a transition in the palette, drag the transition up or down to a new location in the list.

• To order the transitions in the palette by name, choose Sort by Name from the palette menu.

—From the Adobe Premiere User Guide, Chapter 5

Previewing the transition at the intended frame rate

So far, you have used two preview methods: clicking the Play button in the Program view and scrubbing in the Timeline ruler (see "Previewing" on page 100). The Play button, however, is intended for previews of only the video clips; transitions (and other effects) are not shown, as this would take too long to process.

Holding down the modifier key and scrubbing in the Timeline ruler does display the transition but cannot give you a precise speed. To preview transitions (and other effects) at the intended frame rate, you need to use a third method that generates a preview file on your hard disk. Premiere then plays this file in the Program view of the Monitor window.

Before you generate a preview in this way, however, you need to set the work area bar. This bar specifies the portion of your project that you want to preview or export as a movie file.

1 Drag the arrow on the right end of the work area bar to cover the Solar1.mov and Earth.mov clips.

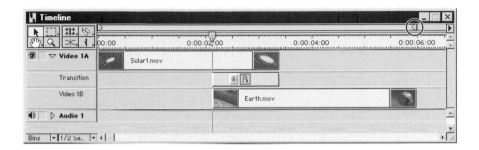

💡 *To make the work area bar cover all contiguous clips, press Alt (Windows) or Option (Mac OS) as you click the work area bar.*

2 Choose Project > Preview, or press Enter (Windows) or Return (Mac OS) on the keyboard.

Premiere generates the preview, displaying a status bar. When it has finished, the two clips and the transition between them are played in the Program view.

Adding the Cross Zoom transition

Now you'll add a third clip (Eye.mov) and use the Cross Zoom transition, which zooms into one clip and zooms out of the other. Here, the Cross Zoom transition zooms into the end of the Earth.mov clip and then zooms out at the start of the Eye.mov clip.

1 From the Time Units pop-up menu in the Timeline window, choose 1 Second.

2 Underneath the Program view of the Monitor window, drag the shuttle slider until the location timecode reads 05:04.

3 From the Project window, drag the Eye.mov clip into the Video1A track, snapping its In point to the edit line.

The Earth.mov and Eye.mov clips now overlap for a duration of about 1 second.

4 From the Transitions palette, drag the Cross Zoom transition into the Transition track, in the area where the Earth.mov and Eye.mov clips overlap.

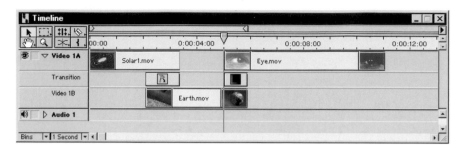

This time, you'll modify the transition somewhat.

5 In the Timeline window, double-click the transition you just placed to open the Cross Zoom Settings dialog box.

6 Select the Show Actual Sources option.

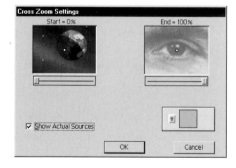

7 Leave the Start and End settings as they are, and make sure the Track Selector is pointing up (⬆).

When the arrow points up, the transition will start zooming into the clip in the Video 1B track (Earth.mov), and then zoom out of the clip in the Video 1A track (Eye.mov), ending with the eye.

This transition also lets you specify the location in each clip where the zoom begins. You'll specify that now.

8 In the End view, drag the small white square from the center of the image into the reflection in the upper right of the pupil of the eye.

This square determines where the zoom ends.

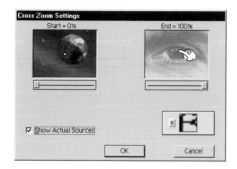

9 In the Start view, drag the white square to approximately the same position as in the End view.

10 Click OK.

11 Preview the Cross Zoom transition by scrubbing in the Timeline ruler while holding down the Alt key (Windows) or the Option key (Mac OS).

If you like, you can also generate a preview at the precise frame rate by setting the work area to cover the new transition and pressing Enter (Windows) or Return (Mac OS).

Adding multiple transitions

To create other effects, you can place two or more transitions together. You'll do this now to give the last clip in the sequence a dream-like quality.

1 Drag the edit line to the end of the Eye.mov clip.

2 From the Project window, drag the Solar2.mov clip into the Video1B track, snapping its Out point to the edit line marked by the edit line.

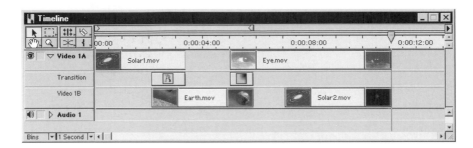

Before you place the transition, take a look at both clips to see what they look like individually.

3 Double-click the Eye.mov clip in the Timeline window so that it appears in the Source view. Then click the Source view Play button.

4 Do the same for the Solar2.mov clip.

5 From the Transitions palette, drag the Sliding Bands transition into the Transition track, between the Eye.mov and Solar2.mov clips, so that it snaps to the beginning of the Solar2.mov clip.

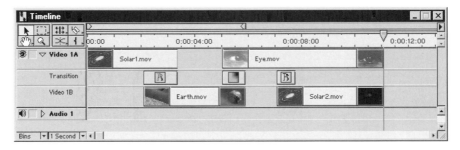

You'll now shorten this transition so you can add others to the same overlapping area. First, let's change our view of the transition area.

6 From the Time Units pop-up menu in the Timeline window, choose 8 Frames. This will make it easier to precisely resize the transition you just placed. Scroll the Timeline until you can see the transition you just added.

7 If the Info palette is not visible, choose Windows > Show Info.

8 Select the selection tool ( ) (if necessary) and position it on the right edge of the Sliding Bands transition so that it turns into a trim pointer ( ). Now drag the edge until the Cursor At display in the Info palette reads 7:20.

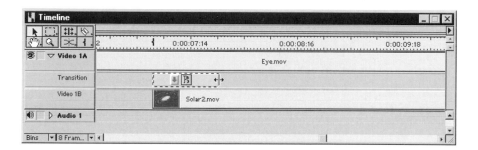

9 From the Time Units pop-up menu in the Timeline window, choose 4 Frames. Then drag the scroll bar in the Timeline window so that the Sliding Bands transition is visible again.

10 Make sure the Track Selector in the Sliding Bands transition icon is pointing down ( ). If it isn't, click it.

The transition begins with the Eye.mov clip and ends with Solar2.mov clip. Let's preview this.

11 Hold down the Alt key (Windows) or the Option key (Mac OS) and scrub in the ruler across the Sliding Bands transition.

Copying transitions

Now you'll duplicate three more versions of the Sliding Bands transition to create a longer and more varied effect.

1 In the Timeline window, select the Sliding Bands transition and choose Edit > Copy.

2 Click in the Transition track just after the Sliding Bands transition, selecting the empty area.

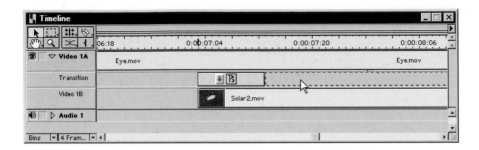

3 Choose Edit > Paste.

A copy of the same transition appears just after the first.

4 In the copy, click the Track Selector to make the arrow point upward (↑). This creates a transition that moves from the Video 1B track to the Video 1A track.

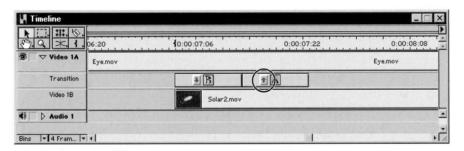

Now let's preview what you've done.

5 In the Timeline window, hold down the Alt or Option key and scrub in the Timeline ruler across the two copies of the Sliding Bands transition.

In the first one, the transition starts with the Eye.mov clip and ends with the Solar2.mov clip. In the second, it begins with the Solar2.mov clip and ends with Eye.mov. As viewed in the Timeline window, therefore, the transitions follow the direction specified by the Track Selector arrows.

Reversing the bands

Now you'll create two more copies of the same transition, but this time, you'll reverse the movement of the sliding bands, making them slide from right to left.

1 Click in the area of the Transition track just after the second Sliding Bands transition.

The empty area is now selected.

2 Choose Edit > Paste.

The Sliding Bands transition that you previously copied is pasted into the track.

3 Double-click this copy to open the Sliding Bands Settings dialog box.

4 Select the Show Actual Sources option.

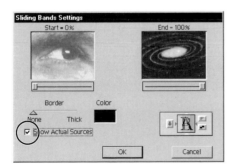

Since the previous Sliding Bands transition finished with the Eye.mov clip, you want this one to finish with the Solar2.mov clip.

5 Make sure the Track Selector to the left of the animating icon is pointing down (↓).

6 To reverse the movement of the sliding bands, click the Forward/Reverse Selector (F) to the right of the animating icon.

The F (forward) changes into an R (reverse), and the animating icon shows the bands moving in the opposite direction.

You'll notice a couple of other controls near the animating icon. Surrounding the icon itself are four triangles, called Edge Selectors; two are red and two are white. Clicking the Edge Selectors sets the orientation of the sliding bands. The Edge Selectors on the left and right sides of the icon, which are red, specify that the sliding bands move horizontally; those on the top and bottom specify vertical movement. The red ones are selected.

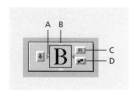

A. Horizontal movement
B. Vertical movement
C. Forward or reverse
D. Anti-aliasing low, high, or off

Below the Forward/Reverse Selector is another button. This controls whether the transition uses anti-aliasing or not. Anti-aliasing blends the edges of the bands, smoothing the hard edges. Anti-aliasing is turned off when you see the (←) icon; it's set to Low when you see the (←) icon; and it's set to High when you see the (←) icon. You'll leave it off.

These controls are available for only certain transitions.

7 In the Setting dialog box, click OK.

Finally, to repeat the Sliding Bands to mirror the first two, you'll copy and paste it one more time.

8 The third version of the Sliding Bands transition (the one you just modified) should still be selected. If it isn't, select it. Then choose Edit > Copy.

9 Select the empty area in the Transition track after the third transition. Then choose Edit > Paste.

Another copy of the transition appears in the Transition track.

10 In the Timeline window, click the Track Selector in the transition icon so that it points up.

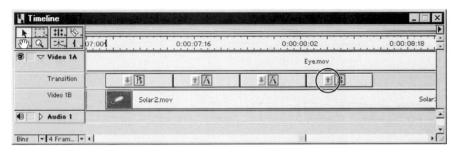

Let's briefly look at what you've done. You've created four copies of the same transition, alternating its direction— down, up, down, up—and changing the motion of the bands for the second two. Let's preview it at the precise frame rate.

11 From the Time Units pop-up menu in the Timeline window, choose 1 Second. This will make it easier to find the work area bar.

12 Drag either end of the work area bar to cover the entire length of the Solar2.mov and Eye.mov clips. Then press Enter (Windows) or Return (Mac OS).

Premiere generates the preview and then plays it in the Program view.

13 To watch it again, press Enter (Windows) or Return (Mac OS).

Since Premiere does not need to generate it again, the preview plays in the Program view immediately.

14 Save the project.

Adding the Zoom transition

To complete the project, you'll add the Zoom transition, which works a little differently from the Cross Zoom. While the Cross Zoom zooms on an element within the clip, the Zoom transition zooms one entire clip into or out of the second clip, playing both at the same time. You'll use the Zoom transition to create a centered inset of the eye (Eye.mov in Video 1A) inside the stars (Solar2.mov in Video 1B).

1 From the Time Units pop-up menu in the Timeline window, choose 8 Frames. This will make it easier to work with the transition you are about to add.

2 From the Transitions palette, drag the Zoom transition into the remaining overlapping area between the Eye.mov and Solar2.mov clips.

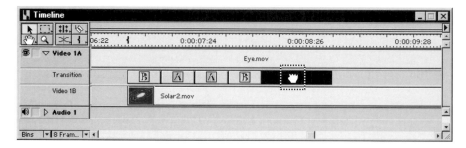

3 Using the selection tool ( ), drag the right edge of the Zoom transition so that it fills about 2/3 of the remaining overlap between the Eye.mov and Solar2.mov clips.

4 In the Timeline window, double-click the Zoom transition.

5 In the Zoom Settings dialog box, select the Show Actual Sources option.

6 To make the Eye.mov clip shrink in size and play on top of the Solar2.mov clip, make sure the Track Selector is pointing down ( ), and click the Forward/Reverse Selector so that it is set to Reverse (R).

7 To shrink the Eye.mov clip, drag the slider below the End view to 68%.

The Eye.mov clip shrinks to 68% of its size, centered within the Solar2.clip.

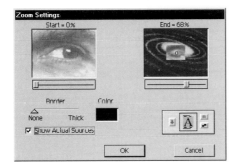

8 Click OK.

Let's preview it.

9 Hold down the Alt key or the Option key and drag in the ruler across the Zoom transition.

The project currently ends as soon as the eye reaches 68%. To finish our project, we'll hold the eye at the end of the zoom as an inset within the stars. To do this, you need to create another version of the Zoom transition, keeping the Start and End percentages the same.

10 From the Transitions palette, drag the Zoom transition into the remaining overlapping area between the Eye.mov and Solar2.mov clips.

11 If the right edge of the second Zoom transition does not quite match the Out point of both the Eye.mov and Solar2.mov clips, drag it to the left or right until it does.

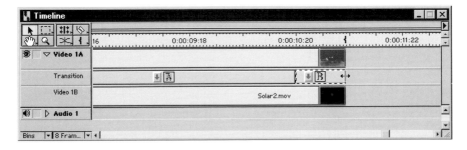

12 Double-click the second Zoom transition to open the Zoom Settings dialog box.

13 If you like, select the Show Actual Sources option.

14 Make sure the Track Selector is pointing down, and click the Forward/Reverse Selector so that it is set to Reverse.

15 Drag the slider underneath the Start view to 68%.

Setting the Start value to 68% continues the inset from the previous instance of the Zoom transition.

16 Drag the slider underneath the End view to 68%.

Setting the End to 68% keeps the Eye.mov clip at its current size as an inset, while both it and the Solar2.mov clip continue to play for about another second. Keep the other settings the same.

💡 *To set the Start value and the End value to the same setting in the Zoom Settings dialog box, press and hold the Shift key and then drag either slider.*

17 Click OK.

18 To preview the end of the project, hold down the Alt key or the Option key and scrub in the Timeline ruler across the final portion.

Alt/Option-scrubbing in the Timeline ruler gives a quick preview of your work but is not time accurate. For a more accurate look at your work, let's generate a preview of the entire project.

19 Extend the work area bar to cover the entire duration of the project and press Enter (Windows) or Return (Mac OS).

Exporting the movie

1 Click anywhere in the Timeline window to make it active. This ensures that Premiere exports the entire project. If the Monitor window and the Source view are selected instead of the Timeline window, Premiere will export only the clip displayed in the Source view.

2 Choose File > Export > Movie.

3 In the Export Movie dialog box, click the Settings button.

4 Make sure QuickTime is selected for the File Type and Entire Project is selected for the Range.

5 Also make sure that the Export Video is selected and Export Audio is not selected. The default values for other settings, including those for compression, are fine for this project. You already set the frame size and frame rate when you started the project.

6 Click OK to close the Export Movie Settings dialog box.

7 In the Export Movie dialog box, type **Dream.mov** for the name of the video program. Click Save (Windows) or OK (Mac OS).

Premiere starts making the movie, displaying a status bar that provides an estimate for the amount of time it will take. When the movie is ready, it opens in the Source view.

8 Click the Play button to watch what you've just created. You may notice that some frames are dropped during playback. This depends on the system you are using and also the frame rate at which the movie was exported.

Congratulations on completing the transitions lesson!

Exploring on your own

Feel free to experiment with the project you have just created. Here are some suggestions:

• Try changing the direction of the transition (click the Track Selector), and then preview the results.

• Open the settings dialog box for one of the transitions (double-click on the transition) and see how the options affect the transition.

• Look at the differences in the appearance of transition icons when you change the icon size in the Timeline Window Options dialog box (make the Timeline window active and then choose Window > Timeline Window Options).

• Use the shortcuts listed in the Premiere Quick Reference Card and in Premiere Help to preview in the Monitor window and the Timeline window.

Review questions

1 What are two ways to preview transitions?

2 What does the Track Selector button do in a transition?

3 What is the purpose of the anti-aliasing feature available in a number of transitions?

4 What does the Forward/Reverse button do in a transition?

5 What are two ways to get more information within the Transition palette about the function of a specific transition?

Answers

1 Scrubbing in the Timeline ruler while holding down the Alt key (Windows) or the Option key (Mac OS), or generating a preview of the work by pressing Enter (Windows) or Return (Mac OS).

2 The Track Selector button sets the direction of the transition, for example, from the Video1A track to the Video 1B track.

3 Anti-aliasing smoothes the edges of an effect, reducing the rough appearance of the edge.

4 The Forward/Reverse button sets the direction of the effect used in the transition. For example, in the Zoom transition, F zooms in and R zooms out.

5 Deselect (uncheck) Hide Descriptions in the Transition Palette menu, or select (check) Animate in the Transition Palette menu.

Lesson 5

Adding Audio

The right music or sound effects adds impact to your video program. Adobe Premiere makes it easy to add additional audio, blend the sound on each, and carefully control the volume for maximum effect.

To learn about working with sound in Premiere, you'll create a promotional spot for a film festival, using a number of basic audio techniques. Specifically, you'll learn how to do the following:

- Place audio clips.
- Adjust audio fades and volume levels.
- Unlink audio and video clips.
- Synchronize audio and video tracks.

Getting started

Because you'll need to listen to audio clips in this lesson, first make sure that your computer's speakers or headphones are set up to play sounds at an appropriate volume. In addition, make sure you know the location of the files used in this lesson. Insert the CD-ROM disc if necessary. For help, see "Using the Classroom in a Book files" on page 4.

To ensure that the Premiere preferences are set to the default values, exit Premiere, and then delete the preferences file as explained in "Restoring default preferences" on page 5.

1 Start Premiere. If it is already running, choose File > New > Project.

2 In the New Project Settings window, choose QuickTime for the Editing Mode, and choose 30 for the Timebase.

Let's set some options Premiere will use when you export a movie at the end of this lesson.

3 Click the Next button to display the video settings.

4 (Windows only) Choose Video for the Compressor.

5 Type **240** in the first Frame Size box. Premiere automatically inserts 180 in the second field.

6 Choose 15 for the Frame Rate.

7 Click the Next button to display the audio settings.

8 Set Rate to 11 kHz and set Format to 8 bit - Mono.

9 Click OK to close the New Project Settings dialog box.

Viewing the finished movie

If you'd like to see what you'll be creating, you can take a look at the finished movie. Because parts of the lesson let you make your own editing decisions, your video program may be slightly different.

1 Choose File > Open and double-click the 05Final.mov file in the Final folder, inside the 05Lesson folder.

The video program opens in the Source view of the Monitor window.

2 Click the Play button (►)to view the video program.

Importing and organizing clips

Now you're ready to import source files. To keep things organized, you'll create a bin for sound files, and then move those files into the sound bin.

1 Import files in one of the following ways, depending on your system:

• In Mac OS, choose File > Import > Multiple, open the 05Lesson folder, select Danger.aif, and then click Import. Do the same for the remaining files, but do not import the Final folder. Then click Done.

• In Windows, Choose File > Import > File and open the 05Lesson folder. Select all the files (but not the Final folder) by selecting the first file, holding down the Shift key, and then selecting the last file. Click Open.

The video and sound files are added to the Project window.

Bins are containers you can create for storing and organizing your clip files. You'll create a bin for the sound files.

2 Click the Project window to make it active. Then choose Project > Create > Bin, type **Sounds,** and click OK.

3 In the Project window, hold down the Control key (Windows) or Shift key (Mac OS) and click the Sounds bin icon (to deselect it), and click the Danger.aif, Horror.aif, Shadow.aif, and Suspense.aif icons to select them. Then drag the icons to the Sounds bin icon.

To make the clips in the Project window easier to identify, let's change the view for the window.

4 Choose Window > Project Window Options, select Thumbnail View from the menu at the top of the dialog box, and then click OK.

Finally, you'll save and name the project.

5 Choose File > Save, type **Mystery.ppj** for the name. Then click Save.

In Windows, the default file extension for Premiere projects, ppj, is added to your filename automatically. In Mac OS, type the extension as part of the filename.

Creating an L-cut

Video and film often use a technique called a *split edit* to create an audio transition between scenes. In a split edit, the audio that belongs to one clip extends into one or both adjacent clips. The audio from a quiet forest scene, for example, could extend into the scene of a crowd. One specific type of split edit, called an *L-cut*, extends the audio only into the following clip.

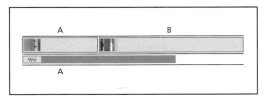

*An L-cut allows the sound from one clip (**A**) to extend into the next clip (**B**).*

Unlinking the video and audio

Typically, when you shoot a scene with your camera, you capture both video and audio at the same time. When you digitize the footage, the video and audio are linked together in one file. In Premiere, this is known as a *hard link*. You can break these links to replace or edit audio and video independently. In a later lesson, you'll temporarily override linked clips instead of breaking the link (see "Creating a split edit" on page 185).

You'll start by assembling the first two video clips of the project.

1 Click the title bar of the Timeline window to make it active. Choose Window > Timeline Window Options. Select the medium-sized icon for the Icon Size and then click OK.

2 In the Timeline window, make sure the Video1 track is expanded so that the Video1A track, the Transition track, and the Video1B track are displayed. If it's not expanded, click the arrow to the left of the Video1 track.

3 From the Project window, drag Door.mov into the Video1B track, placing it at the starting point of the Timeline. Here, you have placed the clip in the Video 1B track because later you will be overlaying clips in the Video 1A track.

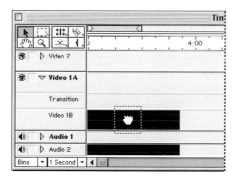 

When you place a clip in the Video 1B track, the audio portion of the clip is automatically placed in Audio 2 track. When you add clips with audio to the Video 1A track, the sound appears in the Audio 1 track. Notice that as you move the clip in the Timeline, the audio portion moves with it.

4 Drag Hall1.mov from the Project window into the Video1B track, placing it so that it snaps to the end of Door.mov.

Let's take a look at what you've assembled so far.

5 Make the work area bar cover all contiguous clips by pressing Alt (Windows) or Option (Mac OS) as you click the work area bar. Then press Enter (Windows) or Return (Mac OS).

The audio plays along with the video. Because the audio in Hall1.mov was recorded further from the door than the audio in Door.mov, it is difficult to hear the door being opened. Instead, you'll delete the Hall1.mov audio and let the audio from Door.mov extend into this clip.

6 Click the audio portion of Hall1.mov to select it.

7 Press the Delete key on the keyboard to delete the audio.

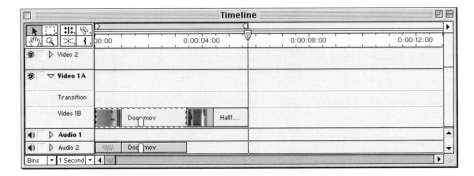

The Door.mov clip you added to the Timeline window contains linked audio and video. In this lesson, you will unlink the audio and video to edit them separately.

8 Select either the video or the audio portion of the Door.mov clip.

9 Choose Edit > Break Link.

The video and audio portions of the clip are no longer linked; they can be moved and trimmed separately.

Trimming the video

Next, you'll trim the first clip so that the action matches that in the Hall1.mov that follows it. This will also permit you to extend the audio from Door.mov into the second clip.

1 Drag the shuttle slider underneath the Program view to find the frame in Door.mov just before the man's coat starts to obscure the door knob (at 2:03).

2 In the Timeline window, select the ripple edit tool.

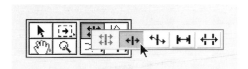

3 In the Timeline window, position the pointer on the end of the Door.mov video clip. The pointer turns into the ripple edit tool.

4 Trim the video portion by dragging it to the left until it snaps to the edit line.

You have just completed an L-cut, in which the audio from one clip extends into the following clip.

5 Select the selection tool (▶) to deselect the ripple edit tool.

Now you'll add a new video clip.

6 Drag the Feet1.mov clip just to the right of the Hall1.mov clip in the Video 1B track.

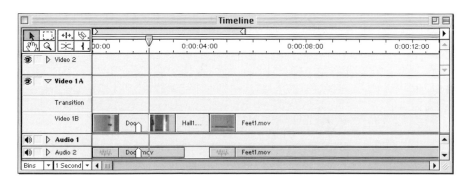

7 Extend the work area bar to span the clips you just added, and then press Enter (Windows) or Return (Mac OS) to preview it.

8 Save the project by choosing File > Save.

Using markers

Markers provide a way to indicate important points in time. They help you position and arrange clips. The Timeline and each clip can contain its own set of up to ten markers numbered from 0 to 9. In addition, the Timeline and each clip can individually contain up to 999 unnumbered markers. You work with markers in much the same way you work with In and Out points, but unlike In and Out points, markers are only for reference and do not alter the video program. In general, add a marker to a clip for important points within an individual clip, and add a marker to the Timeline for significant time points that affect multiple clips, such as synchronizing video and audio on different clips.

When you add a marker to a clip in Source view, it and any existing markers in the master clip will be included with the clip when you add it to the Timeline. However, if you open a clip from the Project window and add a marker to it, the marker won't be added to any instances of the clip already in the Timeline.

When you add a marker to the Timeline or the Program view, it appears in both the Timeline and in the Program view, but it is not added to any master clips. A marker you add to a clip in the Timeline appears with the clip, and a marker you add to the Timeline itself appears on the time ruler.

—From the Adobe Premiere User Guide, Chapter 4

Using markers to synchronize clips

When working with audio clips that are not linked to video, you'll occasionally encounter situations where you need to synchronize the audio to the video clip. In this part of the lesson, you'll cut together two clips of a man walking, filmed from different angles. One clip doesn't have audio, so you need to position it so that the footsteps in it match the sound of footsteps in the audio portion of the other walking clip. The most straightforward method of synchronizing these clips is to insert markers at matching events in both clips.

You'll start by marking a footstep in the clip that will be overlaid.

1 Double-click the Feet2.mov clip in the Project window to display it in the Source view.

2 Play the clip by clicking the Play button (▶).

3 Drag the shuttle slider under the Source view to locate the first footstep of the man's right foot. Find the first frame in which the right heel makes contact with the floor.

`00:00:01:04    Δ2:24`

Now you'll mark this position. Premiere lets you use numbered or unnumbered markers. Numbered markers are convenient because they let you quickly jump to the marker by pressing Control (Windows) or Command (Mac OS) followed by the marker number. Each clip can have up to ten numbered markers.

4 Mark this point in the clip by selecting Clip > Set Marker > 0. The marker appears at the top of the image in the Source view.

Now you'll insert a marker into the Timeline, using the Program view of the Feet1.mov clip as a guide.

To quickly locate or synchronize sounds in an audio clip, view the clip as a waveform. Simply expand the audio track by clicking the arrow next to the track. Sounds are visible as pulses in the waveform displayed at the bottom of the audio track.

5 Drag the shuttle slider below the Program view until the Source and Program views display the same moment in the action (at 14:11 below the Program view). In the Program view, click the Frame Forward (▮▶) and Frame Back (◀▮) buttons to find the frame in which the right heel contacts the floor. (You can also use the left and right arrow keys on your keyboard.)

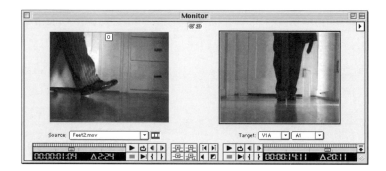

6 Mark this point in the Timeline by selecting Clip > Set Marker > 0.

A marker appears in the Timeline at the edit line and on the clip in the Program view. It doesn't matter what number you choose from the Set Marker menu as long as you haven't already used that number in the same clip. Choosing a marker number previously used in the same clip moves that marker to the current frame.

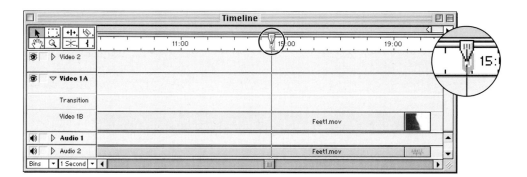

Now you can synchronize the two clips by lining up the markers. You'll do this by placing the Feet2.mov clip in the Video 1A track. Any video in upper tracks covers or hides video in lower tracks, except when a higher track has a Transparency setting. Here, you'll place a clip in the Video 1A track to cover a portion of the video in the Video 1B track. (Because the overlaid clip has no sound, the underlying audio is unaffected.) The result is similar to that of using the Overlay button (see "Trimming, inserting, and overlaying" on page 107). An advantage of this method is that it is easier to locate and position your overlaid clips.

7 In the lower left corner of the Timeline window, choose 1/2 second from the time units pop-up menu.

8 Drag the Feet2.mov clip from the Source view into the Video1A track.

9 Position the pointer over the marker in the Feet2.mov clip and drag the clip so that the marker in the clip snaps to the edit line, which is on the other marker in the Timeline.

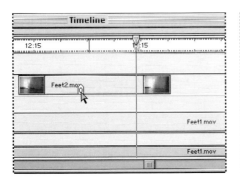 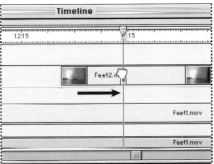

10 Drag the work area bar to span the overlay you just created, and then press Enter (Windows) or Return (Mac OS) to preview it.

The footsteps in the Feet2.mov clip should match the audio track of the Feet1.mov clip. If your markers were not placed correctly, however, the video and the audio may be slightly out of sync. You can easily correct this.

11 If the sound of the footstep occurs before or after the heel contacts the floor, move the Feet2.mov clip slightly one way or the other and preview it again.

💡 *To move a clip in the Timeline one frame at a time, click on the clip to select it, and then press the left or right arrow key to move the clip in the desired direction. Each time you press an arrow key, the clip moves one frame.*

12 When you're satisfied that the clip is in sync with the audio, save the project.

💡 *To jump to a numbered marker, press and hold down Control (Windows) or Command (Mac OS), and then press the number key that corresponds to the marker number.*

Overlaying video without sound

Now that you have positioned and synchronized the second walking clip to the audio, you'll overlay additional clips that don't need to be synchronized and that don't have audio linked to them. As before, you'll place clips in the Video 1A track. The audio from Feet1.mov will continue to play underneath.

1 In the Project window, hold down the Control key (Windows) or the Shift key (Mac OS) and click Hall2.mov, Man.mov, Woman1.mov, and Woman2.mov, to select them all. Then drag them to the Source view in the Monitors window.

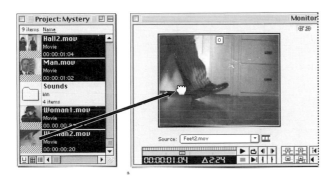

Note: *A clip in the Timeline can include the clip name, but it may not be displayed if the clip is too short or if you select the track format that does not include a name. To see the name of a clip in the Timeline, click the Timeline title bar to activate it, if necessary, and then simply position the pointer on the clip.*

2 From the Source menu below the Source view, select Woman1.mov.

The Woman1.mov clip appears in the Source view.

3 Click the Play button (▶) to preview the clip.

4 Drag the Timeline scroll box to display the center of the Feet2.mov clip.

5 Drag the Woman1.mov clip from the Source view into the Video1A track, so that it ends at the beginning of the Feet2.mov clip you inserted earlier.

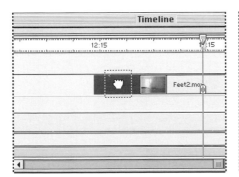
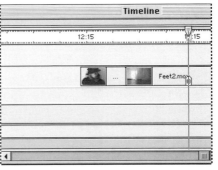

6 From the Source menu, select Woman2.mov, and then click the Play button to preview it.

7 Drag the Woman2.mov clip from the Source view into the Video1A track, positioning it at the end of the Feet2.mov clip.

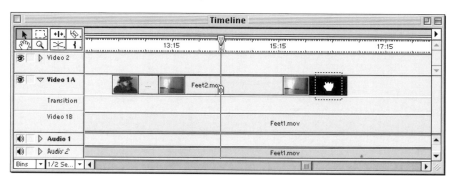

You now have three clips covering part of Feet1.mov. At this point, we want to let some of Feet1.mov "show through," so we'll place the next clip so that it starts a few seconds after the end of Woman2.mov.

8 In the lower left corner of the Timeline window, choose 1 second from the time units pop-up menu.

9 From the Source menu, select Hall2.mov, and then click the Play button to preview it.

10 Drag the edit line in the Timeline to 19:00.

11 Drag the Hall2.mov clip into the Video1A track and let its beginning snap to the edit line.

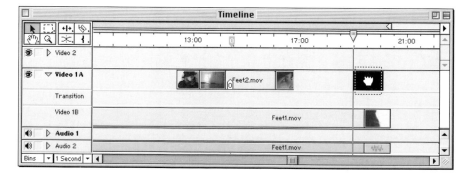

You can now insert the last clip of the video.

Because you want all audio to end at the end of the last video clip, you'll need to trim the Horror.aif audio clip.

16 Move the pointer to the end of the Horror.aif clip, and then drag to trim until it snaps to align with the end of the last video clip.

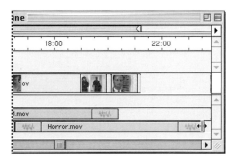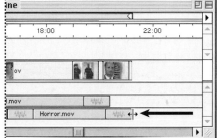

17 Save the project.

Fading audio in and out

In Premiere, you can fade audio in and out to create more subtle transitions between clips. First, let's fade out the end of the audio track linked to the Feet1.mov video clip.

1 In the lower left corner of the Timeline window, choose 1/2 Second from the Time Unit pop-up menu.

2 In the Timeline window, click the arrow to the left of the Audio 2 track to expand it.

Running through the center of the waveform is a red line called the *fade control*, sometimes known as a *rubber band*. The fade control specifies the relative volume of the audio. By default, the fade control is a straight line, meaning that the volume is constant across the clip. To add a fade, you move one end of the fade control up or down.

Note: *The blue line running through the waveform is the* pan control, *which lets you adjust the degree to which sound plays in the left or right stereo channel. You will not change the pan control in this lesson.*

3 In the Feet1.mov audio track, click on the fade control at a point that corresponds to the middle of the Hall2.mov video clip.

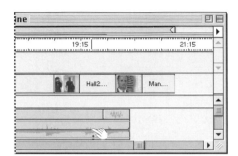 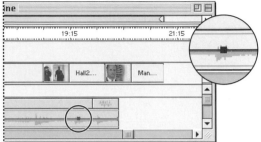

Clicking creates a small red square, called a *handle*. A handle breaks the fade control into separate segments so that you can adjust portions of the audio. The fade control always includes a handle at either end, so you don't have to create those handles.

4 At the end of the audio clip, drag the handle down as far as it will go.

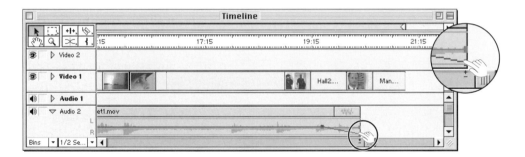

This creates a downward slope from the first handle you created. A downward slope fades out the audio. In this case, because you dragged the handle down to the bottom, the audio fades out to no sound at all.

The audio in the Horror.aif clip starts too abruptly and we want to fade it up at the end to build suspense. To make these changes, you'll fade in the audio by creating two separate handles.

5 Click the arrow next to the Audio 3 track to expand that track.

6 In the Horror.aif audio clip, click the fade control about 1/2 second from the In point. Then drag the handle at the In point all the way down.

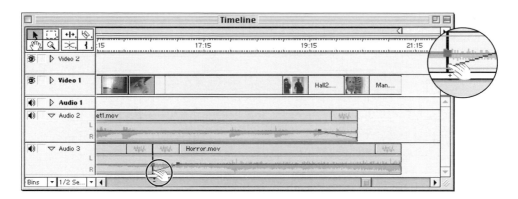

The upward slope fades in the audio. Now let's slowly raise the volume.

7 Click on the Fade Control in Horror.aif at a point that corresponds to the handle you created in the Audio 2 track. Another handle is created.

8 Drag the handle at the right end of the Fade Control all the way up to increase the volume at the end of the clip.

The volume in this audio clip will now fade in to full-level, maintain that level for about two seconds, and then slowly rise to an even higher level at the end of the clip.

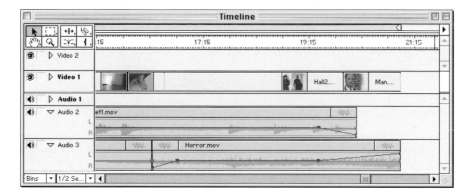

Let's preview this.

9 Make sure the work area bar covers the entire video program, and then press Enter (Windows) or Return (Mac OS).

In about the middle of the piece, you may have noticed that the man calls out a name, but the volume is too low for it to be heard clearly. You'll need to boost just that portion of the audio clip.

10 Drag the edit line through the middle of the video program to locate "Marilyn" in the audio portion of the Feet1.mov clip.

11 Click on the Fade Control on either side of the pulse that forms the word "Marilyn" (at 11:12 and 12:03).

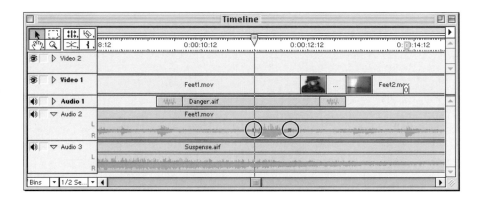

12 Just to the right of the first handle click and drag upward to create and move a handle in one step.

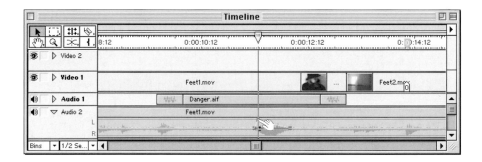

13 Position the pointer just to the left of the handle you created at the end of the pulse. Then click and drag upward to create and move a handle in one step.

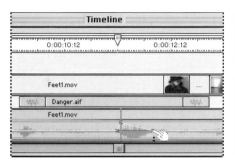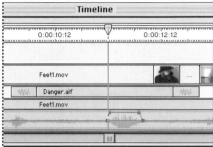

Check the level by playing this part of the project.

14 Make sure the work area bar covers the area of the clip you just changed, and then press Enter (Windows) or Return (Mac OS).

Finally, the sound effect we added before the man turns is a little too loud. You'll use a new technique to change the volume throughout the clip.

15 Click the arrow next to the Audio 1 track to expand it.

16 Locate Danger.aif in the Audio 1 track. Position the pointer on the fade control anywhere between the two handles. Hold down the Shift key and drag the segment downward until the level indication reads about –5 db. Notice that Premiere lets you drag outside the audio track so that you can make fine adjustments in the level.

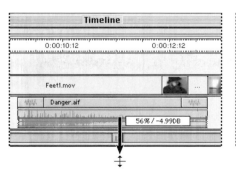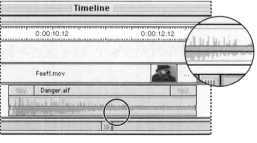

The entire segment moves, adjusting its volume.

17 To preview the project, make sure the work area bar covers all your clips. Then press Enter (Windows) or Return (Mac OS).

18 Save the project.

Exporting the movie

You've finished editing, but your video program is still composed of several video and audio files and a Premiere project file. In order to distribute it as a single file, you need to export it to a movie file.

1 Choose File > Export > Movie.

2 In the Export Movie dialog box, click Settings.

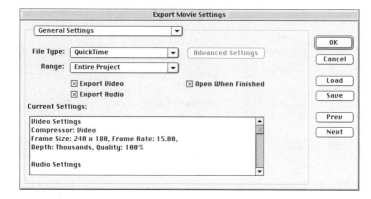

3 Make sure QuickTime is selected for the File Type and Entire Project is selected for the Range.

4 Also make sure that the Export Video and Export Audio options are selected. You can leave the rest of the settings as they are because you set them when you started the project.

5 Click OK to close the Export Movie Settings dialog box.

6 In the Export Movie dialog box, specify the 05Lesson folder for the location and type **Mystery.mov** for the name of the video program. Click Save (Windows) or OK (Mac OS).

Premiere starts making the movie, displaying a status bar that provides an estimate for the amount of time it will take.

7 When the movie is complete, it opens in its own window.

8 Click the Play button (▶) to play the movie.

Exploring on your own

Feel free to experiment with the project you have just created. Here are some suggestions:

• Try inserting numbered markers throughout the project and jumping to them by pressing Control (Windows) or Command (Mac OS) followed by the marker number.

• From the Project Window Options dialog box, select each of the views and view the options for the Project window and look at the results.

• Using the Feet1.mov clip, break the link between video and audio portions, trim the video portion on both ends, and then try to resync the two and relink them.

• Use the shortcuts listed in the Premiere Quick Reference Card and in Premiere Help to move clips in the Timeline.

Review questions

1 What major advantage does a numbered marker have over an unnumbered marker?

2 What is the Fade Control used for?

3 What purpose do the handles on the Fade Control serve?

4 What must you do to see the waveform of an audio clip?

5 Which command might you need to use before editing an audio clip containing linked sound?

Answers

1 You can jump to a numbered marker by pressing and holding down Control (Windows) or Command (Mac OS) while pressing the number key that corresponds to the marker number.

2 The Fade Control changes the volume level of an audio clip.

3 Handles on the Fade Control create segments, which enable you to create fades.

4 To see audio events in an audio clip, you must first expand the track by clicking the arrow to the left of the track name.

5 Chose Edit > Break Link to unlink a video clip from an audio clip before editing the audio clip.

Lesson 6

Additional Editing Techniques

Complex editing situations demand specialized tools. This lesson provides the tools and techniques you need to whip your projects into shape.

You'll fine-tune a segment for a documentary on glassblowing. In editing this segment, you'll learn the following techniques:

- Making three-point and four-point edits.
- Targeting video and audio tracks
- Linking, unlinking, and synchronizing video and audio clips.
- Creating a split edit using the link override tool.
- Closing a gap with the Ripple Delete command.

Getting started

For this lesson you'll open an existing project with the clips roughly assembled in the Timeline. Make sure you know the location of the files used in this lesson. Insert the CD-ROM disc if necessary. For help, see "Using the Classroom in a Book files" on page 4.

To ensure that the Premiere preferences are set to the default values, exit Premiere, and then delete the preferences file as explained in "Restoring default preferences" on page 5.

1 Double-click 06Lesson.ppj in the 06Lesson folder to open it in Premiere.

2 When the project opens, choose File > Save As, open the appropriate lesson folder on your hard disk if necessary, type **Glass1.ppj**, and press Enter (Windows) or Return (Mac OS).

Viewing the finished movie

To see what you'll be creating, take a look at the complete movie.

1 Choose File > Open and double-click the 06Final.mov file in the Final folder, inside the 06Lesson folder.

The movie opens in the Source view of the Monitor window.

2 Click the Play button (▶) to view the movie.

Viewing the assembled project

Let's take a look at the project as it has been assembled so far. Because there are no transitions, filters, or other effects used in this project, you do not need to generate a preview to view the project.

1 Ensure the edit line is at the beginning of the Timeline. To move it to the beginning, click the Timeline window title bar and then press the Home key.

2 To view the project, click the Play button (▶) under the Program view of the Monitor window.

The project plays in the Program view. Although the assembled project looks much like the finished movie you viewed earlier, you may notice some small problems that could be solved by further editing. In this lesson, you'll use some editing tools that are especially useful in fine-tuning a project.

Much of this lesson deals with editing techniques that preserve the length or duration of a project or of a range of frames.

Understanding three-point and four-point editing

In some situations, you may want to replace a range of frames in the program with a range of frames from a source clip. In Premiere, you can do this using a three-point edit or a four-point edit; both are standard techniques in video editing.

In previous lessons, you have worked with *source In and Out points*—the first and last frames of a clip that will be added to the video program. In addition, it's important to understand *program In and Out points*—the location in your video program where you will apply some editing technique. Being able to specify In and Out points for source and program gives you more control so your edits are as precise as possible. You'll need to set source and program In and Out points for three- and four-point editing.

Three-point editing Use three-point editing when at least one end point (In or Out) of the source material or the program material it replaces is not critical. The three-point edit is more common than the four-point edit because you set only three points and the ranges do not have to be the same duration. Premiere automatically trims the point you don't set so that the source and program material are the same length. This is called a three-point edit because you specify three points: any combination of In and Out points in the program material being replaced and in the source material being added.

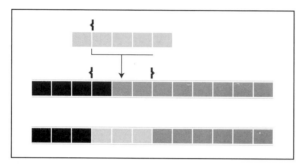

In a three-point edit, you set three points and Premiere sets the fourth point.

Four-point editing Use four-point editing when you want to replace a range of frames in the program with a range of frames of equal duration in the source. This is called a four-point edit because you specify all four points: the In and Out points both for the source material being added and for the program material being replaced.

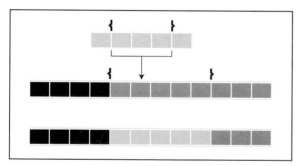

In a four-point edit, you set all four points. If source and target material have different lengths, you can tell Premiere to make the source material fit the target area (as shown above).

If the source material you've selected is not exactly the same duration as the material you're replacing, Premiere gives you one of two options for completing the replacement, depending on the situation: *fit to fill* or *trim source*. If you select Fit to Fill, the duration and speed of the source frames change to fit into the duration of the frames being replaced. If you select Trim Source, Premiere changes the Out point of the source frames, effectively making this a three-point edit instead of a four-point edit.

In the next exercise, you'll make a three-point edit.

Making a three-point edit

You'll use a three-point edit to overlay a scene with linked sound, Talk.mov, replacing parts of Shape.mov and Heat-1.mov in the program. As part of this edit, you'll also eliminate some unwanted camera movement at the beginning of Talk.mov. First, you'll open the source clip in the Source view and preview it.

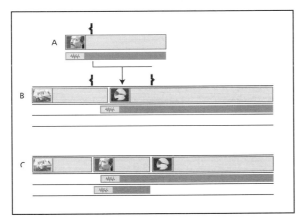

After setting an In point in the source material (A) and In and Out points in the program (B), you overlay the source material into the program (C).

1 In the Navigator palette, use the zoom-out (⌃) button or the zoom-in (⌄) button to set the Time Unit menu (in the Timeline) to 1 Second.

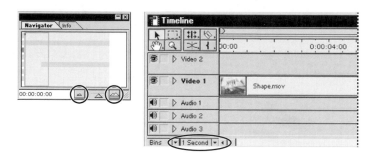

2 In the Project window, double-click Talk.mov to open it in the Source view of the Monitor window.

3 Preview a bit of the clip by clicking the Play button. Notice the camera movement at the beginning of the clip.

You'll set the In point in Talk.mov to remove the camera movement.

4 Under the Source view, double-click the location timecode (the left set of green numbers), type **516**, and press Enter (Windows) or Return (Mac OS).

5 Click the In button (ɬ) to set the source In point in Talk.mov.

Now you'll indicate where you want to place this clip in the program by setting the program In point within Shape.mov and the program Out point within Heat-1.mov.

6 In the Navigator, drag the green box all the way to the left so that the first two clips are visible in the Timeline.

7 Double-click the location timecode under the Program view to highlight it; if necessary, click in the Program view first. Type **625**, and press Enter/Return.

8 In the Program view, click the In button (‍‍) to set the In point. An In icon appears in the Timeline time ruler and the Program view shuttle bar.

9 Under the Program view, double-click the location timecode, type **1018**, and press Enter (Windows) or Return (Mac OS).

10 Click the Out button (‍‍) to set the Out point in the Program view. An Out icon appears in the Timeline time ruler and the Program view shuttle bar.

At this point, the duration timecode (Δ) should read 3:23, which is the duration from program In point to program Out point in the Program view.

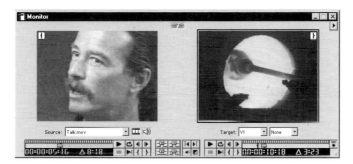

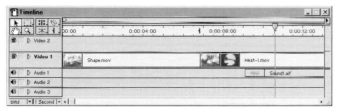

Whenever you add clips to the Timeline using the keyboard or Monitor window controls (as you're about to do), you need to tell Premiere which tracks you want to use. To do that, you'll use the targeting controls immediately below the Source and Program views. Because a sound file already exists in the Audio 1 track, you need to tell Premiere to put the Talk.mov audio in the Audio 2 track so as not to disturb Audio 1.

11 Under the Program view in the Monitor window, select A2 for Target.

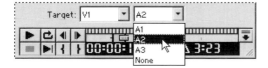

Now that you have specified a source In Point and program In and Out points (for a total of three points) and set the target tracks for your edits, you are ready to replace the program material with the source material.

12 In the Monitor window, click the overlay button (⬚).

The range of frames marked in Shape.mov and Heat-1.mov is replaced with an equal duration of Talk.mov.

13 Save the project.

Specifying source and target tracks

When you add clips to the Timeline by dragging, the clip is added to the track and time position where you drop it. However, when you add clips to the Timeline using Monitor window controls or by using the keyboard, you must specify in advance the way video and audio tracks are added to the Timeline. By default, both source audio and video are added; in the Timeline, the Video 1A and Audio 1 tracks are the default target, or destination, video and audio tracks. In the Timeline, the names of the target video and audio tracks are bold. You control how source video and audio are added to the Timeline using the Take icons and Target menus:

• The Take Video icon (▦) and Take Audio icon (◀)) (under the Source view) control the source clips. They let you control whether a particular source clip's video or audio track is added to the Timeline. For example, if one clip contains video you don't want to use, you can specify that the source clip will provide only audio to the Timeline.

• The video and audio Target menus control the video program in the Timeline. They govern which Timeline video or audio track is set to receive the video or audio track from the source clip. It is possible to target no Timeline track for either video or audio. For example, if you build a rough cut of a music video and the only audio you want to use is a music clip separate from any of your video clips, you may want to target no audio tracks so that your program receives no audio from any source video clip. In this case, no audio is added to the program regardless of how you set the Take icons for the source, and the same is true for targeting video tracks.

• For predictable results, watch out for cases where the target tracks don't make sense compared to the settings for the source video and audio. For example, if you turn on Take Video but turn off Take Audio for the source clip, but Timeline tracks are targeted for both video and audio, the video goes to the target video track as expected, but the source clip audio duration is inserted in the target audio track as blank space. This is because targeting a track always adds the duration of the source clip even if the corresponding source track (audio or video) is not available to the target. If you don't want the blank audio, specify no target audio tracks.

—From the Adobe Premiere User Guide, Chapter 4

Linking and unlinking clips

In Premiere, you can link a video clip to an audio clip, which is useful when you want to move previously unlinked tracks together. This is called a *soft link*. Sound recorded on a video camera can be captured and imported into a Premiere project already linked to its video clip. This is called a *hard link*.

Breaking a link is useful when you want to edit In or Out points independently. You used this technique in the previous lesson to create an L-cut (see "Creating an L-cut" on page 148). You can also override a link temporarily to edit linked clips without breaking the link.

In this exercise, you'll perform three separate tasks. First, you'll soft-link a video clip with an audio clip. Then you'll resynchronize a pair of hard-linked clips. Finally, you'll use the link override tool to create a *split edit*. A standard video editing technique, the split edit contains audio that starts before the associated or linked video.

Linking clips

You'll start by aligning an audio clip to a video clip, and then you'll link them. You want Music.aif to start at the beginning of Oven.mov.

♡ *To quickly display or hide open palettes, press the Tab key.*

1 In the Navigator, use the zoom-out (⌒) button or the zoom-in (⌒) button to set the Time Unit menu (in the Timeline) to 2 Seconds. Scroll the Timeline all the way to the beginning.

2 In the Monitor window, click the next edit button (▸ɪ) until the edit line moves to the beginning of Oven.mov.

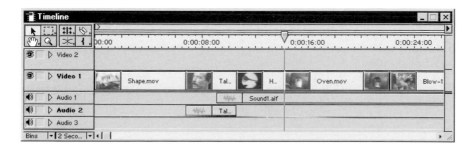

3 Drag Music.aif from the Project window into the Audio 2 track so that it snaps to the edit line at the beginning of Oven.mov.

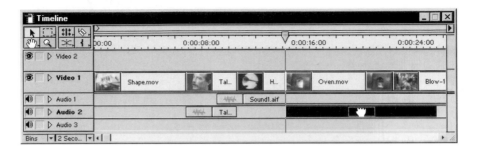

4 In the Timeline window, select the soft link tool.

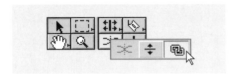

5 Click Oven.mov. Position the pointer on Music.aif so it changes to the soft link tool ( ) and then click.

Oven.mov and Music.aif flash, indicating they are linked. In the next exercise, you'll more clearly see the effect of linking.

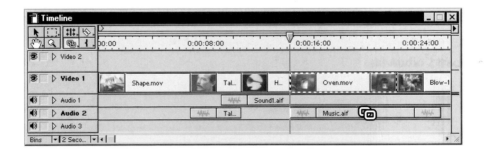

 A shortcut to linking clips without selecting the soft link tool is to click one clip and then hold down the Shift key while clicking the other clip. This works only when the selection tool is selected.

Closing a gap with the Ripple Delete command

Earlier in this lesson, you moved Oven.mov, leaving a gap in the video track between Heat-1.mov and Blow-2.mov. You'll use the Ripple Delete command to remove this gap. The Ripple Delete command eliminates the selected gap by moving all clips that are on the right of the gap. Unlike the ripple edit tool, you must select either a gap or one or more clips in the Timeline before choosing the Ripple Delete command.

It's important to understand that you can use the Ripple Delete command only on one or more clips or a gap—you cannot use it to delete a range of frames marked by In and Out points as you can with the Extract button (discussed in the next lesson). Also, the Ripple Delete command has no effect on clips in locked tracks.

Because the audio in Audio 1 and Audio 2 tracks extend into the portion of the program that will be affected by Ripple Delete, you need to lock these audio tracks to keep them unaffected. Locking a track prevents further changes until the track is unlocked.

1 Click the box next to the speaker icon on the far left of the Audio 1 track. Repeat for Audio 2 track.

2 In the Timeline, select the gap between Heat1.mov and Blow-1.mov.

3 Choose Edit > Ripple Delete.

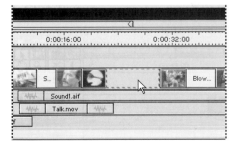 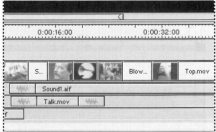

The gap is closed and Blow-1.mov is moved left, next to Heat-1.mov.

4 Alt-click or Option-click just below the Timeline title bar to extend the work area bar over all clips. Then press Enter (Windows) or Return (Mac OS) to preview your work. Save the project.

Exporting the movie

Now that you've finished your editing, it's time to generate a movie file.

1 If you turned off audio previewing earlier in the lesson, make sure you turn it on again by clicking the icon at the at the left edge of each audio track so that it changes to the speaker icon (◀).

2 Choose File > Export > Movie.

3 In the Export Movie dialog box, click Settings.

4 Make sure QuickTime is selected for the File Type and Entire Project is selected for the Range.

5 Also make sure that the Export Video and Export Audio options are selected. You can leave the rest of the settings as they are.

6 Click OK to close the Export Movie Settings dialog box.

7 In the Export Movie dialog box, specify the 06Lesson folder for the location and type **Glass1.mov** for the name of the movie. Click Save (Windows) or OK (Mac OS).

Premiere starts making the movie, displaying a status bar that provides an estimate for the amount of time it will take.

8 When the movie is complete, it is opened in the Source view of the Monitors window.

9 Click the Play button to play the movie.

Exploring on your own

Feel free to experiment with the project you have just created. Here are some suggestions:

• Move the edit line in the Timeline by pressing Shift and dragging the red line in the Navigator palette representing the edit line.

• Perform a four-point edit, but make the source material shorter than the program material. Experiment with the options Premiere gives you to complete the edit.

Review questions

1 In addition to the Timeline window, which two Premiere windows let you move the edit line?

2 What is one advantage of using a three-point edit?

3 To edit linked video and audio clips separately without permanently destroying the link, what tool would you need to use before you begin editing?

4 What is one easy step that helps prevent accidental edits?

Answers

1 You can move the edit line from the Monitor window using the Program view controls, and from the Navigator by pressing the Shift key and dragging.

2 In a three-point edit, Premiere trims the unspecified point for you.

3 The link override tool temporarily breaks the link.

4 Deselecting a tool prevents using it accidentally. Locking a track is another way to prevent accidental edits.

Lesson 7

Advanced Editing Techniques

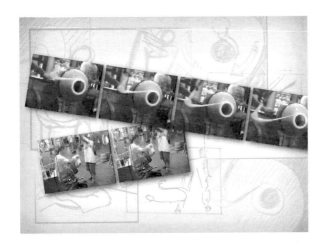

Finishing a project can mean fine-tuning edits while preserving the duration of individual clips and the overall program. The techniques covered in this lesson will help prepare you for the detailed editing needed to polish a project.

You'll complete the introductory segment for a documentary on glassblowing that you started in the previous lesson. This segment must be kept to a finished length of 60 seconds. In editing this segment, you'll learn the following techniques:

- Removing frames using the Extract and Lift buttons.
- Pasting a clip using the Paste Custom command.
- Using the slip and slide tools to adjust edits.
- Editing in the Trim View.
- Changing a clip's rate.

Getting started

For this lesson you'll open an existing project with all of the necessary files imported. Make sure you know the location of the files used in this lesson. Insert the CD-ROM disc if necessary. For help, see "Using the Classroom in a Book files" on page 4.

To ensure that the Premiere preferences are set to the default values, exit Premiere, and then delete the preferences file as explained in "Restoring default preferences" on page 5.

1 Double-click 07Lesson.ppj in the 07Lesson folder to open it in Premiere.

2 When the project opens, choose File > Save As, open the appropriate lesson folder on your hard disk if necessary, type **Glass2.ppj**, and press Enter (Windows) or Return (Mac OS).

Viewing the finished movie

To see what you'll be creating, take a look at the finished movie.

1 Choose File > Open and double-click the 07Final.mov file in the Final folder, inside the 07Lesson folder.

The movie opens in the Source view of the Monitor window.

2 Click the Play button (▶) to view the movie.

Viewing the assembled project

Let's take a look at the project as it has been assembled so far. Because there are no transitions, filters, or other effects used in this project, you do not need to generate a preview to view the project.

Note: This project is a continuation of the project you worked on in Lesson 6, "Additional Editing Techniques." The project you just opened reflects the tasks covered in that lesson. In addition, several clips have been added to the end of the project.

1 Ensure the edit line is at the beginning of the Timeline. To move it to the beginning, make sure the Timeline window is active and no clips are selected. Then press the Home key.

2 To view the project, click the Play button (►) under the Program view of the Monitor window.

The project plays in the Program view. Although the assembled project looks much like the final project you viewed earlier, you may notice some small problems that could be solved by further editing, such as correcting a cut where the action is not synchronized. In addition, you'll make some changes to improve the look of the project, inserting, for example, a close-up to show detail. In this lesson, you'll use some editing tools that are especially useful in fine-tuning a project.

Much of this lesson deals with editing techniques that tune edits to match action while preserving the length or duration of clips.

Understanding the extract and lift functions

Premiere provides two methods of removing a range of frames or a gap from the Timeline: *extracting* and *lifting*.

Extracting   Removes frames from the Timeline, closing the gap like a ripple deletion. These frames can be within a single clip or can span multiple clips, but it is important to understand that extracting removes the selected range of frames from all unlocked tracks. You can also extract a gap from the Timeline. This feature works only with a range of frames that you have identified with In and Out points in the Program view.

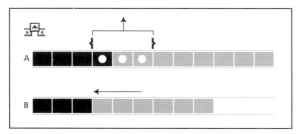

*Frames are marked in the Program view with In and Out points (**A**). The marked portion of the program is deleted and the gap is closed up (**B**).*

Lifting   Removes a range of frames from the Timeline, leaving a gap. These frames can be within a single clip or can span multiple clips and are removed only from the target track. As in extracting, you select which frames you want to remove by setting In and Out points in the Program view of the Monitor window. The Lift button has no effect on clips selected in the Timeline.

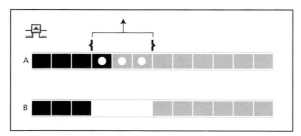

*Frames are marked in the Program view with In and Out points (**A**). The marked portion of the program is deleted, leaving a gap (**B**).*

Removing frames with the Extract button

Here, you'll use the extract feature to remove some camera movement in the middle of the Top.mov clip. Extracting the frames splits the clip into two separate clips.

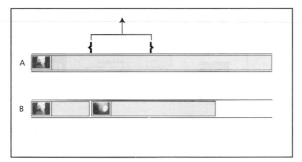

*Top.mov before (**A**) and after (**B**) extracting frames.*

To begin, you'll set In and Out points in the Program view to define the portion of Top.mov you want to extract from the Timeline. But first you'll use the Locate Clip command to find Top.mov in the Timeline.

1 Select Top.mov in the Project window, choose Clip > Locate Clip, and click Done.

Premiere selects the clip in the Timeline.

2 Scrub in the Timeline ruler to preview Top.mov, noting the camera movement near the beginning of the clip. Leave the edit line at about where the movement starts.

3 Under the Program view, use the controls to locate the frame before the sphere and the camera start moving (at 35:12).

4 In the Program view, click the Mark In button ( ) to set the In point for the frames you will extract.

5 Find the frame in which the camera has stopped moving, the image is in focus, and the tool doesn't obscure the sphere (at 42:10).

6 Click the Mark Out button ( ) to set the Out point.

7 To prevent unwanted deletion of audio, lock the Audio 1 and Audio 2 tracks by clicking the lock icon in the Timeline so that it is crossed out.

Now, you'll extract the frames you've just marked.

8 In the Monitor window, click the Extract button.

The portion of Top.mov you marked is removed, breaking Top.mov into two clips. The gap in the track is closed, shortening the program.

9 Preview the video you just edited.

10 Save the project.

💡 *To turn off audio previewing temporarily, make audio tracks shy by clicking the speaker icon (🔊) at the left edge of any audio track that contains audio clips.*

Removing frames with the Lift button

You'll use the Lift button in the Monitor window to remove the middle portion of Closeup1.mov, making two clips. You'll set the In and Out points to keep specific frames in the two remaining clips. Later, you'll fill the gap with a similar scene taken from a different point of view with a second camera.

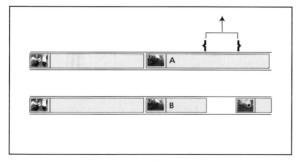

*Closeup1.mov before (**A**) and after (**B**) lifting frames.*

First, you'll define the range of frames you want to remove.

1 In the Navigator palette, click the zoom-in (right) button once to magnify the Timeline view. The Time Unit menu in the Timeline should be set to 2 Seconds.

Now you'll locate Closeup1.mov in the Timeline.

2 Select Closeup1.mov in the Project window, choose Clip > Locate Clip, and click Done. Premiere selects the clip in the Timeline.

3 Scrub in the Timeline ruler to preview Closeup1.mov.

4 Use the controls under the Program view to locate the point several seconds before the molten glass meets to form a circle (at 55:28). This is where you'll cut to a new scene. Click the Mark In button (⨍) to set the In point in Closeup1.mov.

5 In the Program view, find the frame just before the glob of molten glass meets the left edge of the frame (at 56:27). This is where you'll cut back to this scene. Click the Mark Out button (⨍) to set the Out point.

Now that you've defined the range of frames you want to remove, you'll lift it from the Timeline.

6 In the Monitor window, click the Lift button.

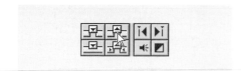

The portion of Closeup1.mov you marked is removed, leaving the other clips in the track undisturbed and preserving the program's duration. In the next exercise, you'll use the Paste Custom command to fill this gap.

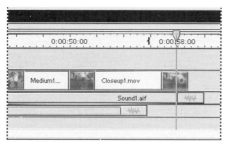 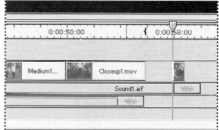

To prevent confusion, let's give a new name, or *alias*, to the fragment of Closeup1.mov to the right of the gap. Giving an alias to an *instance* (a copy of a clip in the Timeline) doesn't affect the *master clip* in the Project window or other instances of the clip.

7 Select the second fragment of Closeup1.mov and choose Clip > Alias.

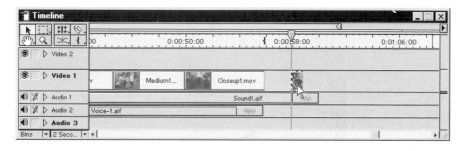

8 When prompted, type **Closeup2** and click OK.

9 Save the project.

Understanding Paste Custom

With the Paste Custom command, you can paste either the content or the settings of the clip you have copied. If Content is selected in the Paste Custom Settings dialog box, this command pastes the copied clip into a clip or an empty space that you have selected in a track. You can choose from a list of options for manipulating the clips at the edit point, such as moving the In or Out point of the source or destination, changing speed, or shifting tracks. As when using a three-point edit, you should select an option that preserves the critical In and Out points involved in the edit. The option you select is dependent on the durations of the source material and the gap.

In a later lesson, you'll use the Paste Custom command to copy settings from one clip to another ("Copying filters and settings" on page 322).

Pasting into a gap

There are a number of ways to insert material into a gap in the project, including using 3-point and 4-point edits. In this exercise, you'll use Paste Custom to paste a copy of Medium1.mov into the gap you just created with the Lift button. Medium1.mov, Closeup1.mov, and Closeup2 contain the same scene shot with two cameras.

Before pasting the copy into the gap, you'll need to determine which of the four points involved in this procedure can be moved without negatively affecting the edit. Because you want to use frames near the end of this clip, moving the In point in the copy makes the most sense in this case. The position of this new In point is not critical here; you'll fine-tune it later. Premiere adjusts the duration of this clip to fit the gap when you paste it.

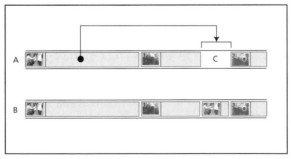

*Closeup2 before (**A**) and after (**B**) pasting a copy of Medium1.mov into the gap (**C**).*

3 Position the pointer on Closeup1.mov, and then press and hold down the mouse button.

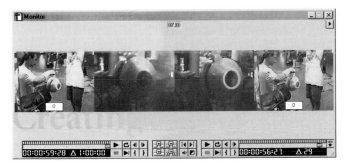

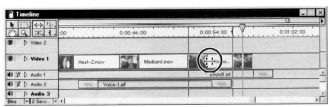

When you hold down the mouse button with the slide tool selected, the Monitor window changes to show critical frames of three clips. It displays four frames: the Out point of the adjacent clip on the left (Medium1.mov), the In point and the Out point of the clip under the tool (Closeup1.mov), and the In point of the adjacent clip on the right (Medium2). While synchronizing the action, you'll be comparing the two frames in the left half of the Monitor window.

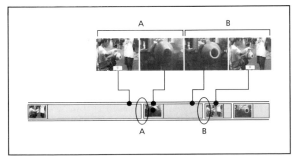

*You can view the edit between Medium1.mov and Closeup1.mov (**A**) and the edit between Closeup1.mov and Medium2 (**B**). Here, you'll fix the first edit (**A**).*

4 With the mouse button still held down, notice the flash of light on the right edge of Closeup1.mov (the second frame from the left in the Monitors window). You want to synchronize this flash with the corresponding flash in Medium1.mov. Drag left to trim Medium1.mov until you see the flash in the first frame (Medium1.mov Out point). The numeric display in the first frame should show -122, indicating you have moved Closeup1.mov 122 frames earlier. Release the mouse button.

Match the action between Medium1.mov (A) and Closeup1.mov (B), ignoring the other two frames.

5 Preview the change.

The action in the first and second frames should match.

6 Save the project.

Using the Slip tool

You'll use the slip tool to match the action between Closeup1.mov and Medium2. To do this, you'll move the In point of Medium2 while preserving the clip's duration. The In and Out points of Medium2 will appear in the two middle frames in the Monitor window as you use the slip tool.

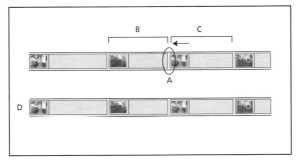

*Use the slip tool to match action at the edit point (**A**) between Closeup1.mov (**B**) and Medium2 (**C**). The tool changes the In and Out points of Medium2 while preserving its duration. Adjacent clips, such as Closeup1.mov, are unaffected. The result can be seen in (**D**).*

1 In the Timeline, select the slip tool.

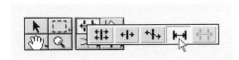

2 Position the pointer on the Medium2 clip in the Timeline, and then press and hold down the mouse button.

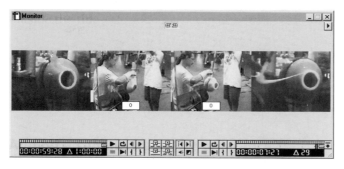

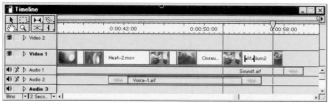

As it did when the slide tool was activated, the Monitor window changes, this time showing the Out point of Closeup1.mov, the In and Out points of Medium2, and the In point of Closeup2.

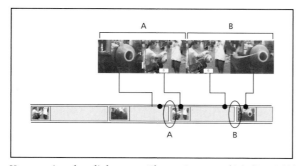

*You can view the edit between Closeup1.mov and Medium2 (A)
and the edit between Medium2 and Closeup2 (B). Here, you'll
fix the first edit (A).*

3 Drag right until the action in the first frame (the Out point of Closeup1.mov) matches the action in the second frame (the In point of Medium2).

Match the action between Closeup1.mov (A) and Medium2 (B), ignoring the other two frames.

4 Release the mouse button.

The Monitor window changes back to the usual configuration.

5 Select the selection tool (⬉) to deselect the slip tool.

6 Preview the change.

The action in the first and second frames should match.

7 Save the project.

Understanding the Trim view

The Trim view is used to trim individual frames on either side of an edit while viewing those frames so you can view the edit as you work. The Trim view provides the same function as the ripple tool, but it provides finer control and a better view of program material. When you select Trim Mode in the Monitor window menu, the Source and

Program views are replaced by two views in which 1, 3, or 5 frames of adjacent clips are displayed. Being able to see frames on either side of the edit enables you to precisely trim each clip. You can also perform a rolling edit in the Trim view. This view is useful for fine-tuning the edit between two clips in which the action must match or timing is critical.

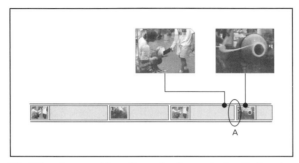

*The Trim view provides a frame-by-frame ripple edit function and a view of each clip at the edit point (**A**).*

Editing in the Trim view

At this point, the action in Medium2 and Closeup2 is out of sync because of the edit you performed with the slide tool. You'll use the Trim view to match the action in these clips so that the action at the Out point of Medium2 is the same as at the In point of Closeup2. First, you'll trim Medium2 to match the action in Closeup2, and then you'll use a rolling edit to move the edit point between them for the most effective edit. The rolling edit preserves the combined duration of the two clips.

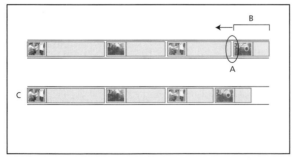

*The Trim view will be used to match action at the edit point (**A**) between Medium2 and Closeup2 while preserving the In and Out points and duration of Closeup2 (**B**). The result can be seen in (**C**).*

1 Under the Program view, use the controls to set the edit line between the last two clips in the program: Medium2 and Closeup2 (at 56:27).

2 In the Monitor window menu, choose Monitor Window Options.

3 Under Trim Mode Options, ensure that the mode on the left is selected, and then click OK.

4 Choose Trim Mode from the Monitor window menu.

In the Trim view, Premiere displays two frames: the Out point of Medium2 on the left and the In point of Closeup2 on the right.

You'll notice some new buttons in the Trim view.

A. *Cancel Edit (all edits)*
B. *Previous Edit*
C. *Trim Left 5 frames*
D. *Trim Left (one frame)*
E. *Trim Right (one frame)*
F. *Trim Right 5 frames*
G. *Next Edit*
H. *Play Edit*

Now you'll sync up the action in Closeup2 to the matching action in Medium2.

When you select one of the views in the Trim view, the timecode below it changes to green.

5 Click the left frame (Medium2) to select it and click the Trim Left 5 Frames (◀▮) and Trim Left (single-frame) (◀▮) buttons to adjust Medium2 until the action in the Medium2 Out point matches that in the Closeup2 In point. If you go too far, use the Trim Right 5 Frames (▮▶) and Trim Right (single-frame) (▮▶) buttons to reverse the trim.

💡 *To undo all edits made in the Trim view, click the cancel Edit button (✖).*

The action in both clips is now in sync. Next you'll move the edit between the clips using a rolling edit in the Trim view.

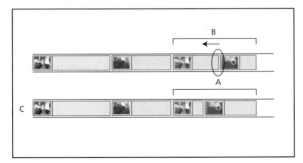

*You'll use a rolling edit in the Trim view to move the edit (**A**) between Medium2 and Closeup2 while preserving the combined duration of both clips (**B**). The result can be seen in (**C**).*

You'll change the edit to the close-up to show a better look at the instrument pulling away from the rim.

6 Position the pointer between the two views so that it changes to the rolling edit tool, and then drag the tool icon left until the instrument just starts to pull away. Use the illustration below as a guide.

7 Scrub in the Timeline ruler to preview the change. Scrubbing automatically exits Trim Mode and returns the Monitor window to its normal view.

Note: *You can also exit Trim Mode by choosing Trim Mode from the Monitor window menu to remove the checkmark from the command.*

8 Preview the last four clips.

9 Save the project.

Changing clip duration and speed

The duration of a video or audio clip is the length of time it plays—the difference in time between a clip's In point and Out point. The initial duration of a clip is the same as it was when the clip was imported or captured. If you alter the beginning and ending of a clip by editing the source In and Out points, its duration will change. You can also set the duration of a clip by specifying a length of time from its current source In point. A still image can also have a duration when you want to display it for a specific length of time. You can set the default duration of the still images you import by choosing File > Preferences > General / Still Image.

The speed of a clip is the playback rate of the action or audio compared to the rate at which it was recorded. Speed is initially the same as it was when the clip was imported or captured. Changing a clip's speed alters its source frame rate and may cause some frames to be omitted or repeated. In addition, changing the speed of a clip requires playing the same number of frames in a different length of time, which also changes the duration (moves the Out point) of the clip. When you change the speed of a clip containing interlaced fields, you may need to adjust how Premiere treats the fields, especially when speed drops below 100% of the original speed.

—From the Adobe Premiere User Guide, Chapter 4

Changing a clip's rate

To polish the end of this project, you'll change the frame rate of the last two clips to create a slow motion effect. At the same time, you'll use the change in clip duration to get the project to exactly 60 seconds (1:00), the specified length for this segment of the documentary. To do this, you'll use two different tools: the Clip Speed dialog box and the rate stretch tool.

First, you'll use the Clip Speed dialog box to make Closeup2 play at exactly one-quarter speed. Then, you'll use the rate stretch tool on Medium2 to provide our required program length.

1 In the Navigator, click the zoom-in (⌂) button until the Time Unit menu is set to 1/2 Second. Then drag the green box to view Medium2 and Closeup2 in the Timeline.

2 Click Closeup2 and choose Clip > Speed to open the Clip Speed dialog box.

3 In the New Rate box, type **25**, and then click OK.

Closeup2 is now plays at one-quarter speed, which means it is four times as long as it was originally. Now you'll move the edit line to 01:00:00 (60 seconds), where you want the project to end.

4 Double-click the location timecode under the Program view, type **10000**, and press the Enter (Windows) or Return (Mac OS).

5 In the Navigator, use the slider or zoom buttons to set the Time Unit menu to 1 Second.

6 Drag Closeup2 until the end snaps to the edit line. Don't worry about the gap; you'll reunite the edit between Closeup2 and Medium 2 shortly.

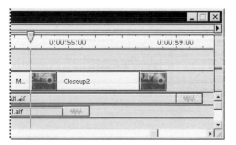 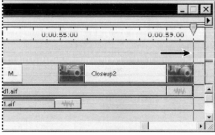

Now you'll stretch Medium2.

7 In the Timeline, select the rate stretch tool.

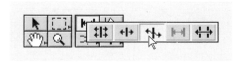

8 Position the pointer over the right end of Medium2 until the pointer turns into the rate stretch tool. Drag right until the end of Medium2 snaps to Closeup2.

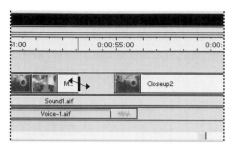 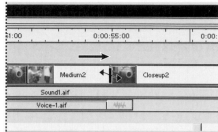

9 Preview Medium2 and Closeup2 at their new frame rate, and then save the project.

Exporting the movie

Now that you've finished your editing, it's time to generate a movie file.

1 If you turned off audio previewing earlier in the lesson, make sure you turn it on again by clicking the blank box at the at the left edge of each audio track so it changes to the speaker icon (🔊).

2 Choose File > Export > Movie.

3 In the Export Movie dialog box, click Settings.

4 Make sure QuickTime is selected for the File Type and Entire Project is selected for the Range.

5 Also make sure that the Export Video and Export Audio options are selected. You can leave the rest of the settings as they are. Click OK to close the Export Movie Settings dialog box.

6 In the Export Movie dialog box, move to the 07Lesson folder to set the location and type **Glass2.mov** for the name of the movie. Click Save (Windows) or OK (Mac OS).

Premiere starts making the movie, displaying a status bar that provides an estimate for the amount of time it will take.

7 When the movie is complete, it is opened in the Source view of the Monitors window.

8 Click the Play button to play the movie.

Exploring on your own

Feel free to experiment with the project you have just created. Here are some suggestions:

• Try changing the name of a clip in the Project window without using Clip > Alias. Here's a hint: You don't need to use any menu items, icons, or buttons, but the Project window must be in List View. Once you've changed the name, observe what effect it has on instances in the Timeline.

• Try using a freeze frame on Closeup2 at the end of this lesson instead of changing the frame rate. Set marker 0 on the frame you want to freeze and then choose Clip > Video > Hold Frame. Experiment with extending a hold frame to see how it differs from a still image.

• Replace the middle of Closeup1.mov with Medium2 using a three-point edit instead of using the Lift button and Paste Custom.

Review questions

1 The Ripple Delete command and the Extract button offer similar functions. What is the key difference between them?

2 Which tool would you use to change the In and Out points of a clip while preserving its duration?

3 What features does the Trim Mode offer that make it well suited to fine-tuning edits?

4 What are two ways to change the frame rate of a clip?

Answers

1 Ripple Delete works on one or more whole clips or on a gap; the extract function works on a range of frames in one or more clips.

2 The slip tool changes the In and Out points of a clip while preserving its duration.

3 The Trim Mode enables you to trim individual frames on either side of an edit point, while viewing those frames.

4 You can change a clip's frame rate using either the Clip Speed dialog box (choose Clip > Speed) or the rate stretch tool (↔).

Lesson 8

Creating a Title

Text and graphics play an integral role in conveying information in a video program. Premiere's Title window lets you create text and graphics, which you can import and superimpose over existing video.

In this lesson you'll use Premiere's Title window to create a 14-second cartoon for a children's educational Web site. You'll create three different titles using text, rolling text, and graphic tools; then you'll superimpose them over a movie clip in Premiere's Timeline. Specifically you'll learn how to do the following:

- Enter text and change text attributes.

- Kern text.

- Add shadows and color.

- Create graphics.

- Apply opacity to graphics and text.

- Create and preview rolling type.

- Add titles to a project.

- Superimpose a title over a video clip.

- Edit titles.

Getting started

To begin, you'll open an existing Premiere project and create a new title. Make sure you have installed the News Gothic font. For help, see "Installing lesson fonts" on page 4. Also make sure you know the location of the files used in this lesson. Insert the CD-ROM disc if necessary. For help, see "Using the Classroom in a Book files" on page 4.

To ensure that the Premiere preferences are set to default values, exit Premiere, and then delete the preferences file as explained in "Restoring default preferences" on page 5.

1 Double-click 08Lesson.ppj in the 08Lesson folder to start Premiere and open the project.

2 When the project opens, choose File > Save As. If necessary, open the appropriate lesson folder on your hard disk and type **Cartoon.ppj**. Press Enter (Windows) or Return (Mac OS).

Viewing the finished movie

If you'd like to see what you'll be creating in this lesson, you can look at the completed movie. Because you'll be making your own drawings in the Title window, your movie will look slightly different.

1 Choose File > Open and select 08Final.mov in the Final folder in the 08Lesson folder, and then click Open. The movie opens in the Source view of the Monitor window.

2 Click the Play button (▶) in the Source view to view the movie.

About titles

Adobe Premiere's Title window lets you create text and simple graphic image files, called *titles*, that can be used only in Premiere. To use the Title window, you do not need to open an existing project or create a new project.

Let's open the Title window and review the basics.

Choose File > New > Title to open the Title window.

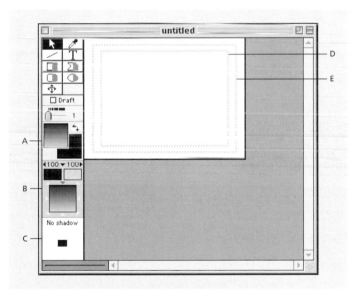

A. Color swatches B. Gradient and Transparency settings
C. Shadow Offset control D. Title-safe zone E. Action-safe zone

When you open the Title window, Premiere adds the Title menu to the menu bar. This menu contains all of the Title window's commands and options. You can also access these options by right-clicking (Windows) or Control-clicking (Mac OS) in the Title window. However, if you want to change the window size or background color, you need to open the Title Window Options dialog box by either choosing the Window menu or by right-clicking (Windows) or Control-clicking (Mac OS) the Title window title bar.

The Title window contains two dotted-line boxes. The inner box represents the title-safe zone and the outer box represents the action-safe zone. If you draw graphic images outside of the action-safe zone, they may not be visible on some NTSC monitors. Text outside the title-safe zone may appear blurry or distorted on a NTSC monitor.

Creating a simple title

Here you'll create a simple, text-only title. You will add a sample frame to the Title window, add text, change the text attributes, add a shadow, and kern the text.

Adding a sample frame for reference

Before you enter text, you'll add a sample background frame to the Title window. This sample frame will help you determine the best complementary colors to use for the title text. Sample frames are only for reference and do not become part of the title. When you save and close the title, the reference frame is not saved with the file.

1 Move the Title window so that is not overlapping the Project window.

Notice that Water.mov is already in the Project window. You'll use this movie as a background reference frame for your title.

2 Drag the Water.mov icon from the Project window to the Title window and release the mouse. The background of the Title window is now the first frame from Water.mov.

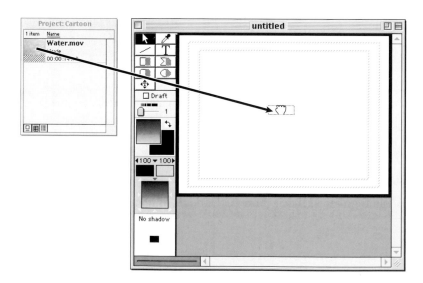

Creating text objects

Compared to paper, video displays at a much lower resolution and is viewed from much farther away (often from across a room). For maximum legibility, use the following guidelines when specifying type for video:

• Use large sans-serif fonts. Avoid small type and serif fonts; the thin strokes of some small or serif characters do not display well on interlaced television sets, causing them to flicker.

• Use semibold and bold type weights, which are generally easier to read on television than regular or light type weights.

• Use few words in your titles. Long paragraphs of small type are difficult to read on television.

• When designing a title to be superimposed, use colors that contrast well with the background video. You can import a sample frame to check a title against its background. If the background is complex, consider adding a shadow or a semitransparent shape behind the type.

—From the Adobe Premiere User Guide, Chapter 7

Creating text and changing text attributes

Premiere lets you change the text attributes of words and individual characters within a word using any font available to your operating system.

1 Select the text tool ('T') and click the top left corner of the Title window, within the title safe zone (innermost dotted line).

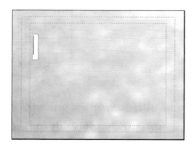

Note: *As a general rule for video, use fonts that are at least 16 points. Anything smaller may not be visible on a TV monitor.*

2 Change the font using the method appropriate for your operating system:

• In Mac OS, choose Title > Font and select News Gothic Bold. Then choose Title > Size, select Other, and type **30** in the text box.

• In Windows, choose Title > Font, select News Gothic for the Font, Bold for the Font Style, and type **30** in the Size text box. Then click OK.

3 Type **Otto**.

4 Choose File > Save, open the 08Lesson folder if necessary, and then type **Otto.ptl** for the name, and click Save.

Changing the text color

The Object Color swatch in the Title window displays the color of the currently selected object.

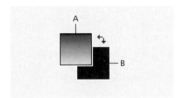

A. Object Color swatch *B.* Shadow Color swatch

The shadow color is determined by the color of the Shadow Color swatch, which is located to the right of the Object Color swatch. To switch the object and shadow colors, click the arrow between the swatches.

Clicking a swatch opens Premiere's Color Picker. You can choose colors in the Color Picker by simply clicking on the color in the color box, or by entering values in the Red, Green, and Blue text boxes. The black, white, and gray values are located along the left side of the color box.

Let's change the color of the word "Otto."

1 Using the selection tool (▶), select "Otto," if not already selected. If it is selected, a small box or handle appears on each of the four corners of the bounding box.

2 Click the Object Color swatch.

Premiere's Color Picker appears with a default color of black.

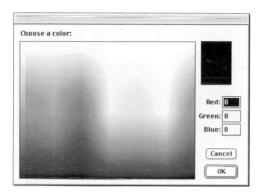

3 Click in the color box to select a deep blue.

If an exclamation point appears next to the color swatch in the upper right corner of the Color Picker, the color you chose is not NTSC-safe. Such colors may bleed or blur when displayed on a NTSC monitor. Because the movie you are creating now will only be played on a computer monitor, you do not need to be concerned with the NTSC-safe warning; however, if you were creating a movie that would ultimately be played from a NTSC monitor, you would need to make sure all your colors were NTSC-safe.

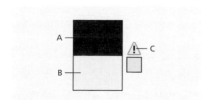

A. Original color swatch ***B.*** *Selected color swatch* ***C.*** *NTSC warning symbol*

4 If you want to use the same color we used for our text, type **51** for Red, **0** for Green, and **176** for Blue. Then click OK to close the Color Picker.

Adding a shadow

You can add a shadow to any image or text object in the Title window by simply selecting the object and then moving the Shadow Offset control (T).

Here you'll create a shadow and then change its color afterward. You can change the color of an object or shadow at any time by selecting the object and clicking the color swatch.

1 With the word "Otto" still selected, drag the Shadow Offset control down and to the right until the shadow value shown above the control is about 4 x 4.

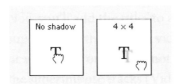

The default color of the shadow is gray. Let's change it to yellow.

2 While the word "Otto" is still selected, double-click (Windows) or click (Mac OS) the Shadow Color swatch to open the Color Picker.

3 Pick a light yellow. To use the same color we used, type **242** for Red, **255** for Green, and **176** for Blue, and then click OK.

By default, Premiere creates soft shadows. You'll change the shadow to a solid shadow, making it more prominent against the aqua-colored background.

4 With the text still selected, choose Title > Shadow > Solid.

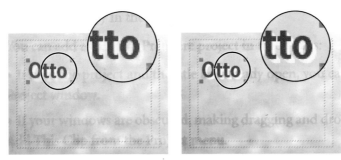

Soft shadow and solid shadow

5 Click anywhere in the Title window to deselect the text.

6 Save the title.

Changing opacity

The opacity slider in the Premiere Title window lets you set different levels of transparency for graphics, text, and shadows. To access the opacity slider, you simply click and hold one of the small black arrows below the Object and Shadow Color swatches.

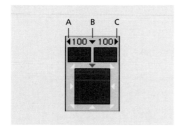

A. *Start transparency* **B.** *Overall transparency* **C.** *End transparency*

You can set the opacity for an entire image by clicking the center arrow (Overall Transparency), or you can vary the opacity by choosing different values using the left arrow (Start Transparency) and the right arrow (End Transparency). See "Using color, transparency, and gradients" in the *Adobe Premiere 5.0 User Guide* for information on varying opacity in the Title window.

Shadows have a default opacity value of 50%. Here you'll increase the overall opacity of the shadow, making it less transparent.

1 Using the selection tool (▶), select the word "Otto."

2 Make sure the Shadow Color swatch is active (is in the foreground). If it isn't, click it to bring it forward.

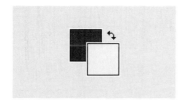

3 Click the center arrow and drag the Overall Transparency slider to approximately 80%. The shadow becomes darker because less of the aqua-colored background is showing through.

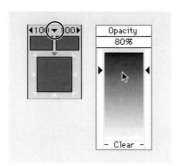

4 Save the title.

Kerning text

Kerning means changing the distance between two characters in a word. To kern text in Premiere's Title window, use the text tool to either highlight the two adjacent letters you want to kern or place the text tool icon between the two letters you want to kern, and then click a kerning button.

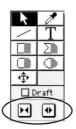

The left kerning button decreases the distance between two letters and the right kerning button increases the distance.

You must use the text tool, not the selection tool, to access the kerning buttons. When you use the text tool, you can kern and edit text, or highlight individual characters to change their font or font attributes.

When you use the selection tool to select text, you select everything within the text's bounding box. If you change the font, color, opacity, shadow, or gradient while the bounding box is selected, all of the text is affected.

Use the selection tool to edit all text. Use the text tool to edit just selected text.

1 Select the text tool (T) and then click between the two Ts in the word "Otto."

2 Click the right kerning button twice to widen the space between the letters.

Because kerning changes letter spacing, it may cause the line to break, splitting the word over two lines. If this happens, you can simply resize the word's bounding box by dragging any of the four corner handles.

3 If kerning caused the word "Otto" to split over two lines in your Title window, click the selection tool, then drag the lower right corner handle of the bounding box up and to the right. When you release the mouse, the two sections of the word reunite on one line.

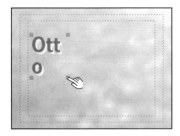 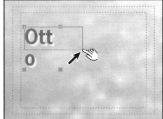

Aligning text

You can align text two ways in Premiere's Title window. You can align the text inside its own bounding box, and you can align the text's bounding box inside the window. Here you'll align the word "Otto" using both alignment methods.

First you'll align the text within the bounding box. This will be especially noticeable if you resized the box in the last exercise.

1 With the word "Otto" still selected, choose Title > Justify > Center. Notice how the word shifts to the center of the bounding box.

Now, before you center the bounding box, let's move it to the top of the window.

2 Using the selection tool (⬏), drag the word "Otto" to the top of the window, so the letters are just inside the title-safe zone. You can also use the arrow keys to reposition the word in the Title window.

Now you can center the bounding box in the window.

3 With the word "Otto" still selected, choose Title > Center Horizontally. Notice how the whole bounding box shifts to the center of the window.

4 Save the title.

Adding more text

Now you'll add more text to the title.

1 Select the text tool (T) and click just below the word "Otto." If you accidently open the text box for the word "Otto," click lower in the window.

💡 *To use a Title window tool one time and then revert to the selection tool, click it once to select it. If you want to use it repeatedly, double-click it. If you don't double-click the tool, it changes back to the selection tool after one use.*

2 Choose Title > Size >18.

3 Type **the octopus**, and then click the selection tool.

Notice the text has a shadow. This text doesn't require a shadow, so you'll remove it.

4 With "the octopus" still selected, drag the Shadow Offset control out of the Shadow area to return the shadow setting to No Shadow.

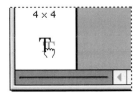 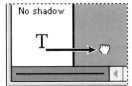

5 Using the selection tool, move the text so that it is positioned in the top one-third of the Title window, directly under the word "Otto." You can also move selected text (or a selected image) by pressing the arrow keys.

6 Choose Title > Center Horizontally.

7 Save the title.

Creating a graphic image in the Title window

Premiere's Title window lets you create simple graphics. You can use the drawing tools to create rectangles, squares, rounded squares, circles, ovals, lines, and polygons.

Adding a title as a background frame

Before you start drawing the graphic, you'll import the title you just created as the sample frame for this new title. The sample frame will provide a reference of exactly where the Otto title text is located so that you don't draw over the top of it.

1 Choose File > New > Title.

2 Move the new Title window to the side of the Otto.ptl Title window so that you can see both windows.

3 Drag the center of the Otto.ptl Title window to the center of the new Title window.

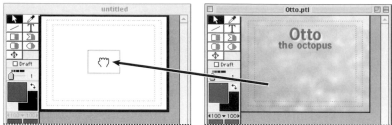

The Otto title appears as a background for your new title. The water background does not transfer to your new title because it is only a sample frame, not a saved component of the Otto.ptl file.

4 Click the new Title window's title bar to make it the active window, and then choose File > Save.

5 Make sure the 08Lesson folder is open, and then type **Octopus.ptl** for the name, and click Save.

6 Close Otto.ptl.

Changing the default color before you draw

When nothing is selected in the Title window and you change the color of the Object Color swatch, the new color becomes the default color for everything you draw or type.

Let's change the default color in the Object Color swatch from the deep blue you used for the text to a different blue before drawing.

1 Using the selection tool, click the Object Color swatch.

2 Pick a different blue color in the color box. To use the color we used, Type **52** for Red, **0** for Green, and **226** for Blue. Then click OK.

Drawing an image using the polygon tool

The polygon tool lets you create random shapes by moving the tool in any direction and clicking to create new end points for each line. To close the polygon tool, either click the first point you created, or double-click where you want your last line to end. If you're using the filled tool, as you'll use in this exercise, you can double-click your last point to automatically connect the last point with the first point.

Now you'll draw a wave using the polygon tool.

1 Select the filled (right) side of the polygon tool.

The right side of the drawing tools represents the filled tool. If you select the filled tool, your drawing will result in a solid graphic. If you select the outlined tool, or the left side of the tool, your drawing will result in an outline only.

2 Position the cursor in the lower left corner of the Title window, outside the action-safe zone, and click to make the first point.

3 Move the cursor about one-third of the way up the left side of the window and click to make your second point.

4 Continue to click up and down across the lower third section of the Title window to make a wave effect. You can use the graphic below as a guide.

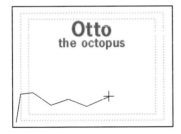 

Note: *If you make a mistake, you can double-click to close the tool and then press Delete to delete all your points, or you can finish drawing your image and then use the selection tool to adjust individual points.*

5 When you reach the right side of the window, double-click anywhere in the lower right corner to close the polygon.

Premiere automatically adds a line from the last point to the first point, closing the image and filling it with blue.

6 With the image still selected, drag the Overall Transparency arrow to 50%.

7 Click anywhere in the Title window, outside the image, to deselect everything; then save the title.

Repositioning objects

You can reposition text and images in the Title window by bringing them to the front or sending them to the back. Here you'll draw another wave with a different opacity setting, and then send it to the back.

1 Select the filled polygon tool ( ).

2 Click the left line of the action-safe zone about halfway up the first wave to create a point.

3 Click to make the second point above the first wave but still in the lower half of the window. You can use the graphic below as a guide.

4 Continue making points up and down across the window as you did with the first wave; however, this time, instead of a flat bottom, draw waves along the bottom of the graphic. Make this wave a little smaller than the first wave.

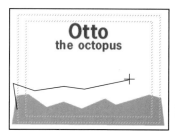 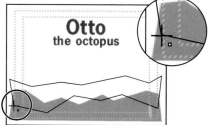

5 When you reach the left side again, close the shape by connecting the last point to the first point. You'll know you're clicking on the first point when you see the "o" next to the pointer.

6 With the second wave selected, set Overall Transparency to 25%.

7 Choose Title > Send to Back. The second wave now sits behind the first wave and shows through slightly.

8 Save the title.

Creating a smooth polygon

Now you'll use the polygon tool to draw an octopus. This time you'll smooth the lines because octopuses are round, not pointy.

Before drawing the octopus, let's change the color to orange. To ensure you don't change the color of the objects you just drew, you'll make sure nothing is selected.

1 Using the selection tool ( ), click anywhere inside the Title window (but outside of the waves) to deselect everything.

2 Click the Object Color swatch.

3 Pick a rich orange color from the right side of the color box. To use the exact color we used, type **245** for Red, **42** for Green, and **10** for Blue. Then click OK.

4 Drag the opacity slider to 100% to remove transparency.

5 Select the filled polygon tool ( ) and click under the words "the octopus" to make your first point for the top left corner of the octopus's head. Then, using the image below as a guide, draw your own octopus in the lower two-thirds of the window, making sure not to draw over the text.

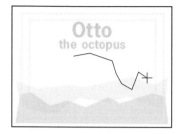 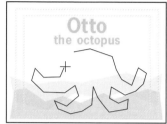

6 Close the shape by clicking your first point. Remember to look for the "o" before clicking your final point to ensure your cursor is directly above the first point.

7 With the octopus selected, choose Title > Smooth Polygon.

8 Save the title.

If you want to adjust any of your images, select the object using the selection tool and drag individual points to reposition them.

Adding an octopus shadow

Now you'll add a light pink shadow to the octopus.

1 If necessary, use the selection tool ( ) to select the octopus image.

2 Drag the Shadow Offset control down and to the right so the dimensions are about 4 x 3.

3 Double-click (Windows) or click (Mac OS) the Shadow Color swatch to open the Color Picker.

4 Click a light pink color between the blues and the reds in the color box. To use the exact color we used, type **255** for Red, **118** for Green, and **174** for Blue. Then click OK.

5 Choose Title > Shadow > Single to remove the shadow's soft edges and create a basic drop shadow that is more apparent against the blue waves.

Repositioning the waves

Now let's move the first wave you drew to the front so that the octopus appears to be floating between the two waves. Because you added transparency to the wave, you'll be able to see the octopus through it.

1 Using the selection tool (➤), select the first wave you drew. To ensure you selected the first wave, check the Transparency settings in the Title window—they should be 50%. If they're at 25%, select the other wave.

2 Choose Title > Bring to Front.

3 To see the shadow effect without the selection points, click an empty area of the Title window to deselect everything.

4 Save the title.

Using the oval tool

Use the oval tool to draw ovals and circles of any size. To make a circle using the oval tool, constrain the tool by pressing the Shift key while drawing. You can also make squares, rounded squares, and 45-degree lines by pressing the Shift key while using the rectangle, rounded rectangle, or line tools.

Before you draw the circles, let's change the object color to green.

1 To ensure you don't change the currently selected object's color, click an empty area of the window, and then click the Object Color swatch to open the Color Picker.

2 Pick a bright green color in the color box. To use the same color we used, type **64** for Red, **255** for Green, and **131** for Blue. Then click OK.

3 Drag the opacity slider to 100%.

Now you'll draw one octopus eye, and then copy and paste it to create a second eye.

4 Select the filled oval tool.

5 Press Shift and draw a small circle on the octopus's head.

6 Choose Edit > Copy and then Edit > Paste. Premiere pastes a copy of the circle directly on top of the original.

7 Position the selection tool ( ) over the eye, making sure the icon is a pointer, not a finger icon, and then drag the center of the new circle beside the first circle.

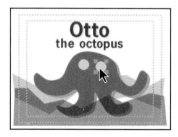

 If you accidently stretch the circle instead of move it, choose Edit > Undo, and then deselect and reselect the circle and use the arrow keys to move it.

8 Click any empty space in the Title window to deselect everything.

9 Save the title.

Leave Octopus.ptl open in the background; you'll be using it again soon.

Creating rolling titles

Using Premiere's rolling titles feature you can create text that rolls onto and off of the screen. You can make text roll up or down, or you can make it crawl across the screen from left to right or from right to left. In this lesson you'll create text that rolls up the screen.

To create rolling titles, you must use the rolling title tool and enter text in a rolling title scroll box.

First you'll open a new title and set the default color to the same deep blue as the text in Otto.ptl.

1 Choose File > New > Title.

2 Click the Object Color swatch.

3 The default color should be the blue you used earlier for the word Otto. If it isn't, type **51** for Red, **0** for Green, and **176** for Blue, and then click OK.

4 If a shadow value is selected, drag the Shadow Offset control out of the Shadow area so no shadow is selected.

Now you're ready to create the rolling title.

5 Select the rolling title tool.

6 Staying within the title-safe zone, drag to define a box from the upper left corner down and to the right about one-third of the way down the window.

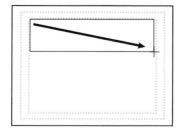

The rolling title scroll box appears with a blinking text cursor at the top. In this box you enter the text you want to roll or crawl across the screen.

7 Change the font size by choosing Title > Size > 18.

The text is still center-justified from the last title you created, so let's left justify it.

8 Choose Title > Justify > Left.

Now you'll enter the poem text.

9 Type **Octopus,** and then press Enter (Windows) or Return (Mac OS) twice.

10 Type **Octopus,** again, and press Enter/Return twice.

11 Type the remaining text and press Enter/Return once at the end of each line and twice where the larger spaces appear.

how squishy
are thee!

With your
eyes
so bright,

and tentacles
of might,

swimming
the deep

blue

sea.

12 Highlight the word "sea" to select it and choose Title > Justify > Center.

13 Choose Title > Rolling Title Options and make sure Direction is set to Move Up; then click OK.

14 Choose File > Save, open the 08Lesson folder if necessary, and then type **Poem.ptl** for the name and click Save.

Previewing the rolling title text

You can preview the rolling text by dragging the preview slider bar at the bottom of the Title window's toolbox.

1 Using the selection tool ( ), click to select the rolling title bounding box.

2 Click the preview slider button on the slider bar and drag to the right.

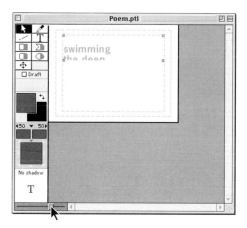

What you see is what will display in your movie. Notice how the text is on the screen at the beginning of the roll and rolls until the last word appears at the bottom.

To make the text roll onto the screen you'll insert extra carriage returns at the beginning of the text. You can also add extra carriage returns to the end of the text if you want the text to roll all the way off screen before stopping. For this lesson you want the text to stop on screen.

3 Select the text tool and click anywhere in the text area.

4 Scroll to the top of the text and make an insertion point before the first letter of the first word.

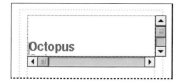

5 Press Enter (Windows) or Return (Mac OS) three times.

Note: Even though it doesn't appear to move the text off the screen, the carriage returns will create the desired effect when you preview.

6 Click anywhere in the Title window to deselect the text box, and then preview the changes by dragging the preview slider bar.

7 Save the title.

Using titles in a Premiere project

Now you'll add the titles to a simple project, and then place them in the Timeline and superimpose them over a video clip. *Superimpose* means playing a clip, such as a title, still, or video clip, on top of another clip. To superimpose clips in Premiere, you add them to the superimpose tracks (Video 2 track and higher) in the Timeline. Clips in superimpose tracks play over the clips in the lower tracks.

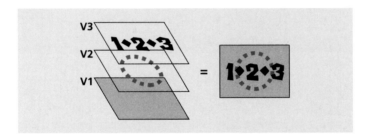

When using titles, Premiere automatically assigns transparency, so clips on the lower tracks display through the title's background. You'll learn more about superimpose tracks and transparency in the next lesson.

You can add a title to a Premiere project in three ways:

• If both the project and the title are already open, you can simply drag the title to the Project window.

• If your windows are obscured, making dragging and dropping difficult, you can choose Add This Clip from the Project menu.

• If the title is not open at the time you want to add it, you can import it to your project the same way you import other clips, by choosing File > Import > File.

Adding titles to a project

Here you'll add the titles you just created.

1 If necessary, move the Title windows on the desktop so they do not overlap each other or the Project window.

2 Click the Poem Title window to make it active, then drag the title to the Project window and release the mouse. You can drag from anywhere in the Title window, except the title bar or the tool bar.

The title file, Poem.ptl, now appears in the Project window.

3 Close the Poem.ptl Title window.

Now you'll add the Octopus title to the project using the menu option.

4 Click the Octopus.ptl Title window to activate it.

5 Choose Project > Add This Clip. The Octopus.ptl title now appears in the Project window.

6 Close the Octopus.ptl Title window.

Because you closed Otto.ptl earlier, you'll have to import it the way you import other video clips.

7 Choose File > Import > File.

8 Select Otto.ptl from the 08Lesson folder; then click Open (Windows) or OK (Mac OS). Otto.ptl now appears in the Project window.

Adding tracks to the Timeline

To superimpose two titles over the Water.mov video clip, you'll need to add another superimpose track to the Timeline. You can have up to 98 superimpose tracks to the Timeline, but you'll just be adding one now.

1 Select Track Options from the Timeline window menu.

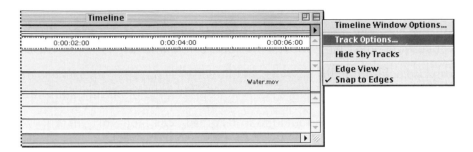

2 Click Add to open the Add Tracks dialog box. By default, 1 video and 1 audio track are selected.

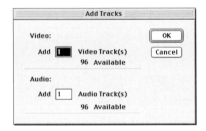

3 Because you don't need to add another Audio track, change the value in the Add Audio track to 0.

4 Click OK to add 1 Video Track; then click OK again to close the Track Options dialog box.

A new track, Video 3, now appears on the Timeline.

Adding titles to the Timeline

Titles are still images with a default duration of one second. You can change the duration by dragging either edge of the clip using the selection tool in the Timeline or by choosing Clip > Duration and entering a new duration. For information on changing the still image duration preference, see Lesson 12 "Assembling the final video program" on page 360.

1 Drag Octopus.ptl from the Project window to the beginning of the Video 2 track.

2 Choose Window > Show Info to display the Info palette. You'll need to refer to this palette when editing the size of the clips in this exercise.

3 Position the selection tool icon on the right edge of the Octopus.ptl clip so it turns into a trim tool (↔).

4 Drag the edge to the right and, using the Info palette as a guide, extend the Out point to 10 seconds (00:00:10:00).

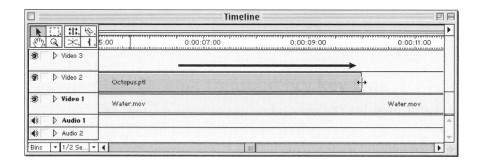

5 Drag Otto.ptl from the Project window to the beginning of the Video 3 track.

6 Select Otto.ptl, and choose Clip > Duration.

7 Type **200** for the new duration and click OK. Otto.ptl is now two seconds long.

8 Drag Poem.ptl from the Project window to the Video 3 track, immediately following Otto.ptl. It should snap to the end of the Otto.ptl clip.

9 Using the selection tool, drag the right edge of Poem.ptl so its Out point is at 10 seconds. It should snap to the end of Octopus.ptl.

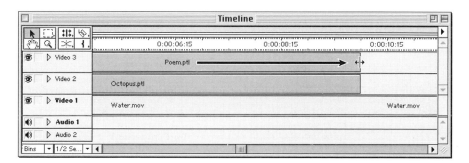

Because titles created in Premiere are automatically transparent, you don't need to apply transparency. So let's build a preview and view the results.

10 Save the project.

11 Press Enter (Windows) or Return (Mac OS) to preview the project.

Changing the speed of a rolling title in the Timeline

You can change the speed of a rolling title by changing its duration: The shorter the duration, the faster the title plays; the longer the duration, the slower the title plays.

When you preview the rolling title script, you may notice that it plays rather quickly. To make it play slower, you'll increase the duration of the clip.

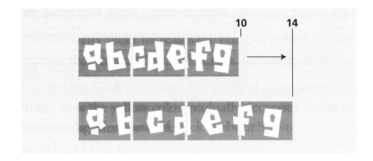

1 Drag the right side Poem.ptl in the Timeline to 14 seconds so that it snaps to the end of Water.mov.

2 Drag the right side of Octopus.ptl to 14 seconds so that it also snaps to the end of Water.mov.

3 Press Enter (Windows) or Return (Mac OS) to preview the project again. Now the title scrolls much slower and is easier to read.

Updating a title in the Title window

You can open the Title window and update a title by double-clicking the title in either the Timeline or Project window. As soon as you save your changes to the title, Premiere updates all the references to it in your project.

Here you will adjust the rolling text of the Poem title so that it doesn't overlap the octopus graphic. To make this adjustment, you'll open Poem.ptl and adjust the size of the rolling text window using the selection tool.

1 Double-click Poem.ptl in the Timeline.

When the Title window opens, nothing appears in the window because you entered carriage returns at the beginning of the text. To see the bounding box, click in the top third of the window.

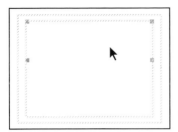

Because you need to make an edit that relies on the position of an object in Octopus.ptl, you'll first import a sample frame to the Title window and use it as a reference.

2 Move the Title window so that it is not obscuring the Project window.

3 Drag Octopus.ptl from the Project window to the Title window. The Octopus title now appears as the background for the Poem title.

Now you can see exactly how high up in the Title window you need to move the Poem title bounding box.

4 Using the selection tool, select one of the lower handles on the poem bounding box and move it up just a little so it doesn't touch the octopus's head.

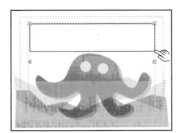

5 Choose File > Save and then close the Title window.

6 Press Enter (Windows) or Return (Mac OS) to preview the project.

7 Save the project.

Exporting the movie

Now let's export the project into a QuickTime movie for the Internet.

1 Click the Timeline title bar to activate it.

2 Choose File > Export > Movie; then click Settings.

3 Choose QuickTime for the File Type and Entire Project for the Range.

4 Make sure that Export Video and Open When Finished are selected, and that Export Audio is not selected. Then click Next.

5 Choose Cinepak for Compressor.

6 Make sure the Frame Rate is set to 15 fps. This frame rate is lower than most movies because you want to maintain the best playback quality without making the file too big for playback from the Internet.

7 Click Limit Data Rate to select it, and then type **500** in the K/sec text box. Limiting the data rate creates a file that requires fewer resources to play, thus enabling it to play back at a higher quality from a variety of systems.

8 Click OK.

9 Type **Otto.mov** for the name, then click Save (Windows) or OK (Mac OS) to export the file.

A progress bar appears, reporting the time remaining, and then the movie opens in a separate Clip window.

10 Click the Play button in the player window to view your animation.

Exploring on your own

Take some time to experiment with the Title window and the project you just created. Here are some suggestions:

• Apply a gradient fill to the word "Otto" in the Otto.ptl title file. A gradient fill requires a different color in the Start and End Transparency color swatches.

• Create a new title and make text that crawls across the screen. Add necessary insertion points to ensure the text starts completely off screen, crawls on to the screen, and then crawls completely off of the screen.

• Use the Rolling Title Options and apply special timing options to the crawling text so that it slows down as it exits the screen.

• Change the octopus graphic to a framed and filled object. Change the color and line weight of the frame.

• If you have a Web browser, export the project as an Animated GIF file, then double-click the file to open and view it in your browser. Animated GIFs are optimized for the Web and quickly open and play.

Review questions

1 How do you create a new title?

2 How do you change the color of title text?

3 How do you add a shadow?

4 How do you change the opacity of text or a graphic?

5 How do you adjust the speed of a rolling title?

6 What is a reference frame?

7 What are the different ways rolling text can move over a frame?

8 How do you add a title to a video program?

9 How do you add video tracks to a project?

Answers

1 Choose File > New > Title.

2 Select the text, click the Object Color swatch and pick a new color from the Color Picker.

3 Select the object and then move the Shadow Offset control.

4 Select the text or graphic and then drag a Transparency slider to a new setting.

5 Change the duration of the title clip.

6 A reference frame is a frame from another title, still image, or video clip that you can copy to your title and use as a reference to help determine what colors to use, to precisely position text over an image, or to provide a guideline for drawing an image.

7 Text can roll across a screen from left to right or right to left, and it can roll up or down the screen.

8 Drag it to the Project window, choose File > Add This Clip, or choose File > Import > File.

9 Choose Track Options from the Timeline window menu and then click Add Tracks.

Lesson 9

Superimposing

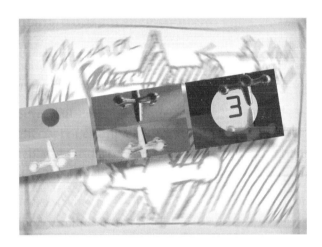

Using Premiere's Timeline, you can create up to 98 different video tracks for endless combinations of layered movies and stills. With the generous selection of transparency keys, you can key out (remove) specific areas of a movie and create customized effects.

In this lesson you'll create a promotional video for CD-ROM distribution. You'll use the superimpose tracks in Premiere's Timeline to create transparencies, fades, and other special effects. Specifically, you'll learn how to perform these tasks:

• Create a split screen.

• Apply transparency key types and adjust settings.

• Create a storyboard and specify the order of display on the Timeline.

• Use the Shy and Exclude track options.

• Use the fade tools.

Getting started

For this lesson you'll open an existing project and add clips to the Timeline. Make sure you know the location of the files used in this lesson. Insert the CD-ROM disc if necessary. Because the files used in this lesson contain font information, you also need to make sure that Adobe Type Manager (ATM) is installed on your system. For information on installing ATM, see "Installing lesson fonts" on page 4.

To ensure that the Premiere preferences are set to default values, exit Premiere, and then delete the preferences file as explained in "Restoring default preferences" on page 5.

1 Double-click 09Lesson.ppj in the 09Lesson folder to start Premiere and open the project.

2 When the project opens, choose File > Save As. If necessary, open the appropriate folder on your hard disk and type **Promo.ppj**. Press Enter (Windows) or Return (Mac OS).

You'll be superimposing six layers of clips in this lesson, so we've created a project with seven video tracks. Because so many video tracks are open during this lesson, we set the Timeline to display small icons. If you prefer to work with larger icons, select the medium sized icons after choosing Timeline Window Options from the Timeline window menu.

Viewing the finished movie

If you'd like to see what you'll be creating, you can look at the final movie.

1 Choose File > Open and double-click 09Final.mov in the Final folder inside the 09Lesson folder.

2 Click the Play button in the Source view of the Monitor window.

Superimposing

Superimposing (often called *matting* or *keying* in television and film production) means playing one clip on top of another. In Premiere, you can add clips to the superimpose tracks (Video 2 track and higher) and then add transparency or fades so that the clips lower in the Timeline partially appear as well. If you don't apply transparency to the clip in the highest track, the clips directly below will not appear when you preview or when you play your final movie.

Clips in superimpose tracks with various transparencies applied.

Premiere provides 15 *transparency key types*, which let you control the location and intensity of transparent areas for a clip. When superimposing, you can designate a *matte* (specified area) to be transparent, or you can designate transparent areas based on a color or color quality, such as lightness.

Always plan ahead for superimpositions, especially when editing video footage. For example, if you videotape a person talking and you want to superimpose a different background behind the person, tape the person in front of a solid-color background, such as a blue wall. Otherwise, keying out the background will be difficult, if not impossible.

Creating a split screen

One of the effects you can create using Premiere's transparency settings is a *split screen.*
A split screen displays a portion of one clip on part of the screen and a portion of another
clip on the other part of the screen.

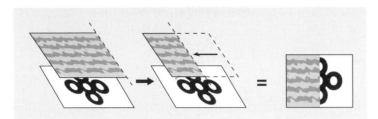

Transparency applied to upper clip; split-screen effect.

Here you'll create a split screen, displaying half of one clip on the top and half of another
clip on the bottom. Let's add the first two clips to the Timeline.

1 Drag Gold.mov from the Project window to the Video 1 track, placing its In point at
the very beginning of the Timeline.

2 Scrub through the Timeline ruler to preview the first clip before applying transparency.

3 Drag Amber.mov from the Project window to Video 2 track, aligning it at the very
beginning of the Timeline.

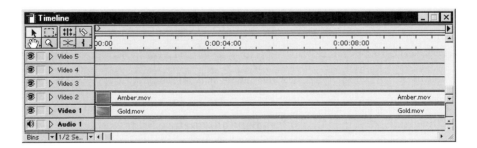

4 Scrub through the Timeline ruler to preview the first two clips before applying
transparency.

Notice how only Amber.mov appears in the Program view. Without transparency,
nothing below this clip displays.

You cannot apply transparency to a clip in the Video 1 track, so you'll apply it to Amber.mov in the Video 2 track. Because Gold.mov is located directly below Amber.mov, once you apply transparency, it will reappear.

5 Select Amber.mov in the Timeline and choose Clip > Video > Transparency.

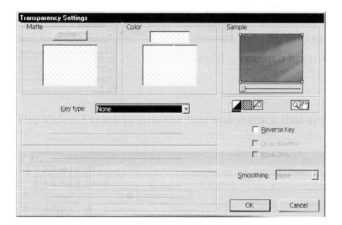

6 Leave the Key Type at None.

When you create a split screen, you don't use a transparency key type; instead, you move the corner points on the Sample area.

7 Position the cursor on the bottom left corner point of the Sample area (located in the top right corner of the dialog box). When the pointer icon changes to a finger icon, drag the point halfway up the left side of the area.

8 Drag the bottom right point of the Sample area halfway up the right side of the area, directly across from the first point, to create a straight line at halfway up the area.

9 Notice that the lower half of the area is white. To see the effect of the split screen, click the page peel icon (🔲) under the Sample area.

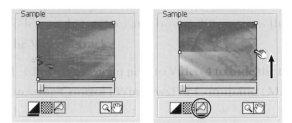

Default Sample area, and Sample area after selecting the page peel icon and moving the two bottom handles.

Now you can see Gold.mov in the bottom half of the screen and Amber.mov in the top half. You can make split screens in diagonal, vertical, and irregular shapes.

10 Click OK to close the Transparency Settings dialog box.

11 Preview the split screen by scrubbing through the Timeline ruler while pressing the Alt key (Windows) or the Option key (Mac OS).

12 Save the project.

If the border between the clips is not straight, you can select Amber.mov, open the Transparency Settings dialog box, and readjust the points in the Sample area.

💡 *You can also achieve a split screen effect using the Push transition between two clips in the Video 1A and 1B tracks; or you can split the screen three ways by combining the Push transition and transparency.*

Applying the Blue Screen transparency key type

The two most commonly used transparency keys are Blue Screens and Green Screens. These keys are generally used to substitute the background of one video clip with another and are favored because they do not interfere with skin tones. For example, TV news programs regularly use blue screens to display footage of the current topic behind the newscaster.

If you use a blue or green background when videotaping footage, and plan to key it out using the Blue or Green Screen key type, make sure everything that is to remain opaque is a color other than your key color. For example, if you film a newscaster in front of a blue backdrop and the newscaster is wearing a blue tie, the tie will become transparent along with the background when you apply the Blue Screen key type to the footage.

Blue Screen transparency with blue tie and with white tie.

Now you'll add clips to the Video 4 and Video 5 tracks and apply the Blue Screen key type and the Chroma key type. We're skipping the Video 3 track intentionally for now—you'll add clips to it later in the lesson.

1 Drag Jacklow.mov from the Project window to the Video 4 track, aligning its In point with the very beginning of the Timeline.

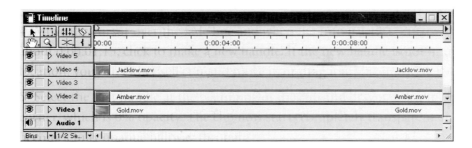

2 Preview this movie by scrubbing through the Timeline ruler. Notice the background, composed of mixed shades of blue. You'll remove this background using the Blue Screen transparency key type.

3 Using the selection tool ( ), select Jacklow.mov in the Timeline, and then choose Clip > Video > Transparency.

4 Select Blue Screen for the Key Type. If necessary, click the page peel icon ( ) and look at the Sample area. Notice that the clip's blue background is replaced by the split screen from the Video 1 track and Video 2 track.

The Threshold and Cutoff sliders at the bottom of the dialog box alter the shadows and the extent of color selected and removed.

5 To see how much of the blue background has been keyed out, click the black and white background icon (◪) under the Sample Area. Notice that a blue-gray shadow still appears.

To enhance the appearance of the clip by removing all of this blue background, you'll adjust the Threshold.

6 Move the Threshold slider bar to 60, or until the background becomes completely white.

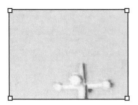 

7 Click the page peel icon (◪) again to see the effect. Notice how the background colors become brighter and more true. This is because you're removing more blue value and shadow from the selected clip.

8 Drag the preview bar in the Sample area to see the effect. Then click OK.

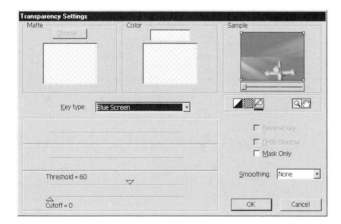

9 Preview the blue screen transparency effect and the split screen by scrubbing through the Timeline ruler while pressing the Alt key (Windows) or the Option key (Mac OS).

10 Save the project.

Applying the Chroma transparency key type

The Chroma key type lets you select any color as your transparent area. If you can't video tape footage using a blue or green background because of conflicting colors in your clip (such as the color of someone's clothes), you can use any solid color background and then use Premiere's Chroma key type to make that color represent your transparent area.

Here you'll use the Chroma key type on a clip with a yellow background.

1 Drag Jackhi.mov from the Project window to the Video 5 track, aligning its In point with the beginning of the Timeline.

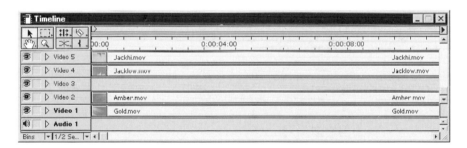

2 Scrub through the Timeline ruler to preview the movie before applying transparency.

3 Using the selection tool ( ), select Jackhi.mov in the Timeline, and then choose Clip > Video > Transparency.

4 Select Chroma for Key Type.

Notice that the Color box in the Transparency Settings dialog box now displays a frame from Jackhi.mov. You can select a key color from this frame, or you can click the white box above the frame and select a key color from the Color Picker. For this lesson you'll select a color from the frame.

5 Position the cursor over the frame in the Color box. The pointer turns into an eyedropper tool.

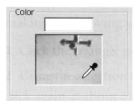

6 Click the yellow background to select it as your key color.

Because the yellow background in Jackhi.mov is dithered (not a solid color), the background color in the Sample area doesn't change much. You'll need to use the Similarity and Blend sliders to make this clip's yellow background transparent.

The Similarity slider increases the range of colors the key uses for transparency. If you increase the similarity for Jackhi.mov, the range of yellows that are transparent increases.

7 Select the black and white background icon (■) and move the Similarity slider to 38. Notice how the yellow color gradually decreases as you increase the similarity, until the entire background is white.

The Blend slider blends the edges of the image with the background by gradually changing the opacity where the color pixels meet.

8 Move the Blend slider to 12. Notice how the edges of the transition between image and background lose their sharpness.

You don't need to use Threshold or Cutoff with this clip.

9 Select the page peel icon (■)to preview the effect with the split screen and Jacklo.mov in the background.

10 Click OK to close the Transparency Settings dialog box.

11 Preview the clips by pressing Alt (Windows) or Option (Mac OS) while scrubbing through the Timeline ruler. Notice how all the clips now appear on-screen, each with its own unique area of transparency.

Adding clips without transparency

Now you'll add clips to the top two tracks of the Timeline. You won't apply a transparency key type to them because you want them to temporarily block the clips below.

1 Drag Ball.mov from the Project window to the Video 6 track, snapping its In point to the beginning of the Timeline.

2 In the Monitor window, drag the Program view shuttle to 0:00:01:00.

3 Drag Excite.ptl from the Project window to the Video 7 track, and snap its In point to the edit line.

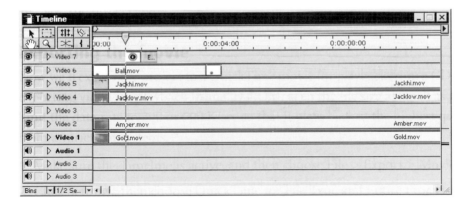

4 Preview the first four seconds of the project by pressing Alt (Windows) or Option (Mac OS) while scrubbing through the Timeline ruler.

Notice how only the bouncing ball and the star graphic appear in the Monitor window. Excite.ptl is a Premiere title file, so its transparency settings are automatic. Ball.mov has no transparency, so nothing below it in the Timeline is visible.

5 Save the project.

You'll adjust the transition between Ball.mov and the rest of the project a little later.

Applying the Track Matte transparency key type

Premiere's Track Matte key type lets you customize and layer movies. When you apply this key type you can play one movie through the matte of another while yet another movie plays in the background.

When you create a track matte effect, the order of your clips is important. Applying the track matte key to different clips and different video tracks results in a wide range of effects. You'll see some of those effects in this lesson. In Lesson 10 you'll apply the Track Matte key type to a moving image and create a traveling matte effect.

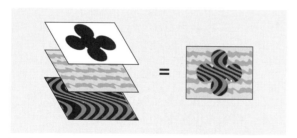

Track Matte transparency key type applied to middle clip.

Track Matte

You can use any clip or still image for the Track Matte key. Areas of white in the matte create opaque areas in the superimposed clip, preventing underlying clips from showing through. Black areas in the matte create transparent areas, and gray areas make partially transparent areas. To retain the original colors in your superimposed clip, use a grayscale image for the matte. Any color in the matte removes the same level of color from the superimposed clip. You can create mattes in a few different ways:

• Use the Title window to create text or shapes (grayscale only), save the title, and then import the file as your matte.

• Create a matte from any clip using the Chroma, RGB Difference, Difference Matte, Blue Screen, Green Screen, or Non-Red key. Then select the Mask Only option.

• Use Adobe Illustrator or Photoshop to create a grayscale image, import it into Premiere, and (optionally) apply motion settings to the image.

— From the Adobe Premiere User Guide, Chapter 8

You'll create a track matte effect with Ball.mov and Excite.ptl so that the ball bounces inside the Excite.ptl graphic and the clips on the lower tracks display in the background.

First you'll add Ball.mov and Excite.mov to the Timeline again and create an alias for each so you don't confuse them with the clips at the beginning of the Timeline. If necessary, use the Navigator palette to quickly move about the Timeline so that you can see the clips.

1 Drag Ball.mov from the Project window to the end of the Video 6 track, snapping its Out point with the Out point for Jackhi.mov (at 0:00:20:00).

2 Select Ball.mov in the Timeline and choose Clip > Alias. Type **Ball2.mov** in the text box, and then click OK.

3 Drag Excite.ptl from the Project window to the end of the Video 7 track, snapping its Out point with Ball2.mov's Out point.

4 Select Excite.ptl in the Timeline and choose Clip > Alias. Type **Excite2.ptl** in the text box, and then click OK.

5 Position the pointer on the left edge of Excite2.ptl and when the cursor turns into the trim tool, drag to the left until the edge aligns with the beginning of Ball2.mov at 0:00:16:00.

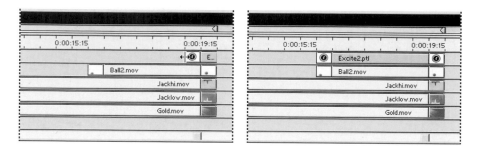

Now let's apply the Track Matte key type.

6 Select Ball2.mov and choose Clip > Video > Transparency.

7 Choose Track Matte for the Key Type.

8 Make sure the page peel icon is selected under the Sample area, and then drag the preview slider bar to view the effect.

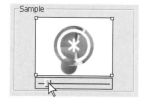

Notice how all the clips in the lower tracks display inside the Excite2.ptl matte (black area). To reverse the effect so that the background remains constant throughout the video program and only the bouncing ball appears inside the matte, you'll apply the Reverse Key option.

9 Select the Reverse Key option. Drag the preview slider bar under the Sample area to view the effect, and then click OK.

10 Save the project.

Adding a series of still images

Here you'll add a series of title files to the Video 3 track. You'll add six clips at once to the Timeline, but first you'll create a storyboard to arrange them in the order you want them to appear in the Timeline.

You can arrange clips in the Project or Bin window in a variety of ways. To arrange clips alphabetically, click the Project or Bin window heading under which you want them to appear. For example, if you want the clips to appear alphabetized by name, click the Name heading in the Project or Bin window; or if you want them to appear alphabetized by type, click Media Type.

To arrange clips in a storyboard, select the Program or Bin window's icon view icon (⬛) and then drag the clip icons around the window in any order you want. We've grouped all the titles into the Titles bin to make it easy to create a storyboard.

1 Double-click the Titles bin icon in the Project window to open it.

2 With the Bin window active, click the Icon view icon (⬛) at the bottom of the window. The titles now appear only as icons, which you can move around the window.

3 Drag the title icons to reposition them in numerical order from left to right. You can resize the window if necessary.

Notice that three of the clips have a white background and three have a black background. The backgrounds vary to create a perceptible transition between clips. Once you apply transparency, the transition from clip to clip will be even more apparent.

Before you drag the clips to the Timeline, you'll set the edit line.

4 Drag the shuttle slider in the Program view of the Monitor window to the In point of Ball2.mov (at 0:00:16:00).

5 Click the Titles Bin title bar to activate it, and then choose Edit > Select All.

6 Drag the files to the Video 3 track, aligning the Out point of the last file with the edit line.

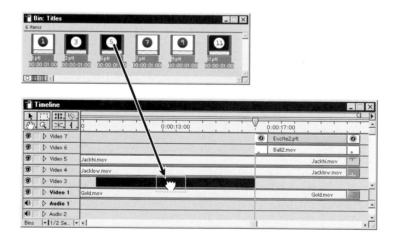

7 If you need to make adjustments to the location of the series of clips in the Timeline, select all the clips using the range select tool (⬚). Then move them as a group. Be careful to only select the clips in the Video 3 track. If you select other clips, click the selection tool to deselect them, then use the range tool again.

Note: You can also use the track select tool (⬚) to select the clips because they are the only clips on the track, but using this tool does not allow you to snap to an edit line or another clip.

8 Close the Titles Bin window.

9 Preview the titles in the project by pressing Alt (Windows) or Option (Mac OS) while scrubbing through the Timeline ruler.

10 Save the project.

Using transparency to blend clips

When you have a group of clips with identical backgrounds located directly above, below, or beside one another on the Timeline, you can select them as a group and apply transparency.

Several of Premiere's transparency key types let you create special blending and fading effects. For example, to brighten a dark clip you can apply the Luminance key type, which replaces the darker colors in the superimposed clip with lighter colors from the clip below it in the Timeline. Here you'll experiment with different key types and their effects.

1 Select the track select tool and then click the first clip in the Video 3 track to select all the title clips in that track.

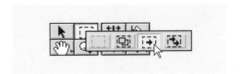

2 Choose Clip > Video > Transparency. Or, if you prefer to use the keyboard shortcut, press Control + G (Windows) or Command + G (Mac OS).

3 Select Screen for Key Type. Make sure the page peel icon is selected so you can preview the effect.

When you apply the Screen key type to a grayscale image, such as 1.ptl, Premiere substitutes the clip's black areas with the color from the clip below it in the Timeline.

4 Move the Cutoff slider to see the different effects that result. This slider lets you gradually change the opacity of the background.

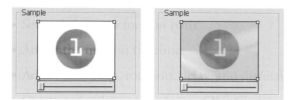

Screen key type with Cutoff slider set to 100% and 50%.

5 Select Multiply for Key Type.

The Multiply key type creates transparency where the clip is bright. Because you applied it to a black and white clip, the white areas are transparent.

6 Move the Cutoff slider and note the different effects. The Cutoff slider adjusts the amount of transparency for the entire clip: As you lower the value, the clip becomes more transparent, and the background begins to appear through the black areas. When the Cutoff is at zero, the selected clip becomes completely transparent.

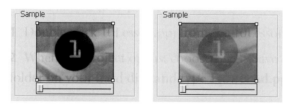

Multiply key type with Cutoff slider set to 100% and 30%.

In addition to these transparency key types, you can also use the Track Matte key type to blend images and colors.

7 Select Track Matte for Key Type. Notice how the transparency affects the clips above and below the selected clip, rather than just below, like most key types.

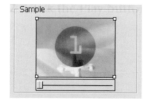

8 Click OK to accept the Track Matte key type and close the Transparency Settings dialog box.

9 Preview the titles transparency effect by scrubbing through the Timeline ruler while pressing the Alt key (Windows) or Option key (Mac OS).

Original titles.

Titles with Track Matte transparency key type applied.

Notice how the alternating black and white backgrounds affect the colors that display in each clip. You can't predict how the Track Matte key type will blend colors; every image generates a different effect. Now you'll make each clip even more distinct by reversing the Track Matte transparency setting on alternating title clips.

10 Using the selection tool, select 3.ptl, and then press Control + G (Windows) or Command + G (Mac OS) to open the Transparency Settings dialog box.

11 Select Reverse Key. Notice once again, the shift in colors. Click OK.

12 Select 7.ptl, press Control + G (Windows) or Command + G (Mac OS), select Reverse Key, and then click OK.

13 Select 11.ptl, press Control + G (Windows) or Command + G (Mac OS), select Reverse Key, and then click OK.

Note: *For information on copying transparency settings from one clip to another, see Lesson 11, "Copying filters and settings" on page 322.*

14 Preview the transparency effect by scrubbing through the Timeline ruler while pressing the Alt key (Windows) or Option key (Mac OS).

15 Save the project.

Making video tracks shy

Now that you have all the clips added to the Timeline, it's time to start managing the video tracks. You won't be editing Gold.mov or Amber.mov again, so you can make the Video 1 and Video 2 tracks shy and make them invisible.

When you make a track shy and then choose Hide Shy Tracks from the Timeline window menu, Premiere makes the tracks invisible, freeing up space to work with clips on other tracks. Although shy tracks don't appear on the Timeline, they are still included when you preview or export the project.

1 Press the Control key (Windows) or Command key (Mac OS) and click the eye icon next to the Video 1 track. Do the same for the Video 2 track.

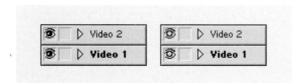

A solid eye icon represents default track; an outlined eye icon represents a shy track.

The eye icon now displays as an outlined eye(☺).

2 From the Timeline window menu, choose Hide Shy Tracks.

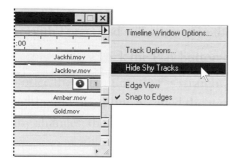

The Video 3 track is now the first video track that appears in the Timeline.

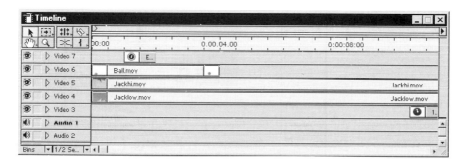

Note: You can also make audio tracks shy and invisible by pressing Control (Windows) or Command (Mac OS) while clicking the speaker icon (◄)) and then choosing Hide Shy Tracks from the Timeline window menu.

3 Preview the project by scrubbing through the Timeline ruler while pressing Alt (Windows) or Option (Mac OS).

Notice how even though you can't see the Video 1 and Video 2 tracks in the Timeline, they do appear in the Program view of the Monitor window when you preview.

When you want the tracks to reappear on the Timeline, you choose Show Shy Tracks from the Timeline window menu. If you want to return the eye icon to its default setting, press Control (Windows) or Command (Mac OS) and click the outlined eye icon. We'll leave these tracks shy for now.

Excluding video tracks

Premiere's exclude feature lets you turn off clips in the Timeline so that they won't appear when you preview or export the project. You won't be using this feature in this lesson. But to learn what it does and how it differs from the shy feature, let's experiment with it on the Video 4 track.

1 Click the eye icon next to Video 4 to hide the track. When you click the eye icon without pressing Control (Windows) or Command (Mac OS), you enable the exclude feature for the track.

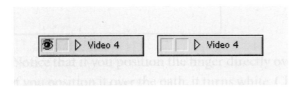

An empty box indicates a hidden track.

2 Scrub through the Timeline while pressing Alt (Windows) or Option (Mac OS) to preview the clips.

The Video 4 track remains visible in the Timeline, but Jacklow.mov does not appear in the Program view window when you preview the project. Also notice that half of the title files display in black and white and half don't appear at all. The Track Matte key type does not create a transparent effect unless there is a clip in the track directly above it.

3 Click the eye icon box for the Video 4 track again to include the track, and then save the project.

Note: You can also exclude audio tracks by clicking the speaker icon ( ).

Fading clips

Premiere's fade controls let you fade in and out of clips on the superimpose tracks, creating shadows, transparencies, and multicamera effects. You'll adjust the fade lines on the top four tracks of the Timeline, starting with the highest track, Video 7.

1 Choose Window > Show Info to open the Info palette so you can use it as a guide; then press the Home key to return the edit line to the beginning of the Timeline.

Note: If a clip is selected in the Timeline, the edit line will return to the beginning of that clip. To deselect the clip, click it again or click the selection tool.

2 Click the triangle to the left of the Video 7 track name to expand the track.

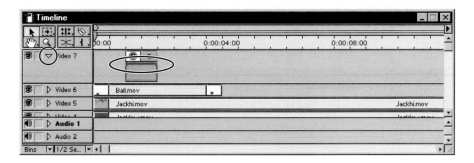

Notice the red line that appears under the clip name and thumbnail; this is the fade line. Every clip has a handle at the beginning and end of the fade line. You can fade in and out of clips by moving these handles or by adding handles to the fade line and moving them up and down. The process is similar to the way you adjusted audio volume in Lesson 5.

3 Using the selection tool, position the pointer over the fade line in the center of the clip until the pointer turns into a finger icon with a plus and minus sign (🖐).

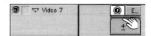

4 Move the cursor over the fade line and when the Info palette's "cursor at" line reads about 0:00:01:15, click to make a new handle. If the new handle is not in the correct location, you can either select it and move it, or drag it off the line to delete it.

5 Select the first handle at the beginning of the clip and drag it down to the bottom left corner, which is 0% opacity. The clip now starts completely transparent and then becomes fully opaque halfway through.

Note: When selecting a handle on the fade line, make sure the finger icon is gray before you click to select it, otherwise, you will create a new handle. If you do create a new handle that you don't want, simply drag it off the fade line to delete it.

6 Drag the last fade handle in the clip to 0% also.

7 Press Alt (Windows) or Option (Mac OS) and scrub through the Timeline ruler to preview the clips. Now when the clip begins playing it is completely transparent; then it gradually becomes completely opaque, and then it gradually dissolves until it's completely transparent again.

8 Click the arrow next to the Video 6 track name to expand the track; then click the fade line to make a handle at 0:00:02:15.

9 Drag the handle at the end of Ball.mov to 0%. Now Ball.mov will play at 100% opacity for 2 seconds and 15 frames, and then it will gradually fade to 0% opacity. As it fades out, all the clips on the lower tracks will fade in.

10 Press Alt (Windows) or Option (Mac OS) and scrub through the Timeline ruler to preview the clips.

11 Click the triangles next to the Video 6 and Video 7 track names to collapse them, and then save the project.

Using the fade adjustment tool

Now you'll use the fade adjustment tool as well as the selection tool to fade in and out of a clip. The fade adjustment tool uniformly moves the fade line between any two handles.

1 Click the triangle next to the Video 5 track name to expand the track.

2 Using the selection tool, click the fade line for Jackhi.mov at about 6:00 to make a new handle; then click again at about 6:05 to make another handle.

Now you'll use the fade adjustment tool to move the line between the first point on the Timeline and the point at 6:00.

3 Select the fade adjustment tool.

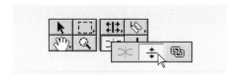

4 Position the tool over the fade line between the handle at 0:00 and the handle at 6:00; then drag the line down to 0% opacity. You can view the opacity setting (Fade Level) in the Info palette as you drag the line.

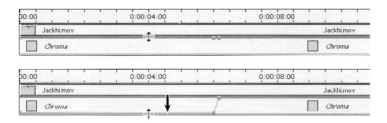

5 Preview the effect by scrubbing through the Timeline ruler while pressing Alt (Windows) or Option (Mac OS).

Jackhi.mov fades in from 0% to 100% over 5 frames. Let's make the fade in effect last longer by extending the distance between the second handle, which is at 0% opacity, and the third handle, which is at 100% opacity.

6 Using the selection tool, select the handle at 6:00 on the fade line, and drag it to the left to about 5:15. Use the Info palette as a guide.

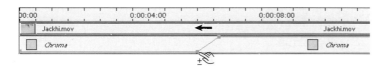

7 Preview the effect by scrubbing through the Timeline ruler while pressing Alt (Windows) or Option (Mac OS).

8 Click the triangle next to the Video 5 track name to collapse the track.

9 Save the project.

Fading Video 4 track

Now you'll adjust the fade line for Jacklow.mov so that it fades in and out without reaching 100% until just before the six titles appear. Use the Info palette as a guide when making and moving your fade handles.

1 Click the triangle next to the Video 4 track name to expand the track.

2 Using the selection tool (⬉), click the fade line at about 4:00 to make a new handle, then click again at about 5:00 to make another handle.

3 Select the fade adjustment tool (↕) and drag the line between the handle at 0:00 and the next handle to 0% opacity.

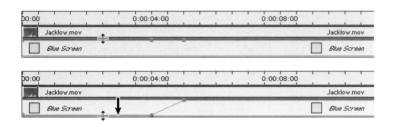

4 Using the selection tool, click at about 5:15 to make a handle. Then click at about 6:00 to make another handle.

You can turn the selection tool into the fade adjustment tool temporarily by positioning the selection tool over a fade line and pressing the Shift key. When you move the fade line using this technique, the opacity value displays on the fade line as you drag.

5 Press Shift and position the selection tool icon (⬉) over the fade line between the handles at 5:00 and 5:15. When it changes to the fade adjustment tool icon (↕), drag the line to 50% opacity.

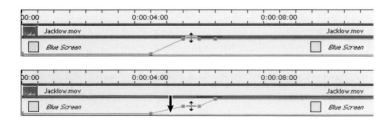

6 Click the fade line at 7:15 and 9:15 to make two new handles.

7 Press Shift and drag the line between the handles at 6:00 and 7:15 to 0% opacity.

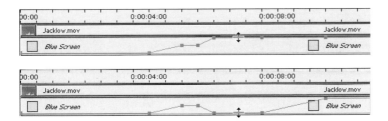

8 Preview the fades by scrubbing through the Timeline ruler while pressing Alt (Windows) or Option (Mac OS).

Notice how all the clips gradually fade in and out, creating a reflection effect.

9 Click the triangle next to the Video 4 track name to collapse the track.

10 Save the project.

Exporting the movie

Now we'll export the project to a QuickTime movie for playback from a CD-ROM. When exporting video for playback from CD-ROM, keep the file size as small as possible, and limit the data rate to 300 or 500 K/sec so that it plays back at the highest quality possible from a variety of systems.

1 Make sure the Timeline is active, and then choose File > Export > Movie.

2 Click Settings; then choose QuickTime for File Type and Entire Project for Range.

3 Make sure Export Video and Open When Finished are selected. Then deselect Export Audio. Click Next.

4 Choose Cinepak for the Compressor. Cinepak is included with QuickTime, and produces high quality output at the limited data rate and high compression rate required for CD-ROM playback.

5 Make sure the Frame Size dimensions are 240 by 180 and the Frame Rate is 15.

6 Select Limit Data Rate and type **300** in the K/sec text box. Limiting the data rate ensures that the movie can play on a variety of operating systems.

7 Click OK to close the Export Movie Settings dialog box.

8 Type **Promo.mov** for the File Name; then click Save (Windows) or OK (Mac OS).

A status bar displays the progress and when Premiere is finished creating the movie it opens in the Clip window.

9 Click Play to view your movie.

Exploring on your own

Feel free to experiment with the project you just created. Here are some suggestions:

• Change the transparency key type for the title files to see the different effects.

• Use the Wipe transition to create a split screen between Amber.mov and Gold.mov.

• Create a three-way split screen using the Wipe transition and the Sample area in the Transparency dialog box.

• Change the transparency for Ball2.mov so that the background clips display through the ball.

• Create a title and add it to the project, superimposing it over all the other clips.

• See what other transparency key types will remove the background of the Jackhi.mov and Jacklo.mov clips.

Review questions

1 How do you create a split screen?

2 What is the difference between the Blue Screen key type and the Chroma key type?

3 Which key type lets you customize and layer movies by playing one movie through the mask of another?

4 How do you make a track shy?

5 What is the difference between a hidden shy track, and an excluded track?

6 What is the difference between the Similarity slider and the Blend slider?

Answers

1 You move the handles in the Sample Area in the Transparency Settings dialog box.

2 The Blue Screen key type only lets you key out the color blue. The Chroma key type lets you key out any color you choose.

3 The Track Matte key type.

4 Press Control (Windows) or Command (Mac OS) and click the eye icon.

5 A hidden shy track does not display on the Timeline, but does display in the preview. An excluded track does display on the Timeline, but does not preview.

6 The Similarity slider increases the range of colors the transparency key type keys out. The Blend slider blends the color pixels around all edges where the transparent pixels meet the opaque pixels.

Lesson 10

Adding Motion

Motion enhances and enriches the effect of still image files in a video program. Premiere's Motion feature lets you move, rotate, distort, and magnify a variety of still image and video files.

In this lesson you'll create a 10-second advertisement for a flower shop. You'll learn how to animate a still image using Premiere's Motion dialog box and a variety of motion settings. In particular you'll learn how to do the following:

- Set and change a motion path.
- Adjust the motion timeline.
- Adjust the zoom, rotation, delay, and distortion settings.
- Create a traveling matte from still images.
- Load a saved motion path.

Getting started

To begin, you'll open an existing project and apply different motion and transparency settings to the clips. Make sure you know the location of the files used in this lesson. Insert the CD-ROM disc if necessary. For help, see "Using the Classroom in a Book files" on page 4.

To ensure that the Premiere preferences are set to the default values, exit Premiere, and then delete the preferences file as explained in "Restoring default preferences" on page 5.

1 Double-click 10Lesson.ppj from the 10Lesson folder to start Premiere and open the file.

2 When the project opens, choose File > Save As. If necessary, open the appropriate folder on your hard disk and type **FlowerAd.ppj**, and then click Save.

Viewing the finished movie

If you'd like to see what you'll be creating, you can open and play the finished movie.

1 Choose File > Open and select 10Final.mov in the Final folder inside the 10Lesson folder.

The movie opens in the Source view of the Monitor window.

2 Click the Play button (▶) to view the movie.

Applying a motion path to a still image

Premiere's motion controls let you create a motion path to animate any still image or video clip. Here you'll add a simple motion path to Forget.psd, a Photoshop file containing an alpha channel. For information on alpha channels, see "Understanding transparency and superimposing" on page 87.

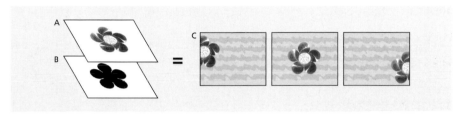

*A. Photoshop file **B.** Alpha channel in Photoshop file **C.** Alpha Channel transparency key type and motion applied*

Applying transparency

Let's begin by adding Backdrop.mov to the Source view, previewing it, and then adding it to the Timeline.

1 Drag Backdrop.mov from the Project window to the Source view of the Monitor window and click the Play button.

2 After you preview it, drag Backdrop.mov from the Source view to the Video 1 track, aligning it with the beginning of the Timeline.

Now you'll add Forget.psd to the Timeline and apply transparency. First you'll move the edit line to a new position, and use it to align the clip in the Timeline.

3 Drag the shuttle slider in the Program view of the Monitor window to about 0:00:00:15.

00:00:00:15   Δ 10:00

4 Drag Forget.psd from the Project window to the Video 2 track, aligning its In point to the edit line.

5 Move the shuttle slider in the Program view to about 0:00:03:00.

6 Drag the right edge of Forget.psd to the edit line. Resizing a clip like this is an easy way to change the duration of a still image.

7 Select Forget.psd in the Timeline and choose Clip > Video > Transparency.

8 Choose Alpha Channel for Key Type. Make sure the page peel icon (⬚) is selected so that you can preview the effect.

When Forget.psd was saved in Adobe Photoshop, the white background was saved as an alpha channel, which is easy to key out using either the Alpha Channel or White Alpha Matte key type.

9 Click OK to accept the transparency settings and close the dialog box.

Applying motion

Now let's add motion.

1 With Forget.psd still selected in the Timeline, choose Clip > Video > Motion.

2 If necessary, click the Play button by the preview thumbnail to view the motion.

Notice the default motion is straight, as represented by the horizontal line in the upper right panel. This line is called the *motion path*. If you were to click OK without making any changes, the selected clip would move in a horizontal line.

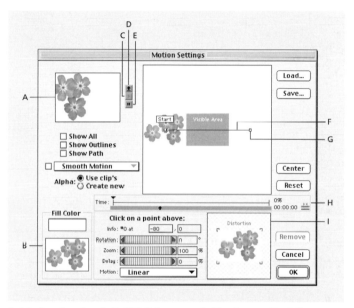

A. Motion thumbnail B. Fill Color area C. Play button D. Collapse icon (Mac OS only) E. Pause button F. Motion path G. Motion point H. Motion timeline I. Distortion area

3 Make sure the Alpha option under the motion thumbnail is set to Use Clip's, and then select Show All to see a preview of the motion superimposed over Backdrop.mov.

When you select Use Clip's, Premiere uses the clip's alpha channel for transparency. When you select Create New, Premiere uses the clip's frame as the transparent border, so a white box surrounds the image.

Notice that each end of the motion path has a small box, called a *motion point*. You use motion points to change the direction and shape of the path.

4 Position the pointer on the start point of the motion path. The pointer icon becomes a pointing finger icon.

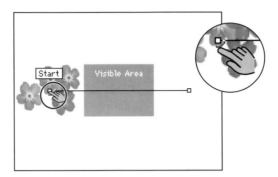

Notice that if you position the finger directly over a point, the finger icon turns gray, and if you position it over the path, it turns white. Clicking while the finger icon is gray selects a motion point and clicking while the finger icon is white creates a new motion point.

Note: The finger icon may flicker when you position it over a point along the motion path because of the constant screen redraw in the preview window or because of memory-related issues. Pausing the preview may help control the flicker.

5 Click the Pause button by the motion thumbnail to stop the preview from playing and to preserve memory.

The motion thumbnail requires memory in order to display the motion settings. Leaving it active all the time may slow your system's performance. Pausing the preview increases the memory available for other functions in Premiere.

6 Drag the first motion point to the lower left corner so that the image is just outside of the Visible Area.

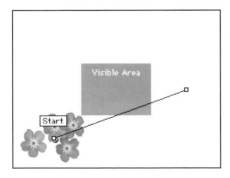

The Visible Area represents what you can see on-screen. Any points or paths outside this area will not be fully visible when you view the video program. When you want clips to gradually enter or exit the screen, place points outside the Visible Area.

7 Drag the last motion point up to the top right corner so that the entire image is outside the Visible Area.

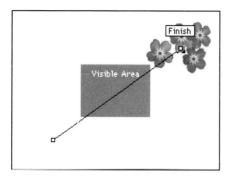

Note: In Windows, the last point on the motion path is labeled End, rather than Finish.

8 Click the Play button by the motion thumbnail to view the motion. When you're finished viewing, click the Pause button.

Adding points and distorting an image

You can add motion points to the motion path in two ways:

• Click directly on the path and drag the point to the desired location.

• Click anywhere along the motion timeline to add a point; then move the point on the motion path.

To move points in space, move them on the motion path; to move points in time, move them on the motion timeline.

You'll add points and move the path using both methods.

1 Click the motion path about one-third of the way from the start point to make a new point, and drag it to the top left corner of the Visible Area.

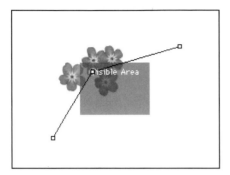

While the point is still selected, you'll distort the image.

2 In the Distortion area, drag the top left corner point up and to the left.

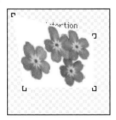

3 Drag the bottom right corner point down and to the right.

4 Drag the top right corner point toward the center of the Distortion area, and then drag the bottom left point toward the center of the area. The image should look something like this:

The clip will gradually return to its original shape.

5 Click the Play button to view the motion, and then click the Pause button.

You'll end the distortion effect sooner by adding another point and returning the clip to its original shape, although smaller, in the Distortion area.

6 Click about two-thirds of the way across the motion path to make another point; then drag it down to the lower right corner of the Visible Area.

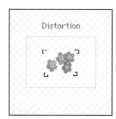

7 While this point is still selected, move the corner points of the clip in the Distortion area back to their original square positions, but make the clip about one-third of its original size. Use the picture below as a guide.

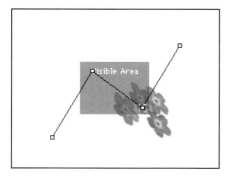

8 Click the Play button in the motion thumbnail to preview the changes.

9 Click OK to close the Motion Settings dialog box.

10 Save the project.

Fine-tuning the position of a point on the motion path

The Motion Settings dialog box lets you set coordinates for each point on the motion path using the Info boxes (just below the motion timeline). The coordinates you enter are specified at the resolution of the sample image (80 x 60 pixels) but scaled at output time to the project output size. A 1-pixel shift at the sample size scales up to a 4-pixel shift if the project output size is 320 x 240, or to an 8-pixel shift if the output size is 640 x 480. You can type fractional decimal values to reposition points with finer precision than 4- or 8-point increments. For example, typing 1.75 in the first text box results in a horizontal shift of 14 pixels at 640 x 480 resolution. To derive the correct value to type for the direction you want to move, first divide the appropriate output dimension (for example, 640) by the corresponding sample image dimension (80), and then divide the distance you want to move (for example, 14 pixels) by the result.

—From the Adobe Premiere User Guide, Chapter 9

Applying motion settings and transparency

Now you'll animate Lotus.psd using the motion path, zoom, and rotation options. First, though, you need to add Lotus.psd to the Timeline and apply transparency.

1 Move the edit line to 0:00:02:15, using the timecode in the Monitor window's Program view as a guide.

2 Drag Lotus.psd from the Project window to the Video 3 track, aligning its In point to the edit line.

3 Move the edit line to about 0:00:06:15.

4 Drag the right edge of Lotus.psd to the edit line.

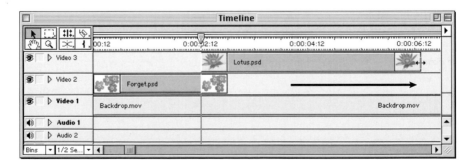

5 Select Lotus.psd in the Timeline and choose Clip > Video > Transparency.

Lotus.psd was created in Adobe Photoshop with a blue-green background (Red= 0, Green = 255, and Blue = 255). With this color, you could make the background transparent using the Blue Screen, Green Screen, Chroma, or RGB Difference transparency key types. See "Applying the Blue Screen transparency key type" on page 262 or "Applying the Chroma transparency key type" on page 265 for more information on these key types.

The RGB Difference key type includes the option to add a drop shadow to the remaining opaque image, so we'll use it on Lotus.psd.

6 Choose RGB Difference for Key Type.

7 In the Color area, click the blue-green background of the thumbnail to select it as the transparent value.

Make sure the black and white icon (⬛) is selected under the Sample area so that you can clearly view the transparency effect.

8 Move the Similarity slider to 60 to increase the range of colors affected by the key type. Click the page peel icon (⬛) to view the transparency in relation to the other clips in the Timeline.

Sample area before and after moving Similarity slider.

9 Select Drop Shadow. Notice the new shadow that appears on the remaining opaque image (the flower).

10 Click OK to close the Transparency Settings dialog box.

Applying motion to a clip with a colored background

Now you'll apply motion to Lotus.psd. Because this clip has a colored background, you'll need to adjust the Fill Color in the Motion Setting dialog box.

1 Select Lotus.psd in the Timeline, if it's not already selected.

2 Choose Clip > Video > Motion.

3 Click the Play button if necessary, and make sure Show All is selected so that you can see the clip on the lower track as you preview the motion.

Notice that as the clip moves across the screen, a white background follows and precedes it. By default, Premiere uses white to fill the area around the clip's frame when the frame does not fill the screen. Because you applied transparency to a color other than white, the white fill area is not transparent. The Fill Color option lets you select the color Premiere uses for the fill area so that it appears transparent.

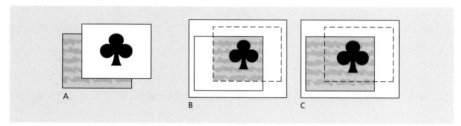

A. Clip with a transparency value other than white B. Before choosing the motion Fill Color
C. After choosing the motion Fill Color

4 Position the pointer on the clip thumbnail in the Fill Color area. The pointer turns to an eyedropper tool (✎).

5 Click the blue-green background to select it. If necessary, click the Play button and notice how the white box disappears from the preview, which now displays with a completely transparent background.

Applying zoom and rotation

Now you'll add points to the motion timeline and apply zoom and rotation. When you add points directly to the motion timeline rather than to the motion path, you can select the exact time you want the effect to occur.

1 If necessary, click the Pause button to stop the preview.

2 Position the pointer over the middle of the motion timeline and when the pointer turns to a solid triangle icon click and drag until the motion timeline percent is at 55%; then release the mouse to make a point.

3 Click the Center button to position the new point directly in the center of the Visible Area. This button centers the point visually, but not chronologically.

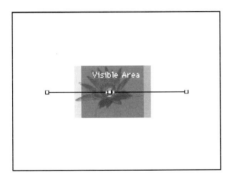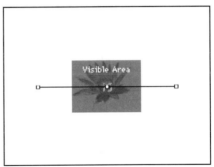

4 With the point still selected, type **300** in the Rotation text box. One complete rotation is 360 degrees. By entering 300, you're rotating the image almost one full rotation.

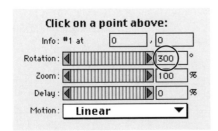

5 Press Tab to move to the Zoom text box and type **180**, and then press Tab again. A zoom value of 100% represents the original size of the clip. Entering a zoom value of 180, increases the image size by 80%.

6 Preview your edits in the motion thumbnail, and then click the Pause button.

Notice how the flower begins rotating clockwise as it moves from the first point to the second point and then turns counter clockwise as it moves from the second point to the last point. Because the first and last points on the motion path have rotation values of 0 (zero), the flower must rotate to 300 degrees by the time it reaches the second point and then return to 0 degrees by the time it reaches the last point; thus creating a backwards rotation effect between the second and last point.

Now you'll edit the first point of the motion path.

7 Select the Start point on the motion path and click Center.

Note: Remember that the finger icon turns gray when it is over a point on the motion path. If the icon is not gray, each click will create a new point rather than select an existing point.

8 Type **0** in the Zoom text box, and then press Tab.

9 Click the Play button by the motion thumbnail and notice how the clip now zooms in from 0 to 180% in the center of the Visible Area. Click the Pause button to stop the preview.

Now let's move the last point of the motion path out of the Visible Area, making the clip move off the screen.

10 Drag the last point of the motion path to the top right corner so the image is just outside of the Visible Area.

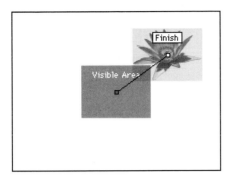

11 With the last point still selected, type 150 in the Rotation text box; then press Tab.

12 Preview the effect by clicking the Play button by the motion thumbnail.

This effect may not be too obvious, but the 150 degree rotation on the last point slows down the spinning flower as it leaves the Visible Area. The image now only needs to return to 150 degrees instead of 0 while traveling from the second point to the last point.

Adjusting points on the motion timeline

You can adjust the speed of motion effects by changing the Motion or Delay option, or by moving the points on the motion timeline.

Here you'll make the zoom effect on the second point appear more realistic by accelerating it with the Motion option.

1 Select the second point on the motion timeline. (The points appear as short vertical lines.)

Note: When selecting a point on the motion timeline, make sure the pointer appears as a finger icon before clicking. If the pointer appears as a triangle, each click will create a new point rather than select an existing point.

2 Choose Accelerate from the Motion menu at the bottom of the dialog box. Click the Play button to preview the results.

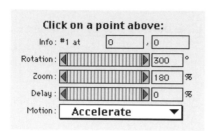

The motion now speeds up as the flower approaches its full magnification of 180%.

💡 *When you zoom out of a point, use the Decelerate Motion option to make it appear more realistic. The Linear option keeps the motion at a constant rate between two points.*

Now you'll adjust the points on the motion timeline to increase the speed at which the clip moves off the screen.

3 Click the Pause button to stop the preview.

4 Drag the second point on the motion timeline to the left until it is at 46%.

Now the time it takes the flower to get from the first point to the second point is less than what it takes to get from the second point to the last point.

5 Click OK to close the Motion Settings dialog box, and then save the project.

6 Drag the work area bar over Forget.psd and Lotus.psd, and then press Enter (Windows) or Return (Mac OS) to preview the new motion settings.

Creating a traveling matte

Traveling mattes are moving track mattes. You can create a traveling matte by using a still image with applied motion or by using a black-and-white or grayscale video clip. The motion applied to a still image can be as simple as a zoom or it can be complex, involving rotations, distortions, and delays.

First let's add two more clips to the Timeline.

1 Drag Logo.ai from the Project window to the Video 3 track, aligning its In point with the end of Lotus.psd.

2 Drag the right edge of Logo.ai until its Out point snaps to the end of Backdrop.mov.

3 Drag Green.psd from the Project window to the Video 2 track, aligning its In point with the In point of Logo.ai.

4 Drag the right edge of Green.psd until its Out point also snaps to the end of Backdrop.mov.

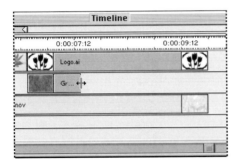 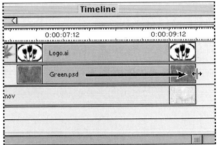

Applying transparency to traveling matte clips

When creating a track or traveling matte transparency effect, always apply the Track Matte key type to the clip located below the matte in the Timeline. Here you'll apply the Track Matte key type to Green.psd so that it will play through the black area (matte) in Logo.ai, which is located above it.

1 Select Green.psd in the Timeline and choose Clip > Video > Transparency.

2 Choose Track Matte for Key Type. Make sure the page peel icon is selected.

Notice how Green.psd becomes the background and Backdrop.mov (the video program's background) displays through Logo.ai's matte. We want to reverse this effect so that the background remains constant throughout the video program and Green.psd plays through Logo.ai's matte.

3 Select Reverse Key.

Before and after selecting Reverse Key.

4 Click OK, and then save the project.

Applying preset motion settings

You can save motion settings and use them repeatedly on different clips and in different projects. Here you'll load a previously saved motion file and apply it to Logo.ai.

1 Select Logo.ai in the Timeline and choose Clip > Video > Motion.

2 Click Load and double-click Logomoti.pmt in the 10Lesson folder.

A motion path appears in the Visible Area.

3 Preview the motion by clicking the Play button.

4 Click the Start point on the motion path (remember to click only when the finger icon turns gray, otherwise you'll create a new point). Notice the different settings for Rotation, Zoom, and Delay.

5 Press Tab to move to each point along the path.

The motion path begins with a zoom value of 450%, shrinks to 37% by the second-to-last point, and ends at 75%. The block at the end of the motion timeline represents a delay on the last point.

6 Click the last point on the motion timeline to see the details of the delay setting. Notice that the delay is set to 7%.

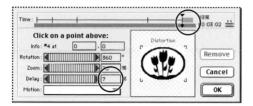

7 Click OK to close the Motion Settings dialog box.

8 Save the project.

Delaying a point on the motion path

Let's preview the motion in the Monitor window and then make some changes to the delay.

1 Drag the work area bar over all the clips in the Timeline; then press Enter (Windows) or Return (Mac OS) to preview the project.

Currently, the logo reaches its final position right before Background.mov stops playing. We want the logo to appear at its last motion point sooner, and remain there longer, so a longer portion of Background.mov plays after the logo stops moving. To achieve this effect, we'll increase the length of the delay on the last point to one-half second, or 15 frames.

2 Select Logo.ai in the Timeline and choose Clip > Video > Motion.

You'll use the motion timeline's time display ( ), located to the right of the motion timeline, to set the delay in the Motion Settings dialog box to exactly 15 frames.

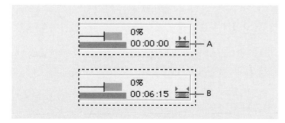

A. Time display showing the timecode for the clip
B. Time display showing the timecode for the entire project

The time display shows you whether the motion timeline timecode represents the timecode for your entire project or for the selected clip. Using this information, you can determine the exact time at which a motion effect occurs in the video program or the video clip.

Let's set the time display to show the timecode for the entire project, which is 10 seconds long. Once it's set, you can accurately set the delay to 9 seconds 15 frames, which is one-half second in from the end of the project.

The time display ( ) is currently set to show the timecode for the selected clip.

3 Click the time display's red arrows to display the location of the selected motion point in relation to the timecode for the entire project ( ).

4 Select the last point on the motion timeline, and notice that the time display reads about 00:09:22. The delay setting stops all motion at this point, and the image remains constant for the last 8 frames of the project.

5 Drag the Delay tread until the time display reads 00:09:15. The Delay text box should be at approximately 14%.

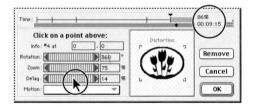

6 Click OK to close the Motion Setting dialog box, and then save the project.

7 Press Enter (Windows) or Return (Mac OS) to preview the project.

Exporting the movie

If you were really creating an advertisement to be broadcast on television, your clips would all be 640 x 480 resolution so that they would display optimally on a NTSC monitor. Your project Timebase would be 29.97, and you'd export your project using a hardware codec and print the final movie to video tape.

However, because 640 x 480 resolution files require an exceptional amount of hard disk space to store and memory to edit, we kept the tutorial files to 240 x 180 resolution. You'll export this project using this smaller file size, a 15 fps Timebase, and a software codec.

1 If necessary, click the Timeline title bar to activate it, and then choose File > Export > Movie.

2 Click Settings.

3 Choose QuickTime for the File Type, and Entire Project for the Range.

4 Deselect Export Audio, and then click Next.

5 Select Cinepak for the Compressor.

6 Choose 15 for the Frame Rate.

7 Click OK to close the Export Movie Settings dialog box.

8 Type **FlowerAd.mov** for the File name, and then click Save to export the movie. Premiere displays a status bar providing the estimated time it will take to process the movie.

When the movie is complete, it opens in a separate Clip window.

9 Click the Play button to play the movie.

Printing to video

When you want to print your finished movie to video tape, you use the Print to Video option. This option lets you display the movie at full screen on your computer monitor. If your movie is not in full screen resolution (640 x 480) you can zoom the movie to fill the screen, or you can display it at its smaller resolution with a black border.

1 With the Clip window still active, choose File > Export > Print to Video.

2 Enter 1 second for Color Bars, 1 second for Play Black, and then select Full Screen (Windows) or Zoom Screen (Mac OS). Click OK.

The movie plays at full screen on your computer or peripheral monitor. Because your movie is not full resolution(640 x 480), it appears pixelated or jaggy.

3 Choose File > Export > Print to Video again and don't select Full Screen. Now the movie plays in high resolution at its smaller size.

Exploring on your own

Take a few minutes to experiment with the project and try out some of your new skills. Here are some suggestions:

• Change the motion path for Forget.psd so that it continually rotates along the path. Save the path as a file.

• Create a one- or two-word title for the flower advertisement. Place the title at the beginning of the project in the Video 3 track and change the duration so it ends when Lotus.psd begins. Add motion to the title, making it zoom in from 10% to 100%.

• At different points along Logo.ai's motion path, set the Motion to Accelerate and Decelerate and notice the effects.

• Apply a zoom effect to Backdrop.mov using only the Center button and the distortion area.

Review questions

1 Under what circumstances would you need to use the Fill Color setting in the Motion dialog box?

2 When should you accelerate a motion path?

3 If you want to set a point on the Motion timeline that matches a specific time in the clip, should the time display's red arrows be close together or far apart?

4 What are two different ways to add points to a motion path?

5 How do you convert a track matte to a traveling matte?

6 How do you adjust the time between two points on the motion path?

Answers

1 When your clip has a colored background, such as blue.

2 When your image zooms in to a larger size.

3 Close together.

4 Clicking on the motion path and clicking on the motion timeline.

5 Add motion to the clip that has the track matte applied.

6 Move the point on the motion timeline. The farther the points arc from each other, the longer the time between them.

Lesson 11

Applying Video and Audio Filters

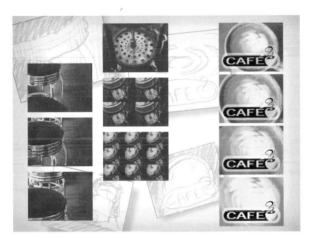

Adobe Premiere provides a broad range of video and audio filters you can use to solve problems and enhance your video project.

To learn about Premiere's filters, you'll create a short promotional spot for a coffee bar. Specifically, you'll learn how to do the following:

- Apply video and audio filters.
- Change filter effects and settings.
- Use multiple filters and change their order.
- Copy filters and settings from one clip to another.
- Change filters over time using keyframes and transitions.
- Apply a filter to part of an image.
- Use the Image Pan filter.

Getting started

For this lesson you'll open an existing project with most of the necessary files imported. Make sure you know the location of the files used in this lesson. Insert the CD-ROM disc if necessary. For help, see "Using the Classroom in a Book files" on page 4.

To ensure that the Premiere preferences are set to the default values, exit Premiere, and then delete the preferences file as explained in "Restoring default preferences" on page 5.

1 Double-click 11Lesson.ppj in the 11Lesson folder to open it in Premiere.

2 When the project opens, choose File > Save As, open the appropriate lesson folder on your hard disk if necessary, type **Coffee.ppj**, and press Enter (Windows) or Return (Mac OS).

Viewing the finished movie

To see what you'll be creating, take a look at the finished movie.

1 Choose File > Open and double-click the 11Final.mov file in the Final folder, inside the 11Lesson folder.

The movie opens in the Source view of the Monitor window.

2 Click the Play button to view the movie.

Why use filters?

Video and audio filters serve many useful purposes in a project. You can use them to fix defects in video or audio material, such as changing the color balance of a video clip or removing noise from dialogue. You might also use audio filters to add an appropriate level of ambiance or echo to dialogue recorded in a studio. Filters are often used to create an effect or mood not present in the raw video or audio clip, such as softening the focus or adding a sunset tint to a scene.

Obtaining video filters

Adobe Premiere includes a variety of video filters that let you distort, blur, sharpen, and add special effects to your clips. You can change filters over time to increase or decrease the effect, and you can apply multiple filters to any clip. You can also create and apply your own custom filters, which you can save and use over again.

In addition to the dozens of filters included with Premiere, many filters are available in the form of plug-ins, which you can purchase or otherwise acquire. For example, Photoshop plug-ins can be copied into the Premiere Plug-ins folder to use on video clips or still-images in your video work.

—From the Adobe Premiere User Guide, Chapter 10

Applying filters

In Premiere, video and audio filters are both applied in the same way. If you selected a video clip, video filters are listed in the Filters dialog box. If you selected an audio clip or the audio portion of a video clip, audio filters are listed.

In this project, you'll create a monochrome appearance using a yellow tint that will be applied to a number of clips. This effect requires three video filters: Black & White, Color Replace, and Tint. You'll start by applying the Tint filter to the Stool.mov clip.

1 Before you begin working in the project, mute the audio tracks to avoid the added distraction of audio while previewing: Click the speaker icon (🔊) on the left side of the Audio 1 and Audio 2 tracks so that the icon disappears.

2 Double-click Stool.mov in the Timeline to open it in the Source view, and then click Play to preview it.

We want to give this clip the feel of an old photograph using a brown tint to simulate the sepia tone of early photographic prints. As you change clips using filters, it will be helpful to keep the original clip displayed in the Source view so that you can compare it to the preview image in the Filters dialog box.

3 Drag the Source view shuttle slider all the way to the left to display the first frame of Stool.mov in the Source view.

4 Click Stool.mov in the Timeline to select it, and then choose Clip > Filters to open the Filters dialog box.

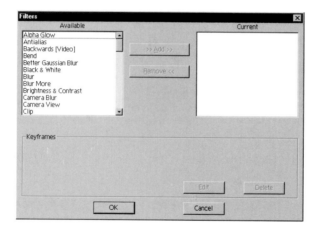

To scroll the Available list in the Filters dialog box to the filter you want to select, type the first letter of the filter name. In Windows, a filter must be selected in the Available list for this shortcut to work.

5 Select Tint in the Available list, and then click Add to add the Tint filter and open its dialog box.

6 In the Tint Settings dialog box, click on the Color swatch to open the Color Picker dialog box.

7 Click on a medium dark brown color for your tint (we used **85** red, **42** green, and **0** blue), and then click OK to close the Color Picker dialog box.

8 Drag the Level slider to about 35%, and then click OK to close the Tint Settings dialog box. Click OK again to close the Filters dialog box.

9 Preview this filter by scrubbing in the Timeline ruler while holding down the Alt key (Windows) or the Option key (Mac OS).

You should see a brown tint applied over a color image, when compared to the original image in the Source view, especially in white areas. Notice the blue-green bar at the top of the clip icon in the Timeline. This indicates that a filter has been applied to the clip.

◯ *You can open the Filters dialog box quickly by pressing Control+F (Windows) or Command+F (Mac OS).*

Applying filters in the right order

When you apply multiple filters to one or more clips, the order in which you apply them can affect the final result. Here, you'll add two more filters to the Stool.mov clip. You'll start by applying the Black & White filter to strip out the original color from the clip, making it look more like an early black-and-white photograph. After that, you'll add the Color Replace filter to change a range of colors.

1 With Stool.mov still selected in the Timeline, open the Filters dialog box. Then double-click Black & White in the Available list to add it to the Current list.

2 Click OK to close the Filters dialog box, and then preview the effect of both filters by scrubbing in the Timeline ruler while holding down the Alt key (Windows) or the Option key (Mac OS).

Instead of seeing a brown tint over a black-and-white image, you see only the black-and-white image. This is because the Black & White filter removed all color from the image after the tint was applied. When applying filters, order is important. It's an easy matter to put these filters in the right order.

3 With Stool.mov still selected, open the Filters dialog box again. In the Current list, make Black & White the first item in the list by dragging Tint below it. Click OK to close the Filters dialog box.

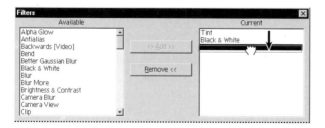

4 Preview the effect of both filters again by scrubbing in the Timeline ruler while holding down the Alt key (Windows) or the Option key (Mac OS).

This time you see a brown tint over a black-and-white image, which is just what you want. Now you'll add the last filter to this clip, with which you'll change highlights to a color.

5 With Stool.mov still selected, open the Filters dialog box again. Double-click Color Replace in the Available list to open the Color Replace Settings dialog box.

To establish which color you'll replace, you'll select a color by using the eye dropper tool in the Color Replace Settings dialog box.

6 Position the pointer in the Clip Sample image so that it turns into an eye dropper icon (🖉). Move the eye dropper over the bright area in the upper left corner and click to capture the color.

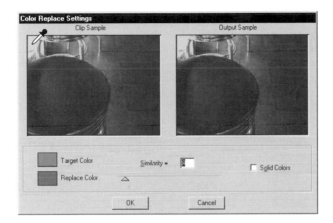

7 Now click the Replace Color swatch, click on a light orange color (we used **255** red, **210** green, and **115** blue) to replace your first color selection, and click OK.

Now you'll set the Similarity slider to indicate the range of colors to be replaced, based on their similarity to the color you selected. This setting determines the smoothness of the transition from original colors to the replaced color.

8 Using the Similarity slider, set Similarity to about 70, and then click OK to close the Color Replace Settings dialog box. Click OK to close the Filters dialog box.

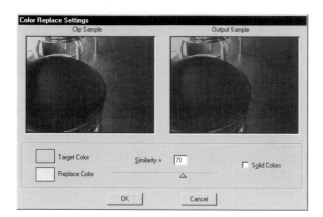

9 Preview the cumulative color effects of the filters you just applied by scrubbing in the Timeline ruler while holding down the Alt key (Windows) or the Option key (Mac OS).

10 Save the project.

Copying filters and settings

Once you have set up and applied one or more filters to a clip, you may want to use the same filters and settings on other clips. Doing this manually would be a lot of work, but there is a much easier way. Using the Paste Custom command, you can apply identical filters and settings to any number of clips. You'll use this technique now to copy the filters from Stool.mov and apply them to Roaster.mov.

1 Make sure Stool.mov is still selected in the Timeline and choose Edit > Copy.

Note: Remember, you can see the complete name of a clip by positioning the pointer over the clip and pausing.

2 Now select Roaster.mov in the Timeline and choose Edit > Paste Custom.

3 In the Paste Custom Settings dialog box, click Settings, and then deselect Fade Control, Transparency Settings, and Motion Settings so that only Filters is selected.

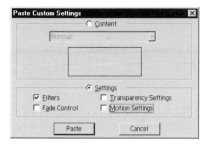

4 Click Paste.

5 Preview Roaster.mov by scrubbing in the Timeline ruler while holding down the Alt key (Windows) or the Option key (Mac OS).

The filters you originally applied to Stool.mov are now also applied to Roaster.mov, along with the settings you selected. You also need to apply the same filters to several other clips, so this time you'll select those clips using the range select tool, which lets you select more than one clip at a time.

6 In the Timeline window, select the range select tool.

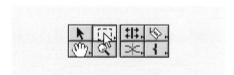

7 Drag over Press.mov and Dessert.mov in the Timeline to select them.

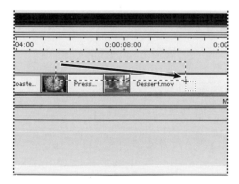

Because you have not used the Copy command since you copied Stool.mov, the Paste command still contains the filters and their settings from that clip. Also, because you already set up the Paste Custom function in the Paste Custom Settings dialog box, you can simply use the Paste Custom Again command to reuse those settings.

8 Choose Edit > Paste Custom Again.

The filters and settings from Stool.mov are now applied to the clips you selected.

9 Deselect the range select tool by selecting the selection tool (▸).

10 Preview the project by scrubbing in the Timeline ruler while holding down the Alt key (Windows) or the Option key (Mac OS).

The first four clips in the project should all have identical filters and settings.

11 Save the project.

Changing filters over time

Some Premiere filters can be changed over time, or *dynamically*. Filters that can be changed dynamically use *keyframes* to tell them when to make changes. Filters that don't have settings associated with them, such as the Black & White filter, don't need or use keyframes, so they can't be changed in this way.

For filters that don't use keyframes, you can often create change over time using transitions, although this technique is not as flexible as using keyframes.

Changing filters using keyframes

A keyframe is a marker in time that contains a video filter's settings for a specific point in a clip. You'll use the Replicate filter to add an effect to Press.mov, and use keyframes to indicate when the filter starts and what its settings are at that point. Then, you'll use another keyframe to change the effect again at a different point in time.

1 Select Press.mov in the Timeline window and then open the Filters dialog box.

2 In the Available list, double-click Replicate.

3 In the Replicate dialog box, drag the slider to see the effects of the settings for this filter. Set the slider back to the 2-by-2 format as shown below, and then click OK to close the dialog box.

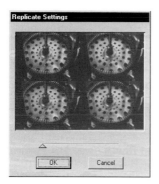

To create and position keyframes and edit their settings, you use the keyframe timeline in the Filters dialog box. Keyframes are represented by triangular markers on the keyframe timeline. By default, the first keyframe is active when you select a filter. The active keyframe is indicated by the blue marker. The keyframe timeline represents the duration of the clip. Below the left end of the keyframe timeline, Premiere displays the number of the active keyframe and the timecode of its location in the video program.

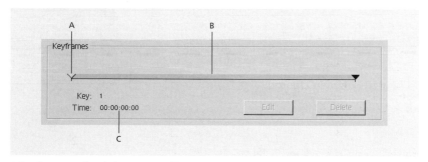

*A keyframe marker (**A**) represents filter settings at a point on the keyframe timeline (**B**), identified by the timecode for that keyframe (**C**).*

Because you want the filter to start near the middle of the clip, you'll move the first keyframe on the keyframe timeline to that point. Then you'll add a new keyframe and change the filter settings for that keyframe. Finally, you'll change the settings for the last keyframe.

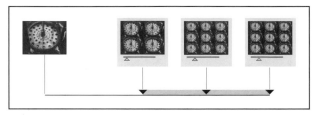

The Replicate filter will change at keyframes along the keyframe timeline, from one image to four to nine.

4 Drag the Filters dialog box so you can see the Program view in the Monitor window.

5 On the keyframe timeline, drag the first marker until just before the point where the shiny lid of the coffee maker enters the frame. This indicates where the filter starts in the clip.

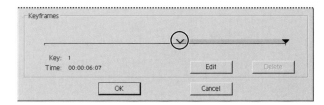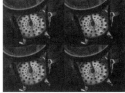

Next, you'll create a new keyframe and set a filter value for that keyframe.

6 Click the keyframe timeline midway between the first and last keyframes to create a new keyframe.

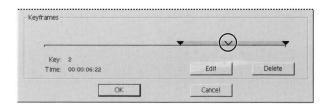

The Replicate Settings dialog box opens with the same settings as the previous keyframe.

7 Drag the slider so that the preview shows the 3-by-3 format, and then click OK.

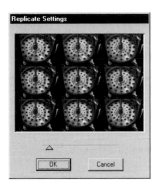

Now you'll select the filter settings you want at the end of the clip. The last keyframe is currently set to the 2-by-2 format. Because the last keyframe affects only the last frame of the clip, a change at that keyframe would cause a distracting one-frame flash of the new settings. To avoid this, let's make it the same as the previous keyframe, the 3-by-3 format.

8 Double-click the keyframe at the right end of the keyframe timeline to open the Replicate Settings dialog box. Drag the slider to select the 3-by-3 format, and then click OK. Click OK again to close the Filters dialog box.

9 Preview this filter by scrubbing in the Timeline ruler while holding down the Alt key (Windows) or the Option key (Mac OS).

The Replicate filter applied to Press.mov maintains a single image throughout the first half of the clip. At that point it changes to four images and then to nine images.

10 Save the project.

Changing filters using transitions

For filters that do not permit using keyframes to change the filter over time, you can sometimes use a transition to do the same thing. Simply position the transition, usually a cross dissolve, between two versions of the same clip, which are identical except for the filter settings.

This method of changing a filter over time works best with certain filters, such as those that affect image quality (for example, hue, saturation, and contrast).

Here, you'll use a cross-dissolve transition to remove the effects of three filters in the Dessert.mov clip over time, returning the clip to its original color. In this case, you need to use a transition to make the change because the Black & White filter applied to Dessert.mov can't be changed dynamically.

You'll start by adding the cross-dissolve transition to the Transition track.

1 Click the arrow on the left side of the Video 1 track to expand it.

2 Drag the Cross Dissolve transition from the Transitions palette to the Transition track so that it snaps to the In point of the Dessert.mov clip.

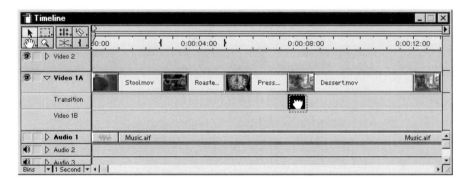

Next, you'll add an instance of Dessert.mov to the Video 1B track.

3 Drag Dessert.mov from the Project window into the Video 1B track in the Timeline, until it snaps to a position directly below the first instance of Dessert.mov.

4 Position the pointer over the right edge of the transition and drag to the right so that it completely spans the Dessert.mov clip.

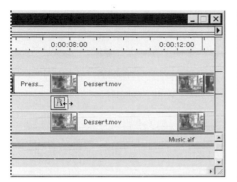 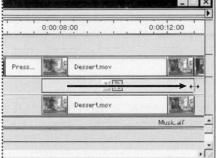

5 Preview Dessert.mov: Resize the work area bar so that it covers the clip you just worked on, and then press Enter (Windows) or Return (Mac OS).

The Dessert.mov clip changes gradually from the effect of yellow highlights on brown shadows into full color over the duration of the clip.

Note: *If your preview shows one image ghosted on another, check both instances of Dessert.mov in the Timeline and be sure they are aligned exactly.*

6 Save the project.

Using the Image Pan and ZigZag filters

Next, you'll animate a still image of a cup of espresso, Latte.tif, by applying the Image Pan filter to create a zoom and applying the ZigZag filter to add a swirling effect. These filters can be set to change gradually over time, in contrast to the Replicate filter you used earlier in this lesson, which can be changed only in discrete steps.

The instance of Latte.tif in the Timeline has a duration of 30 frames. For this project, this clip should be 3:23 long, and you'll want to set the clip to this duration before you apply the Image Pan filter. You'll make this change using the Duration command.

1 In the Project window, select Latte.tif, choose Clip > Locate Clip, and then click Done.

2 Choose Clip > Duration.

3 Type **323** in the duration box, and then click OK to close the dialog box. You've just changed the duration of Latte.tif from 00:30 to 3:22.

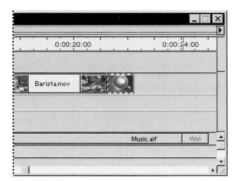 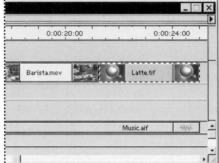

You'll now apply the Image Pan filter to it.

4 With Latte.tif still selected, open the Filters dialog box, and then double-click Image Pan in the Available list.

The Image Pan dialog box includes a preview window that plays the entire clip. You'll use the Image Pan feature to add a zoom, previewing it in the Image Pan dialog box as you work. This dialog box also includes images of the first and last frames of the clip, each with a selection box used to create pan and zoom effects. You can change the size of these selection boxes in two ways: by entering values for width and height, and by dragging the handles at the corners of each box. First, you'll crop the image slightly by entering a new frame size, in pixels.

5 In the Image Pan Settings dialog box, locate the Start settings on the left side. Type **392** in the Width box and type **287** in the Height box.

6 Click the top copy button (>>Copy>>) to set the same size and position on the End image.

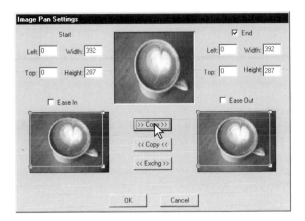

Notice that in the preview, the image is cropped (as indicated by the white selection box) and there is no motion. To introduce motion with the filter, the selection box in the Start view must be a different size or in a different position from the selection box in the End view. The filter then moves from the Start position to the End position. Now you'll add a zoom by dragging the handles of the selection box to size it.

7 In the Start view, locate the lower right handle on the selection box. While holding down the Alt key (Windows) or the Option key (Mac OS), drag this handle so that the bottom right corner of the selection box meets the right edge of the cream in the cup. Dragging while holding down the modifier key maintains the aspect ratio (ratio of height to width) of the original image, and is important because we don't want to distort the image. Use this technique to drag the other handles so the selection box includes only the cream. Drag inside the selection box to center it over the cream.

Now let's change the direction of the zoom, so that it zooms in instead of out. Premiere provides a button to do this so that you don't have to manually change the size and position of the selection boxes.

8 Click the exchange button (<<Exchg>>) to change the direction of the zoom.

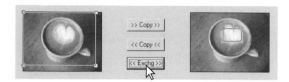

9 When you are satisfied with the pan and zoom you have set up, click OK to close the Image Pan Settings dialog box.

Next you'll add the ZigZag filter to Latte.tif. You'll set the filter to start with no effect and change over time to the desired intensity of effect at the end of the clip.

10 Scroll the Available list to the bottom and double-click ZigZag to open the ZigZag Settings dialog box. By default, the first keyframe is selected, although keyframes are not yet displayed in the dialog box at this point.

Now you'll select the settings for this keyframe.

11 In the ZigZag dialog box, type **0** for Amount, type **1** for Ridges, and set Style to Around Center. With these settings, the filter will have little or no effect on the clip. Click OK to close the ZigZag dialog box.

Finally, you'll select the settings for the last keyframe in this filter.

12 Double-click the keyframe on the right end of the keyframe timeline to select it and open the ZigZag dialog box.

13 Type **41** for Amount, type **5** for Ridges, and then click OK to close the ZigZag dialog box. Click OK to close the Filters dialog box.

14 Preview the filter you just applied: Resize the work area bar so that it covers the clip you just worked on, and then press Enter (Windows) or Return (Mac OS).

The image in Latte.tif zooms in while the ZigZag effect gradually intensifies.

15 Save the project.

Adding a logo

You'll add a logo to the last scene in this project. To do this, you'll simply make the logo clip visible. Logo.tif is already in the Video 3 track, but that track has been made shy and the shy tracks have been hidden to keep them out of your way. To eliminate it from your previews, the track has also been excluded. Note that the eye icon is missing from the left of the track. Its absence indicates that the track is excluded.

For a full description of shy and excluded tracks, see "Hiding tracks" in Premiere online Help or in Chapter 4 of the Premiere User Guide.

1 From the Timeline window menu, choose Show Shy Tracks to display the Video 3 track and Logo.tif. You may need to resize the Timeline window or scroll the video tracks vertically to view this track.

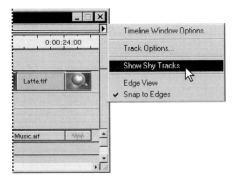

2 Preview Barista.mov and Logo.tif by scrubbing in the Timeline ruler while holding down the Alt key (Windows) or the Option key (Mac OS).

The logo doesn't appear in the preview because the Video 3 track is still excluded, as indicated by the blank box ( ) on the far left edge of the Video 3 track.

3 Click the blank box on the far left side of the Video 3 track so that the outlined eye icon ( ) appears, indicating that the track is still shy but is no longer excluded. This means the track will now be included in previews and exported video.

4 Preview Barista.mov and Logo.tif again by scrubbing in the Timeline ruler while holding down the Alt key (Windows) or the Option key (Mac OS).

The logo is superimposed over Barista.mov and Latte.tif, but it is difficult to see over the clips because the backgrounds are too dark for a black logo. Adding a matte would enable you to use a filter to lighten just the area of Barista.mov under the logo.

Applying a filter to areas of an image

In Lesson 10, "Adding Motion," you used a travelling matte to create a motion effect. Here, you'll use an image matte to apply a filter to just one area of an image. To do this, another instance of the clip must be placed in the superimpose (Video 2) track, and a filter must be applied to one of the clips.

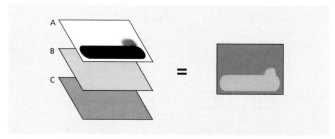

A. Matte
B. Lightened instance of clip with matte applied
C. Original clip

Adding a filter sets up a difference between the two clips so that part of one clip will show through the matte on the other clip. If the clips were identical, the matte would provide no function.

You'll start by adding an instance of Barista.mov to the superimpose track.

1 Drag Barista.mov from the Project window into the Video 2 track, snapping it to the first instance of Barista.mov in the Video 1 track so that the two clips are aligned.

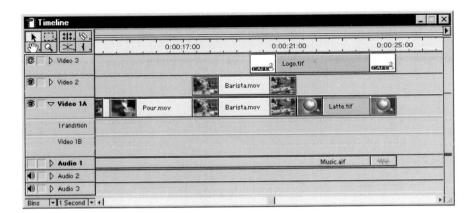

Now you'll apply a filter to lighten the instance of Barista.mov you just added to the Video 2 track.

2 Select Barista.mov in the Video 2 track and then open the Filters dialog box.

3 Double-click Brightness & Contrast in the Available list. Set Brightness to **-37** and set Contrast to **-60**, and then click OK to close the dialog box. Click OK again to close the Filters dialog box.

Now you'll set the transparency options and apply the matte for the instance of Barista.mov that you added to the Video 2 track.

4 With Barista.mov still selected in the Video 2 track, choose
Clip > Video > Transparency to open the Transparency Settings dialog box.

5 For Key type, choose Image Matte.

6 For Matte, click Choose, and then double-click Matte.tif in the 11Lesson folder.

7 Click the page peel icon (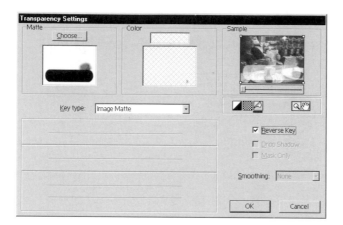), and click Reverse Key to select it.

8 Drag the slider in the Sample box to preview the effect of your settings, and then click OK to close the Transparency Settings dialog box.

9 Preview Barista.mov and Logo.tif by scrubbing in the Timeline ruler while holding down the Alt key (Windows) or the Option key (Mac OS).

The area of the image from the original Barista.mov clip, above the logo, displays normal brightness and contrast values, while the area of the copy below the logo is lighter, to go under our logo.

Right now, the matte starts before the logo, which is unnecessary. To fix this, you'll trim the beginning of the top instance of Barista.mov.

10 Move the pointer to the beginning of Barista.mov in the Video 2 track and drag right until it snaps to the beginning of Logo.tif.

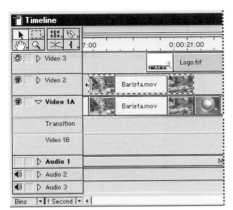 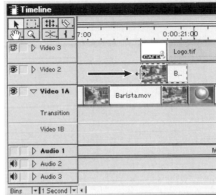

Next, you'll set up Latte.tif the same way you set up Barista.mov so the logo is visible in both clips. To start, you'll add a copy of Latte.tif to the Video 2 track and add a filter to it. Then you'll copy the transparency settings from Barista.mov and paste them into the copy of Latte.tif in the Video 2 track to set up the matte.

11 Select Latte.tif in the Timeline and choose Edit > Copy.

12 Select the Video 2 track by clicking the space to the right of Barista.mov, and then choose Edit > Paste.

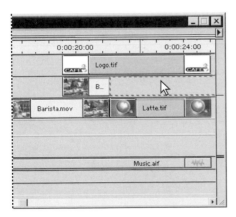 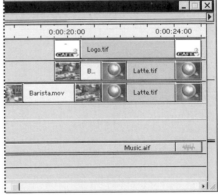

The copy of Latte.tif has the same duration, Image Pan filter, and ZigZag filter you applied earlier to the original Latte.tif.

13 Select the copy of Latte.tif and open the Filters dialog box.

14 Double-click Brightness & Contrast in the Available list. Set Brightness to **-40** and set Contrast to **-50**, and then click OK to close the dialog box. Click OK again to close the Filters dialog box.

Now you'll copy the transparency settings, which include the matte, from Barista.mov to Latte.tif.

15 Select Barista.mov in the Video 2 track, choose Edit > Copy.

16 Select the copy of Latte.tif in the Video 2 track and choose Edit > Paste Custom. Under Settings, deselect Filters and select Transparency Settings, and then click Paste.

You didn't choose Filters in the Paste Custom dialog box because that would have affected the filters already applied to the copy of Latte.tif.

17 To see the completed effect, including the logo, preview Barista.mov and Latte.tif by scrubbing in the Timeline ruler while holding down the Alt key (Windows) or the Option key (Mac OS).

18 Save the project.

Applying audio filters

As you learned earlier, audio filters and video filters are applied in about the same way. Here, you'll first remove noise from an audio clip, and then add some reverberation to the same clip.

1 Set the Time Unit menu in the Timeline to 2 Seconds.

2 Using the scroll bar on the right side of the Timeline, scroll the audio tracks, if necessary, so that Audio 1 and Audio 2 tracks are visible.

3 Drag Voice1.aif from the Project window into the Audio 2 track so that its Out point snaps to the end of the last clips in the project.

You'll need to unmute the Audio 2 track before you work with Voice1.aif.

4 Click the box on the far left of the Audio 2 track so that the speaker icon (🔊) appears.

5 Preview Voice1.aif by moving the edit line to the beginning of the clip and pressing the Play button under the Program view. Notice the constant noise in the clip.

The Notch/Hum filter in Premiere can be used to remove or reduce hum (low-frequency noise) or other single-frequency noise in an audio clip. You'll use the Notch/Hum filter to remove noise from the Voice1.aif clip.

6 In the Timeline, select Voice1.aif and open the Filters dialog box.

7 In the Available list, double-click Notch/Hum Filter.

8 Click the Preview sound box. Premiere plays a short loop of audio from the audio track.

The frequency of the noise in Voice1.aif is 800 Hz.

9 Drag the slider in the Notch/Hum Filter dialog box while listening to the audio preview.

Notice that as the filter setting (to the right of the slider) approaches 800 Hz, the noise is reduced. To set the filter precisely at 800 Hz, you'll enter that value.

10 Type **800** in the Hz box, and then click OK to close the Notch/Hum Filter dialog box. Click OK again to close the Filters dialog box.

11 Preview Voice1.aif again. The noise is now nearly inaudible. Also notice that the audio sounds flat. Let's add some life to it.

Now you'll apply a filter to add reverberation to the same audio clip. The Reverb filter simulates sound bouncing off hard surfaces in either a medium-sized room or a large room.

12 Click in the Timeline window title bar to make it active. With Voice1.aif still selected, open the Filters dialog box and double-click Reverb in the Available list.

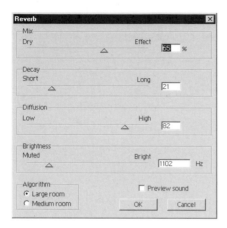

13 Select Preview Sound, select Medium room, and set Mix to about **20%**. Set Decay to a value that makes the audio sounds like it is coming from a medium-sized room (we used **20%**).

14 Click OK to close the Reverb dialog box, and then click OK to close the Filters dialog box.

Before previewing Voice1.aif and Music1.aif together, you'll need to unmute the Audio 1 track.

15 Click Voice1.aif again to deselect it.

16 Click the box on the far left of the Audio 1 track so that the speaker icon (◀)) appears.

17 Preview Voice1.aif and Music1.aif together by moving the edit line to a point several seconds before the beginning of Voice1.aif and pressing the Play button under the Program view. You have just improved the quality of the sound in your project significantly!

18 Save the project.

Exporting the movie

Now that you've finished your editing, it's time to generate a movie file.

1 Click the title bar of the Timeline window to make it active.

2 Choose File > Export > Movie.

3 In the Export Movie dialog box, click Settings.

4 Make sure QuickTime is selected for the File Type and Entire Project is selected for the Range.

5 Also make sure the Export Video and Export Audio options are selected. You can leave the rest of the settings as they are.

6 Click OK to close the Export Movie Settings dialog box.

7 In the Export Movie dialog box, specify the 11Lesson folder for the location and type **Coffee.mov** for the name of the movie. Click Save (Windows) or OK (Mac OS).

Premiere starts making the movie, displaying a status bar that provides an estimate for the amount of time it will take.

8 When the movie is complete, it is opened in the Source view of the Monitor window.

9 Click the Play button to play the movie.

Exploring on your own

Feel free to experiment with the project you have just created. Here are some suggestions:

• Find filters to reverse an image (left-to-right), invert an image (top-to-bottom), and reverse a clip (front-to-back).

• Try this method of making a filter start changing at an exact point in a clip: Set a marker in a clip where you want the change to start. Then drag the keyframe marker in the Filters dialog box so that it snaps to the marker in the clip.

• Split a clip into a number of equal-sized segments using the razor tool, and then apply a filter to every other segment using Paste Custom and Paste Custom Again.

Review questions

1 How can you tell if a filter has been applied to a clip?

2 What does the timecode under Keyframes in the Filters dialog box represent?

3 Why would you need to use a transition to change a filter over time?

4 What is the quickest method of applying identical filters and settings to multiple clips?

5 What does the speaker icon in the Timeline do?

Answers

1 A blue-green bar is displayed at the top of the clip in the Timeline.

2 This timecode represents the position of the active keyframe in relation to the entire video program.

3 Filters that do not use keyframes can be changed over time only by using a transition.

4 Using the Paste Custom command is the quickest way to apply identical filters and settings to multiple clips.

5 The speaker icon can be used to mute the audio track or make it shy.

Lesson 12

1. Create

a. CD-ROM

3. Deliver

Assemble

Acrobat

d. World Wide Web

1. Create

PageMaker

Illustrator

Streamline

Dimensions

Subclips and Virtual Clips

Subclips and virtual clips are powerful tools for assembling a video program in Premiere. Subclips are useful in splitting clips into a number of shorter clips that appear in the Project window. In contrast, you can combine one or more clips, filters, and transitions into a single virtual clip, which simplifies the Timeline and lets you use filters and transitions repeatedly on the same material.

From video clips you import into a Premiere project, you can create two other types of clips: subclips and virtual clips. You'll learn about using subclips and virtual clips in Premiere by creating one component of a television spot for a resort.

In this lesson, you'll learn the following skills:

- Creating and naming subclips.

- Using subclips in a project.

- Creating virtual clips.

- Nesting virtual clips.

- Editing virtual clips.

- Compiling a virtual clip into an actual clip.

Getting started

For this lesson you'll open an existing project with most of the necessary files imported. Make sure you know the location of the files used in this lesson. Insert the CD-ROM disc if necessary. For help, see "Using the Classroom in a Book files" on page 4.

To ensure that the Premiere preferences are set to the default values, exit Premiere, and then delete the preferences file as explained in "Restoring default preferences" on page 5.

1 Double-click 12Lesson.ppj in the 12Lesson folder to open it in Premiere.

2 When the project opens, choose File > Save As, open the appropriate lesson folder on your hard disk if necessary, type **Windsurf.ppj**, and press Enter (Windows) or Return (Mac OS).

Viewing the finished movie

If you'd like to see what you'll be creating, you can take a look at the finished movie. Because parts of the lesson let you make your own editing decisions, your movie may be slightly different.

1 Choose File > Open and double-click the 12Final.mov file in the Final folder, inside the 12Lesson folder.

The movie opens in the Source view of the Monitor window.

2 Click the Play button to view the movie.

Understanding subclips

Each component of a video program has a name that describes its function and location in the Premiere window.

Master clip A *master clip* is a reference to a file containing video that has been digitized. All of the files currently in the Project window of this project are master clips.

Instance You can drag copies of a master clip from the Project window into the Timeline as many times as you want. Each copy you make in this manner is called an *instance*.

Subclip You can also create a *subclip* from a master clip in the Project window. Although a subclip can include all of a master clip, the most useful function of a subclip is creating shorter clips from a master clip. Like a master clip, a subclip appears in the Project window, and is identified by the name you specify when you create it. You can use any number of instances of a subclip in a project. Don't confuse a subclip with an *alias*. Applying an alias to a clip simply changes the name of the clip and doesn't create a new clip.

To create a subclip that is a subset of a master clip, you must first open an instance of the master clip in the Source view to set In and Out points.

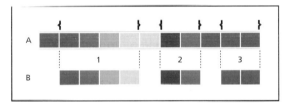

*From a master clip (**A**), you can create multiple subclips (**B**).*

It's important to understand that if the master clip is deleted from the Project window, the instances and subclips created from that master clip will also be deleted, both from the Project window and from the Timeline.

Creating subclips

You'll start this lesson by creating three subclips from the Surf.mov master clip. These subclips are automatically added to the Project window when you create them, and you'll use them in the next exercise to create your program.

1 In the Project window, double-click Surf.mov to open it in the Source view, and then preview it.

Notice that Surf.mov contains a number of separate scenes. You'll make subclips of three of these scenes.

2 In the Source view, set the In point (ᵻ) for the first subclip where the scene changes, at 1:22.

3 Set the Out point (ᵻ) at 9:26.

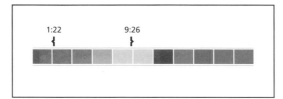

In and Out points define the source of a subclip.

4 Click the loop button (↻) to preview only the portion of Surf.mov defined by the In and Out points you just set. Press the stop button when you are finished previewing.

5 Choose Project > Create > Subclip.

6 In the Name box in the Make Subclip dialog box, type **Surf1.mov** for the subclip name. Make sure the location in the Location box is **Project: Windsurf.ppj**, and then click OK. Surf1.mov now appears in the Project window.

💡 *One way to rename a subclip is to use the Project window. First select the list view in the Project window, if necessary, by clicking the list view icon (▤). Then double-click the subclip name in the Project window, type the correct name, and then press Enter (Windows) or Return (Mac OS).*

Now you'll make the second subclip.

7 Make sure the Source view in the Monitor window is active, and choose Clip > Clear All Markers to clear the In and Out point markers.

8 For the second subclip you're going to create, set the In point at 13:20.

9 Set the Out point at 21:24.

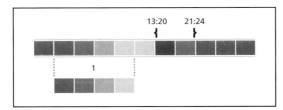

In and Out points for the first subclip are cleared and new ones are set for the second subclip.

10 Click the loop button (⟳) to preview the material you just defined. Press the stop button to end previewing.

11 Choose Project > Create > Subclip.

12 In the Name box in the Make Subclip dialog box, type **Surf2.mov** for the subclip name, and then click OK.

Let's make one last subclip.

13 Choose Clip > Clear All Markers to clear the In and Out point markers.

14 For the third subclip you're going to create, set the In point at 23:10.

15 Set the Out point at 29:04.

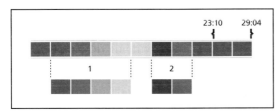

In and Out points are set for the third subclip.

16 Click the loop button (⟳) to preview the material you just defined. Press the stop button to end previewing.

17 Choose Project > Create > Subclip.

18 In the Name box in the Make Subclip dialog box, type **Surf3.mov** for the subclip name, and then click OK.

The Surf1.mov, Surf2.mov, and Surf3.mov subclips are now included in the Project window, ready for you to use in the project.

19 Save the project.

Understanding virtual clips

In creating subclips, you made a number of clips from a single master clip. Virtual clips let you do just the opposite: Create a single clip from a specified area of the Timeline, which can include any number of clips. A virtual clip is much like a clip exported as a movie from a separate project, using multiple clips, tracks, filters, and transitions. The advantage of using virtual clips is that you can do all of this in a single project without having to export movies.

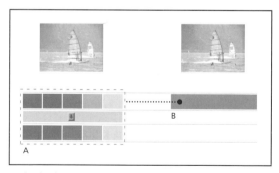

*Multiple clips (**A**) can be combined into a virtual clip (**B**).*

Using virtual clips, you can easily reuse material in the Timeline any number of times in a video program. You can apply filters, transitions, or other settings to the clips in the source area for a virtual clip. If you later make changes to these settings or edit these clips in any way, those changes are automatically applied to all instances of the virtual clip.

As with subclips, each clip in the source area for a virtual clip refers back to a master clip in the Project window. Deleting the master clip or the clip in the source area for the virtual clip will also delete the corresponding portion of each instance of the virtual clip.

The power of virtual clips

Using virtual clips, you can do the following:

• Reuse anything you build. For example, if you create a short sequence involving four superimposed video tracks and three mixed audio tracks, and you want to use the sequence ten times in a project, just build the sequence once, create a virtual clip from it, and add ten instances of the virtual clip to the Timeline.

• Apply different settings to copies of a sequence. For example, if you want a sequence to play back repeatedly but with a different filter each time, you can create a virtual clip and just copy that for each instance where you want it to appear with a different effect.

• Update identical scattered sequences all at once. For example, if you create the virtual clip described above and use the virtual clip in your video program ten times, you can simultaneously update all ten instances of the virtual clip just by editing the clips in the area of the Timeline that defines the virtual clip. And if different effects are applied to each instance of a virtual clip, the different effects are preserved for each instance. If you had copied and pasted the sequence instead of creating a virtual clip, you'd have to update one sequence and then copy and paste the update nine times, or edit each copy individually.

• Apply settings more than once to the same clip. For example, certain effects can be achieved only by combining transitions. However, you cannot apply more than one transition to the same point in time—unless you use a virtual clip. For example, you can apply a transition between two clips in the Timeline outside the main program, create two virtual clips using the clips on either side of that transition, and move the new virtual clips to the Timeline. The first transition you applied is now inside each virtual clip, so now you can apply a second transition between the two virtual clips.

—From the Adobe Premiere User Guide, Chapter 4

Creating virtual clips

In this exercise, you'll use create a virtual clip that will be combined with other clips to make the final project.

Before you can create a virtual clip, you must assemble the clips that will make up the virtual clip. To create a virtual clip, you use the block select tool, which selects material in all tracks in the area defined by the block select marquee. Although you can use any part of the main video program in the Timeline from which to create a virtual clip, the ideal location for the source material is at the beginning of the Timeline, ahead of the main video program. This is because you don't want changes you make in the main video program to shift or otherwise affect the clips in the source area for the virtual clip.

Assembling source clips

You'll now assemble the clips from which you will create a virtual clip. The effect you'll set up in this virtual clip is to combine two clips of windsurfers. You'll set one clip to be partially transparent, and the other clip will show through the transparent clip.

1 Drag Surf1.mov from the Project window into the Video 1B track, at the beginning of the Timeline.

2 Drag Surf2.mov from the Project window into the Video 2 track, also at the beginning of the Timeline.

With your clips in place, you'll select the transparency key type for one of them.

3 Select Surf2.mov in the Timeline, and then choose Clip > Video > Transparency to open the Transparency Settings dialog box.

4 Click the page peel icon (⬛) under the Sample window to view a thumbnail of the actual clip.

5 Select Luminance for the Key Type, and leave Threshold set to 100 and Cutoff set to 0, and then click OK.

Now you'll set up a fade to make Surf2.mov partially transparent.

6 Click the triangle to the left of the Video 2 track name to expand the track.

💡 *To drag the entire fade control line instead of a single handle, simply hold down the Shift key before dragging.*

7 Press and hold down the Shift key, and then drag the red fade control line down to 50%. You will need to drag outside the clip to reach this value.

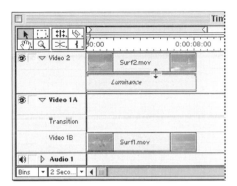 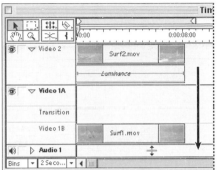

8 Clean up the Timeline by clicking the arrow in the Video 2 track to collapse the track. You have assembled the source clips for the first virtual clip.

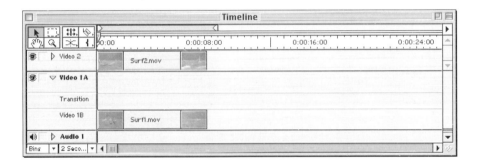

Let's preview your work so far.

9 Preview the assembled clips by scrubbing through the Timeline ruler while pressing the Alt key (Windows) or Option key (Mac OS).

10 Save the project.

Making and positioning the virtual clip

Now that you have assembled the source clips, you are ready to make a virtual clip from them.

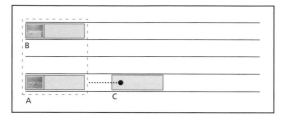

You'll select Surf1 (A) and Surf2 (B) to create a virtual clip (C).

1 In the Timeline, select the block select tool.

💡 *When using the block select tool to select clips at the beginning of the Timeline, the easiest method is to drag from right to left.*

2 Drag to select Surf1.mov and Surf2.mov, from which the virtual clip will be created. Be sure all of both clips are inside the selection marquee. Any part of a clip outside the marquee will not be included in the virtual clip.

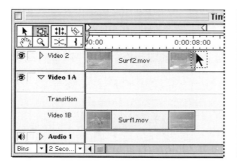 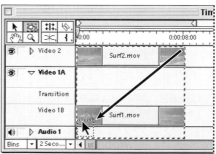

3 Position the pointer inside the selected area so that it changes to the virtual clip tool (🚏).

4 Drag the selected block to the Video 1B track, about a second after the end of the source area so you have space to work.

After you drop the black markers representing the virtual clip at this location, the virtual clip looks like any other clip, except for the color and the name, Virtual Clip, and the numbers below the name. The numbers indicate the beginning and end points of the block you selected in the Timeline. Therefore, the numbers on your virtual clips may vary somewhat from those in the illustrations.

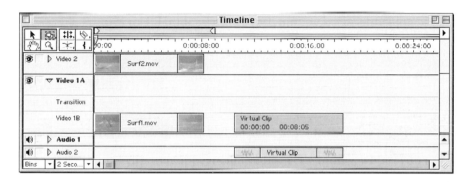

By default, Premiere creates an audio clip along with the video clip. In this case, the audio clip is empty. Because you won't be adding audio in the project, you'll delete the audio clip.

5 Deselect the block select tool by selecting the selection tool ( ).

6 Select the audio portion of the virtual clip and press the Delete key.

7 Preview the virtual clip you just created by scrubbing through the Timeline ruler while pressing the Alt key (Windows) or Option key (Mac OS).

Note: If you included any blank space (without clips) when you selected the source area in the Timeline for the virtual clip, you'll see black frames in that part of the virtual clip.

All virtual clips are named Virtual Clip when they are created. To make this virtual clip easier to distinguish from other virtual clips, you'll give it an alias.

8 Select the virtual clip and choose Clip > Alias.

9 When prompted, type **Background**, and click OK.

The virtual clip's name changes to Background.

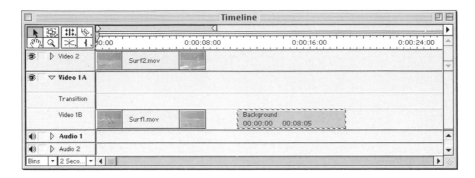

10 Save the project.

You've just created a virtual clip, and, as you'll see in the next exercise, you can use this virtual clip in ways you couldn't use the two clips from which it was created.

Nesting virtual clips

In this exercise, you'll make another virtual clip using the one you just created. When assembling clips to create a virtual clip, you can include other virtual clips in the source material. This process of putting one virtual clip inside another is called *nesting*.

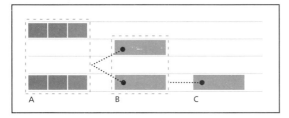

Source areas (A) are selected to make several virtual clips (B), which are nested in a new virtual clip (C).

Here you'll assemble two instances of the virtual clip you just made and apply a filter to one of them. Then you'll add the Image Mask transition between the virtual clips to show both at the same time. Finally, you'll make a nested virtual clip from these clips.

Assembling source clips

First, you'll make a copy of Background and position it in the Timeline.

1 Select Background and choose Edit > Copy.

2 Click the Video 1A track to select it, and choose Edit > Paste. Drag the clip until it snaps to the beginning of Background.

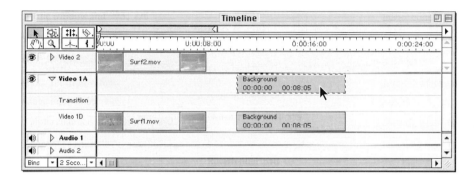

To avoid confusion, let's give a new name to the copy of Background.

3 Select the copy of Background and choose Clip > Alias.

4 When prompted, type **Background 2**, and click OK.

Next, you'll apply a filter to Background and Background 2. When you apply a filter to a virtual clip, it affects all the images that make up the virtual clip but does not affect the source clip. This is an efficient way to apply a filter to more than one clip at a time. Here, you'll set the filters differently for each virtual clip so that when you add the transition, you'll be able to see the difference between the two.

5 With Background 2 still selected, choose Clip > Filters to open the Filters dialog box.

6 Select Brightness & Contrast in the Available list and click Add.

7 Set Brightness to +19 and set Contrast to -20, and then click OK. Click OK again to close the Filters dialog box.

8 Select Background and open the Filters dialog box.

9 Select Brightness & Contrast in the Available list and click Add.

10 Set Brightness to +19 and set Contrast to -5, and then click OK. Click OK again to close the Filters dialog box.

In Lesson 11, "Applying Video and Audio Filters," you used the Transparency Settings dialog box to apply a filter to an area of an image. Here, you'll use the Image Mask transition to do the same thing to Background and Background 2.

11 Drag the Image Mask transition from the Transition palette to the Transition track, positioning it between the two virtual clips.

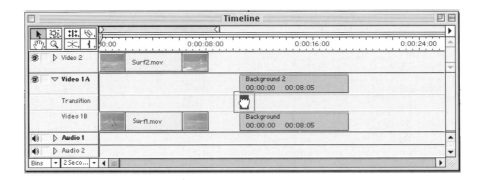

12 In the Image Mask Setting dialog box, click Select Image, locate the 12Lesson folder, and double-click Mask1.tif. Then click OK to close the Image Mask Setting dialog box.

13 To resize the transition, move the pointer to the end of the transition and drag right until it snaps to the end of the virtual clips.

14 Double-click the transition in the Timeline. As you can see in the dialog box previews, the clip in the Video 1A track shows through the black part of the mask, while the clip in the Video 1B track shows through the white part. Click Show Actual Sources to see the effect on the virtual clips. Click OK to close the Image Mask Settings dialog box.

15 Preview the effect you just created by scrubbing through the Timeline ruler while pressing the Alt key (Windows) or Option key (Mac OS).

Next, you'll create a virtual clip from the clips you just assembled.

Making and positioning the virtual clip

1 Scroll the Timeline left or drag in the Navigator palette so that Background and Background 2 are visible on the left side of the Timeline.

2 In the Timeline, select the block select tool (▦).

3 Drag to select all of Background, Background 2, and the transition.

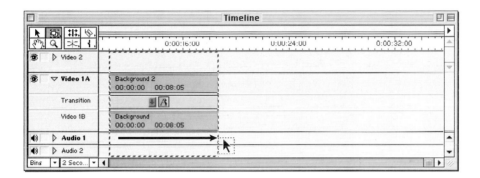

This time, you'll use a key combination to create a virtual clip without audio.

4 Press and hold the Shift key and the Alt key (Windows) or the Shift key and the Option key (Mac OS) and then drag the selected block to the Video 1B track, leaving a small gap between the selected block and the new virtual clip.

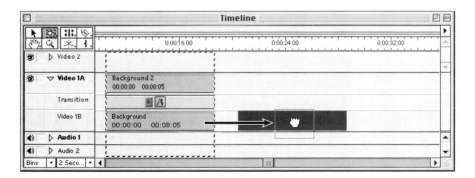

5 Deselect the block select tool by selecting the selection tool (▸).

You now have a new virtual clip with the previous virtual clips nested inside. Because the Timeline contains only one Transition track, you can normally use only one transition at a time. By nesting virtual clips that contain transitions, you can apply multiple transitions to one set of clips for more complex effects. Nesting virtual clips does, however, slow down previewing and exporting movies, especially if you are using transitions, filters, and superimposition.

Let's give the virtual clip an alias that will be a more descriptive clip name.

6 Select this new virtual clip, choose Clip > Alias, type **Masked Background**, and click OK.

7 Preview the virtual clip you just created by scrubbing through the Timeline ruler while pressing the Alt key (Windows) or Option key (Mac OS). The effects of the filters and the transition look just like they did when you previewed the source clips.

8 Save the project.

Assembling the final video program

You'll now nest the virtual clip you just made inside a new virtual clip. In this new virtual clip, you'll combine the Masked Background virtual clip along with another video clip and some still images, adding another Image Mask transition. This time, we'll use this transition to make a clip and a collection of still images play on top of our background effects through our image mask. First, you'll add a new scene to the project.

1 In the Navigator, use the slider or zoom buttons to set the Timeline unit menu to 1 Second so that you can see more detail.

2 Scroll the Timeline or drag in the Navigator palette so that just Masked Background is displayed.

3 Drag Surf3.mov from the Project window into the Video 1A track so that it snaps to the beginning of Masked Background.

The still images you'll be adding to this project will be inserted in the middle of Surf3.mov. To make this insertion possible, you'll use the razor tool to cut the clip in two pieces.

4 In the Timeline window, select the razor tool (✥), and click about in the middle of Surf3.mov.

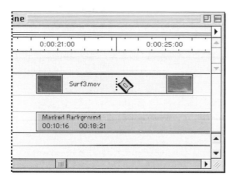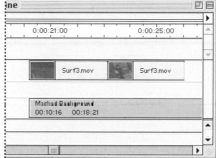

Surf3.mov is split in two pieces.

5 Select the selection tool (↖) to deselect the razor tool.

Before you add the still images to the project, you'll make a change to the preferences that will set the duration of the stills automatically as they are imported. Note that you must make preference change before you import the still images.

6 Choose File > Preferences > General/Still Image. Under Still Image, type **5** for the Default Duration for Frames, then click OK.

7 Choose File > Import > Folder, select the Images folder in the 12Lesson folder, and click OK (Windows) or Select 'Images' (Mac OS).

You'll add all 10 still images at once between the two portions of Surf3.mov you created with the razor tool.

8 In the Project window, double-click the Images bin to open it and choose Edit > Select All to select all 10 files in the bin. Drag these files together into the Video 1A track, between the two segments of Surf3.mov. Close the Images bin.

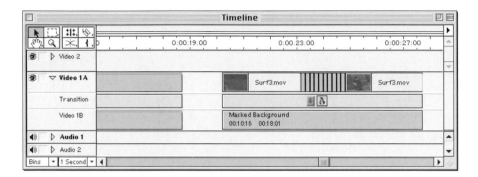

The virtual clip is slightly longer than the clips you've assembled in the Video 1A track. Because you want the material in both the Video 1A and the Video 1B tracks to be the same length, you'll trim the virtual clip, just as you would trim any other clip.

9 With the selection tool (▶) selected, position the pointer on the right end of Masked Background and drag left until it snaps to the end of the last Surf3.mov segment above it.

Next you'll add the Image Mask transition with a new mask shape.

10 From the Transitions palette, drag the Image Mask transition into the Transition track, so it snaps to the beginning of Masked Background.

11 In the Image Mask Settings dialog box, click Select Image, and double-click Mask2.tif in the 12Lesson folder. Then click OK to close the Image Mask Settings dialog box.

12 Resize the transition by moving the pointer to the right end of the transition and dragging right until it snaps to the end of Masked Background and the other clips you just assembled.

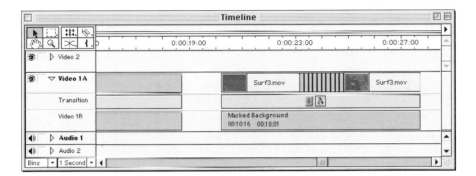

13 Preview the two clips and the transition you just assembled by scrubbing through the Timeline ruler while pressing the Alt key (Windows) or Option key (Mac OS).

With the transition in place, you'll apply the Invert filter to Masked Background and set the keyframe markers so that it affects this clip only when the still images are playing. To make this easier, you'll add two unnumbered markers to aid in setting where the filter starts and ends.

14 In the Program view, drag the shuttle slider to position the edit line near the beginning of Masked Background in the Timeline. Click the next edit button (▸ı) to move the edit line to the beginning of the Still01.tif, and choose Clip > Set Marker > Unnumbered.

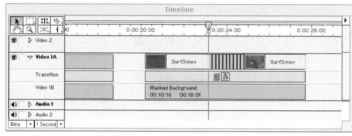

15 In the Program view, drag the shuttle slider to position the edit line in the last segment of Surf3.mov in the Timeline. Click the previous edit button (⁊) to move the edit line to the first frame of the last segment of Surf3.mov. Now click the previous frame button (◀ǀ) under the Program view to move the edit line to the last frame of Still10.tif and choose Clip > Set Marker > Unnumbered. Move the edit line away from the marker so it won't interfere when you align the keyframe to the marker.

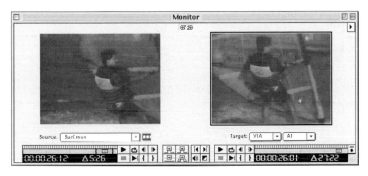

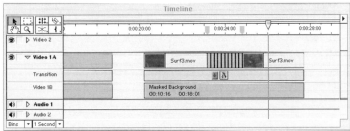

Now you'll apply the Invert filter to Masked Background. This filter inverts each color to its complementary color.

16 Select Masked Background and open the Filters dialog box.

17 Select Invert in the Available list and click Add. Drag the dialog box so you can see the markers in the Timeline and the Program view.

18 Drag the first marker on the Keyframe timeline right until it is aligned with the unnumbered marker at the beginning of Still1.tif.

19 In the same way, drag the end marker on the Keyframe timeline left until it is aligned with the marker at the end of Still10.tif. Click OK to close the Filters dialog box.

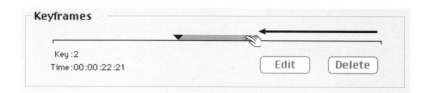

20 Preview the clips you have assembled by scrubbing through the Timeline ruler while pressing the Alt key (Windows) or Option key (Mac OS).

21 Save the project.

Editing virtual clips

Virtual clips can be edited in several ways. Like any other clip, you can trim either end of a virtual clip, change various settings, or apply filters to it, as you did earlier in this lesson. In addition, you can edit the clips in the source area from which the virtual clip was made, and the changes are automatically reflected in all instances of the virtual clip. Since you already modified virtual clips directly by applying filters, we'll use the second method, editing the clips in the source area, to modify the last virtual clip you just created and all previous virtual clips.

Here, you'll add a shadow under the shape you created with the Image Mask transition. To do this, you'll add a clip to the source area of Masked Background.

💡 *To quickly find the source area for a virtual clip, simply double-click the virtual clip.*

1 Double-click Masked Background. The source area is selected by the marquee and the block select tool is active. Select the selection tool (➤).

2 Drag Shadow.tif from the Project window into the Video 2 track, directly above the beginning of Background and Background 2.

We want Shadow.tif to be the same length as Background and Background 2, so you'll change the duration of this clip.

3 Position the pointer over the end of Shadow.tif and drag to extend it until it snaps the end of the virtual clips.

4 Select Shadow.tif, and then choose Clip > Video > Transparency to open the Transparency Settings dialog box.

5 Select Luminance for the Key type, set Threshold to 0 and set Cutoff to 100.

6 Click the page peel icon (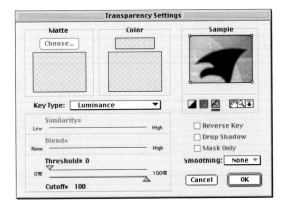) under the Sample window to view a thumbnail of the actual clip, and then click OK.

Now you'll set up a fade to make Shadow.tif partially transparent.

7 Click the triangle to the left of the Video 2 track name to expand the track.

8 Press and hold down the Shift key and then drag the red fade control line down to 50%. You will need to drag outside the clip to reach this value.

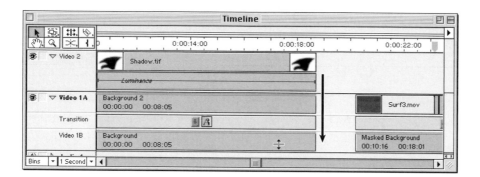

9 Preview the effect you just created by scrubbing through Background and Background 2 in the Timeline ruler while pressing the Alt key (Windows) or Option key (Mac OS).

Adding Shadow.tif to the source area added a shadow effect to Virtual Clip1 and Virtual Clip2.

10 Preview Masked Background and the clips above it in the same way.

Adding Shadow.tif to the source area changed Masked Background. Notice that the filter you applied to Masked Background inverts the shadow.

11 Clean up the Timeline by clicking the arrow in the Video 2 track to collapse the track.

12 Save the project.

Compiling virtual clips

When a virtual clip is in its final form and needs no more changes, you can compile the source components into an actual clip. This step saves time in previewing and eliminates the need to keep the source material in the Timeline. Another advantage is that deleting any of the clips in the source area in the Timeline or deleting associated master clips in the Project window has no effect on the compiled clip.

Now that your second virtual clip is finished, you can compile it. In addition to greatly reducing the time it takes to preview and export movies, compiling a virtual clip prevents further changes at the source clip level. You can still edit the compiled clip as you can any other clip, and if you want to make changes at the source clip level, you can edit the clips and compile again.

1 Select Background in the Timeline.

2 Choose Clip > Replace with Source to display the Export movie dialog box.

3 In the File name box, type **Background.mov** to name the clip you are about to compile.

4 Make sure the Export Movie dialog box is set to save in the appropriate project folder, and then click Save (Windows) or OK (Mac OS).

When Premiere has finished compiling, the virtual clip changes to the new named clip in the Timeline and also appears in the Project window.

5 In the Source view, preview the clip you just compiled.

6 Save the project.

Exporting the movie

Now that you've finished your editing, it's time to generate a movie file. You'll export just the last virtual clip you created, Masked Background, and the clips above it.

1 Scroll the Timeline so that Masked Background is visible.

2 To quickly resize the work area bar to cover Masked Background and the clips above it in the Timeline, hold down the Alt key (Windows) or Option key (Mac OS) and click between the title bar and the ruler, above Masked Background.

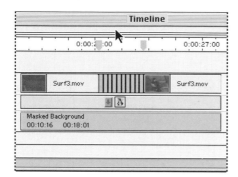 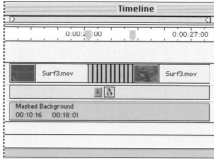

3 Choose File > Export > Movie.

4 In the Export Movie dialog box, click Settings.

5 Make sure QuickTime is selected for the File Type and Work Area is selected for the Range.

6 Also make sure that the Export Video option is selected and the Export Audio option is deselected. You can leave the rest of the settings as they are. Click OK to close the Export Movie Settings dialog box.

7 In the Export Movie dialog box, specify the 12Lesson folder for the location, and type **Windsurf.mov** for the name of the movie. Click Save (Windows) or OK (Mac OS).

Premiere starts making the movie, displaying a status bar that provides an estimate for the amount of time it will take.

8 When the movie is complete, it is opened in a clip window.

9 Click the Play button to play the movie.

Exploring on your own

Feel free to experiment with the project you have just created. Here are some suggestions:

• Use the Paste Custom command to copy just the fade control settings from Surf1.mov to Background 2.

• Use the razor tool to cut one of the virtual clips into several segments and apply different filter settings to each segment.

• Add the Strobe filter (in addition to the Invert filter) to the last virtual clip you created. Set Visible Frames to 4, Hidden Frames to 1, and pick a bright color. Set keyframes identical to the Invert filter.

Review questions

1 What are two ways to rename a clip?

2 What advantage does nesting virtual clips provide in using filters and transitions?

3 To create a new clip that appears in the Project window, would you use a subclip, an alias, or a virtual clip?

4 What are the advantages and disadvantages of compiling a virtual clip?

5 Can a subclip contain more than one source clip?

6 What are three ways to change the duration of a still image?

Answers

1 Assign an alias to it or change the name in the Project window with the list view selected.

2 You can use transitions and filters more than once on the same material.

3 A subclip.

4 Compiling a virtual clip protects it against being accidentally modified, eliminates the need to keep its source material in the project, and shortens preview time. Once a virtual clip is compiled, however, you can't change it by modifying the source material, and if the source area is deleted, you can't identify the source clips by name, or see the filters, transitions, or settings used to create it.

5 A subclip cannot include more than one clip. To achieve this effect, create a virtual clip instead.

6 You can change the duration of a still image in the following ways:

• Before importing the clip, set Default Duration for Still Image in the General/Still Image Preferences dialog box.

• Choose Clip > Duration and then enter a new duration.

• Position the selection tool pointer on the edge of the clip and drag.

Index

Production Notes

This book was created electronically using Adobe FrameMaker®. Art was produced using Adobe Illustrator and Adobe Photoshop. The Minion® and Frutiger® families of typefaces are used throughout the book.

Photography, Audio, Original Graphics

Photographic images, video footage, audio and graphics for use with tutorials only.

Adobe Image Library, Adobe Systems, Incorporated, 345 Park Avenue, San Jose, CA 95110-2704 USA: Lesson 9 (Amber, Gold); Lesson 10 (Flowers, Lotus)

Adobe Image Club Graphics, Suite 800, 833 4th Avenue SW, Calgary, Alberta, Canada T2P 3T5: Lesson 4 (Earth, Solar 1 and 2)

KTZZ Television, WB-22 Cable 10, 945 Dexter Avenue North, Seattle, WA 98109 USA: Lesson 1 (Tower, Ferry, Sailby, Unload)

Music Services, Canary Collection, 121 Pennsylvania Avenue, Wayne, PA 19087-0590 USA: Lesson 1 (Seagulls); Lesson 5 (Danger, Horror, Shadow, Suspense); Lesson 6 & 7 (Music); Lesson 11 (Music1)

Julie Brockmeyer: Lesson 3 (Dressage logo); Lesson 4 (Eye); Lesson 11 (Barista, Cafe, Dessert, Latte, Cafe logo)

Paul Carew: Lesson 7 (Blow-1, Heat-1, Medium, Shape, Talk, Voice-1)

Craig Hoeschen: Lesson 7 (Closeup, Heat-2, Oven, Sound, Top)

Julieanne Kost: Lesson 11 (Press, Roaster, Stool)

Bonnie Lebesch: Lesson 1 (Shiplogo, Sun); Lesson 8 (Octopus); Lesson 9 (1, 3, 5, 7, 9, 11, Excite, Ball, Jackhi, Jacklow); Lesson 10 (Backdrop, Green, Logo); Lesson 11 (Pour)

Susan Bari Price: Lesson 3 (Field, Finish, Ride, Trot); Lesson 5 (Door, Feet1, Feet2, Hall1, Hall2, Man, Woman1, Woman2); Lesson 12 (Surf, Stills)

Special thanks to our acting and voice talent: David Butler, Daniel Monda, Julie Brockmeyer, Eric Brakken, Saloua Laalami, John M. Rajala, Pam Ghambari, Tessa E. Hicks, Bonnie Lebesch, and Bob Fischer